FIFTY KEY FIGURES IN QUEER US THEATRE

Whether creating Broadway musicals, experimental dramas, or outrageous comedies, the performers, directors, playwrights, designers, and producers profiled in this collection have contributed to the representation of LGBTQ lives and culture in a variety of theatrical venues, both within the queer community and across the US theatrical landscape.

Moving from the era of the Stonewall Riots to today, notable scholars in the field bring a wide variety of queer theatre artists into conversation with each other, exploring connections and differences in race, gender, physical ability, national origin, class, generation, aesthetic modes, and political goals, creating a diverse and inclusive study of 50 years of queer theatre.

For readers seeking an introduction to or a deeper understanding of LGBTQ theatre, this volume offers thought-provoking analyses of theatre-makers both celebrated and lesser-known, mainstream and subversive, canonical and new.

Jimmy A. Noriega is Professor of Theatre at the College of Wooster and President of the American Society for Theatre Research. He is the co-editor of *Theatre and Cartographies of Power: Repositioning the Latina/o Americas* (2008), and the founder of Teatro Travieso/ Troublemaker Theatre.

Jordan Schildcrout is Professor of Theatre & Performance at SUNY Purchase and author of *In the Long Run: A Cultural History of Broadway's Hit Plays* (Routledge, 2020) and *Murder Most Queer: The Homicidal Homosexual in the American Theater* (2014).

ROUTLEDGE KEY GUIDES

Fifty Key Theatre Directors
Edited by Shomit Mitter and Maria Shevtsova

Fifty Key Contemporary Thinkers
John Lechte

Art History
The Key Concepts
Jonathan Harris

Fifty Contemporary Choreographers
Edited by Jo Butterworth and Lorna Sanders

Fifty Key Figures in Latinx and Latin American Theatre
Edited by Paola S. Hernández and Analola Santana

Fifty Key Stage Musicals
Edited by Robert W. Schneider and Shannon Agnew

Fifty Key Irish Plays
Edited by Shaun Richards

Fifty Key Figures in Queer US Theatre
Edited by Jimmy A. Noriega and Jordan Schildcrout

For a full list of titles in this series, please visit: https://www.routledge.com/Routledge-Key-Guides/book-series/RKG

FIFTY KEY FIGURES IN QUEER US THEATRE

Edited by
Jimmy A. Noriega and Jordan Schildcrout

LONDON AND NEW YORK

Cover Image: Chitra Ganesh, *Cadre*, 2019. Courtesy the artist. Photo credit: Emily Peacock.

First published 2023
by Routledge
4 Park Square, Milton Park, Abingdon, Oxon OX14 4RN

and by Routledge
605 Third Avenue, New York, NY 10158

Routledge is an imprint of the Taylor & Francis Group, an informa business

© 2023 selection and editorial matter, Jimmy A. Noriega and Jordan Schildcrout; individual chapters, the contributors

The right of Jimmy A. Noriega and Jordan Schildcrout to be identified as the authors of the editorial material, and of the authors for their individual chapters, has been asserted in accordance with sections 77 and 78 of the Copyright, Designs and Patents Act 1988.

All rights reserved. No part of this book may be reprinted or reproduced or utilized in any form or by any electronic, mechanical, or other means, now known or hereafter invented, including photocopying and recording, or in any information storage or retrieval system, without permission in writing from the publishers.

Trademark notice: Product or corporate names may be trademarks or registered trademarks, and are used only for identification and explanation without intent to infringe.

British Library Cataloguing-in-Publication Data
A catalogue record for this book is available from the British Library

Library of Congress Cataloging-in-Publication Data
Names: Noriega, Jimmy A., editor. | Schildcrout, Jordan, editor.
Title: Fifty key figures in queer US theatre / Edited by Jimmy A. Noriega and Jordan Schildcrout.
Description: Abingdon, Oxon ; New York, NY : Routledge, 2022. | Includes bibliographical references and index.
Identifiers: LCCN 2022009953 (print) | LCCN 2022009954 (ebook) | ISBN 9781032067995 (hardback) | ISBN 9781032067964 (paperback) | ISBN 9781003203896 (ebook)
Subjects: LCSH: Gay theater—United States—Biography. | Gay actors—United States—Biography. | Gay theatrical producers and directors—United States—Biography. | Gay dramatists—United States—Biography.
Classification: LCC PN2270.G39 F54 2022 (print) | LCC PN2270.G39 (ebook) | DDC 792.086/640973 [B]—dc23/eng/20220602
LC record available at https://lccn.loc.gov/2022009953
LC ebook record available at https://lccn.loc.gov/2022009954

ISBN: 978-1-032-06799-5 (hbk)
ISBN: 978-1-032-06796-4 (pbk)
ISBN: 978-1-003-20389-6 (ebk)

DOI: 10.4324/9781003203896

Typeset in Times New Roman
by Apex CoVantage, LLC

CONTENTS

List of Contributors	x
Acknowledgments	xx

Introduction 1
Jimmy A. Noriega and Jordan Schildcrout

Reza Abdoh 16
Joseph Cermatori

Luis Alfaro 21
Patricia Ybarra

Kate Bornstein 26
Rye Gentleman

Sharon Bridgforth 30
T. Chester

Charles Busch 35
Sean F. Edgecomb

Jane Chambers 40
Sara Warner

Ellie Covan 44
Jeff McMahon

Will Davis 48
Joshua Bastian Cole

CONTENTS

Ty Defoe (Giizhig) *Courtney Elkin Mohler*	53
Snehal Desai *Dan Bacalzo*	58
Harvey Fierstein *Jordan Schildcrout*	63
William Finn *Ryan Donovan*	67
The Five Lesbian Brothers: Moe Angelos, Babs Davy, Dominique Dibbell, Peg Healey, and Lisa Kron *Lisa Sloan*	72
María Irene Fornés *Gwendolyn Alker*	76
John Glines *Jordan Schildcrout*	81
David Greenspan *Nick Salvato*	85
Jeremy O. Harris *David Román*	90
Rachel Hauck *Stacy Wolf*	94
Chisa Hutchinson *La Donna L. Forsgren*	99
Michael R. Jackson *Aviva Helena Neff*	103
Bill T. Jones *Ariel Nereson*	108

Moisés Kaufman *Bess Rowen*	113
Tony Kushner *Virginia Anderson*	118
Tina Landau *David Román*	123
Nathan Lane *James F. Wilson*	127
Haruna Lee *Jessica Del Vecchio*	132
Joan Lipkin *Gad Guterman*	137
Charles Ludlam *Joe E. Jeffreys*	142
Taylor Mac *Sean F. Edgecomb*	146
Joe Mantello *James F. Wilson*	151
Tarell Alvin McCraney *Isaiah Matthew Wooden*	156
Terrence McNally *Virginia Anderson*	160
Muriel Miguel *Christy Stanlake*	165
Cherríe Moraga *Alicia Arrizón*	170

CONTENTS

Daaimah Mubashshir *Adam Ashraf Elsayigh*	175
The NEA Four: Karen Finley, John Fleck, Holly Hughes, and Tim Miller *Jimmy A. Noriega and Jordan Schildcrout*	179
Robert O'Hara *Faedra Chatard Carpenter*	184
Monica Palacios *Marci R. McMahon*	189
Miguel Piñero *Karen Jaime*	193
Billy Porter *Eric M. Glover*	197
Clint Ramos *Jimmy A. Noriega*	201
Guillermo Reyes *Jimmy A. Noriega*	206
Edwin Sánchez *Analola Santana*	211
Leigh Silverman *Bess Rowen*	215
Ana María Simo *Virginia Baeta*	219
Split Britches: Peggy Shaw, Lois Weaver, and Deb Margolin *Benjamin Gillespie*	223
Paula Vogel *Sara Warner*	228

Ron Whyte *Patrick McKelvey*	233
George C. Wolfe *Charles I. Nero*	238
BD Wong *Esther Kim Lee*	242
Chay Yew *Dan Bacalzo*	246

CONTRIBUTORS

Gwendolyn Alker is an Associate Arts Professor and Director of Theatre Studies in the Department of Drama, Tisch/NYU. She is the former editor of *Theatre Topics* and the former managing editor of *Women & Performance*. As a scholar and dramaturg, she has taught, written about, and advocated for the work of María Irene Fornés over the last two decades.

Virginia Anderson is Associate Professor of Theater at Connecticut College, where she teaches courses concerning theatre and culture and directs for the main stage. Much of her scholarly work concerns the on- and off-stage history of Broadway theatre and the AIDS epidemic; recent essays include "Choreographing a Cause: Broadway Bares as Philanthroproduction and Embodied Index to Changing Attitudes Toward HIV/AIDS," "Performing Interventions: The Politics and Theatre of China's AIDS Crisis in the Early Twenty-First Century," and "'Something Bad [was] Happening': *Falsettos* as an Historical Record of the AIDS Epidemic." www.virginialanderson.com.

Alicia Arrizón is Associate Dean of Student Academic Affairs in the College of Humanities, Arts and Social Sciences and professor of Gender and Sexuality at UC Riverside. She is the author of *Queering Mestizaje: Transculturation and Performance* (2006); *Latina Performance* (1999); and co-editor of *Latinas on Stage* (2000) and *Sensualidades*, a special issue of *Women and Performance: A Journal of Feminist Theory*. Some of her articles have appeared in *TDR*, *Theatre Journal*, *Theatre Research International*, and *Ollantay*.

Dan Bacalzo is Associate Professor of Theatre at Florida Gulf Coast University, where he also serves as Theatre Program Coordinator. He received his Ph.D. in Performance Studies from New York University. He is the former artistic director of Peeling, an Asian American writing/performance collective, and also worked over 15 years as a theatre editor and critic in New York City, including eight years as managing editor of TheaterMania.com. His academic publications include articles and/or reviews in *Embodying Asian/American Sexualities*, *Theatre Journal*, *TDR*, and the *Journal of American Drama and Theatre*.

Virginia Baeta is a New York-based theatre creator and enthusiastic learner of things. This learning side-hustle led to *Out Lines*, an LGBTQ+ theatre/history podcast that she co-hosts with Mark Finley and Jordan Schildcrout. Virginia is a core member of The Queen's Company, a theatre company dedicated to inventive productions of classical plays featuring all-female casts. As an actor, playwright, and director, she also contributes to the LGBTQ+ theatre company TOSOS: The Other Side of Silence.

Faedra Chatard Carpenter is a theatre and performance studies scholar, professional dramaturg, and cultural critic. Her book *Coloring Whiteness: Acts of Critique in Black Performance* (2014) received the Honorable Mention for ATDS' John W. Frick Book Award for the Best Book in American Theatre and Drama as well as the Honorable Mention for ASTR's Errol Hill Award for Outstanding Scholarship in African American Theatre, Drama, and/or Performance Studies. She also received the American Theatre and Drama Society's Betty Jean Jones Award for being an Outstanding Teacher of American Theatre and Drama (2019).

Joseph Cermatori is Associate Professor of English at Skidmore College in Saratoga Springs, New York, where he is also affiliated with the department of theatre and the program in women and gender studies. His teaching and research concentrate on modern literature, drama, and performance, and on the intersections of theatre and philosophy. His first book, *Baroque Modernity: An Aesthetics of Theater* (2021), won the American Comparative Literature Association's Helen Tartar First Book Award. His essays have appeared in numerous publications, including the contemporary arts journal *PAJ*, where he is a contributing editor.

T. Chester (they/them) is a performance studies scholar specializing in gender, sexuality, and religion in the Black diaspora. Their research uses both popular culture and the lived experiences of Black people to explore the development and performance of sexuality and gender identities. Over the last ten years, T. has taught in Black studies, women and gender studies, and theatre departments at the university level. As an artist, scholar, and organizer they center storytelling as a way to understand difference, promote empathy, and create change.

CONTRIBUTORS

Joshua Bastian Cole is a PhD candidate at Cornell University. His multidisciplinary work spans transgender studies, disability and Deaf studies, theatre, dance, puppetry, film, and television. Cole has published on topics ranging from trans men's casting to spectatorship. He holds a BA in Theatre and Dance from James Madison University and an MA in Theatre History and Criticism from CUNY, Brooklyn College. Cole has been a lecturer at CUNY, SUNY, and Cornell.

Jessica Del Vecchio is an Assistant Professor of Theatre at James Madison University in Virginia. She holds a BA in psychology from Princeton University, a MA from the University of Texas, Austin, and a PhD in theatre from the Graduate Center at the City University of New York. Her writing has appeared in *Contemporary Theatre Review*, *Theatre Journal*, *TDR*, and *Modern Drama*. She is currently working on her book manuscript, *Straddling Feminisms: Post-Wave Pop Politics and Contemporary Performance*.

Ryan Donovan is the author of *Broadway Bodies: A Critical History, 1970–2020* (2023), *Queer Approaches in Musical Theatre* (2023), and co-editor of *The Routledge Companion to Musical Theatre* (Routledge, 2023). Ryan is Assistant Professor of Theater Studies at Duke University. His articles appear in the *Journal of American Drama and Theatre* and *Studies in Musical Theatre*. He holds a PhD in Theatre and Performance from The Graduate Center, City University of New York. ryan-donovan.com.

Sean F. Edgecomb is Associate Professor of Theatre and Performance at the CUNY Graduate Center and the College of Staten Island. His first monograph was *Charles Ludlam Lives! Charles Busch, Bradford Louryk and Taylor Mac and the Queer Legacy of the Ridiculous Theatrical Company* (2017). He is currently completing an edited collection on the complete works of Taylor Mac in collaboration with David Román, as well as his second monograph, *A Queer Bestiary: Ritual Anthropomorphism and Animal Symbolism in LGBTQ+ Performance*. Additionally, Sean paints queer folk art under the pseudonym Peter Kunt (peterkunt.com).

Adam Ashraf Elsayigh is an Egyptian writer, theatre maker, and dramaturg. His plays (including *Memorial*, *Jamestown/Williamsburg*, *The Marginalia* and *Drowning in Cairo*) have been developed and seen at The Lark, The Tisch School of the Arts, The LaGuardia Performing Arts Center, and Golden Thread Productions. Adam is a co-founder of The Criminal Queerness Festival with National Queer Theater, and a fellow at Georgetown University's Laboratory for Global Performance. He holds a BA in Theater from NYU Abu Dhabi and is an MFA Candidate in Playwriting at Brooklyn College. He is the Literary Manager and Resident Dramaturg of the Asolo Repertory Theatre. adamaelsayigh.com.

La Donna L. Forsgren is an Associate Professor in the Department of Film, Television, and Theatre at the University of Notre Dame. She is the author of *In Search of Our Warrior Mothers: Women Dramatists of the Black Arts Movement* (2018) and *Sistuhs in the Struggle: An Oral History of Black Arts Movement Theatre and Performance* (2020), a finalist for ATHE's 2021 Outstanding Book Award. In addition, she is the recipient of ASTR's Oscar G. Brockett Essay Prize (2020) and the MATC's Robert A. Schanke Theatre Research Award (2016) for her research in African American theatre.

Rye Gentleman is a PhD candidate in the Theatre Arts and Dance Department at University of Minnesota where he conducts research at the intersection of performance studies, media studies, and transgender studies. His writing has been published in *TDR*, *QED: A Journal in GLBTQ Worldmaking*, and *Text and Performance Quarterly*. He is currently working as a contributor and co-editor on an anthology focused on transfeminist theatre and performance.

Benjamin Gillespie holds a PhD in Theatre & Performance from The Graduate Center, CUNY. His research focuses on the intersections of aging, gender, and queer sexuality in contemporary theatre and drama, especially in the later works of Split Britches. Benjamin currently holds a full-time Lectureship at Baruch College, where he teaches communication and performance studies. He is Associate Editor of *PAJ: A Journal of Performance and Art* and his articles and reviews have been published in *Theatre Journal*, *Modern Drama*, *Theatre Survey*, *Performance Research*, *PAJ*, *Canadian Theatre Review*, *Theatre Research in Canada*, and a number of edited anthologies.

Eric M. Glover is an Assistant Professor Adjunct of dramaturgy and dramatic criticism at the David Geffen School of Drama at Yale University, where he is an expert on Black musical theater. Eric is also working as a production dramaturg for Tarell Alvin McCraney's *Choir Boy* at Yale Repertory Theatre, New Haven, 2022. He serves on the Executive Committee of the American Society for Theatre Research.

Gad Guterman is Associate Professor and Chair of the Sargent Conservatory of Theatre Arts at Webster University. He is the author of *Performance, Identity, and Immigration Law: A Theatre of Undocumentedness* (2014). His essays appear in *Theatre and Cartographies of Power: Repositioning the Latina/o Americas* (2018), and *Critical Insights: American Multicultural Identity* (2014), and journals including *Theatre Survey*, *Theatre Journal*, and *Contemporary Theatre Review*.

Karen Jaime is Assistant Professor of Performing and Media Arts and Latina/o Studies at Cornell University. Karen's monograph *The Queer Nuyorican: Racialized Sexualities and Aesthetics in Loisaida* (2021) argues for a reexamination of the Nuyorican Poets Cafe as a historically queer space in terms of sexualities and performance practices. Her writing has been published in *Women and Performance*, *Small Axe*, *TSQ*, and *Queer Nightlife* (2021). Karen is also an accomplished spoken word artist and published poet, who served as the host/curator of the Friday Night Poetry Slam at the Nuyorican Poets Cafe from 2003 to 2005.

Joe E. Jeffreys is a Ridiculous scholar and drag historian. He teaches theatre and LGBTQ+ studies at New York University and The New School. He is published in encyclopedias, anthologies, journals, and zines. Jeffreys' drag-happy video works have been exhibited at festivals and museums internationally.

Esther Kim Lee is Professor of Theater Studies and the Director of the Asian American and Diaspora Studies at Duke University. She is the author of *A History of Asian American Theatre* (2006), which received the 2007 Award for Outstanding Book given by Association for Theatre in Higher Education. She edited *Seven Contemporary Plays from the Korean Diaspora in the Americas* (2012) and authored *The Theatre of David Henry Hwang* (2015). Her latest book, *Made-Up Asians: Yellowface During the Exclusion Era*, was published in 2022.

Patrick McKelvey is Assistant Professor of Theatre Arts at the University of Pittsburgh, where he teaches courses in performance studies, theatre history, and disability studies. He has published essays in *Theatre Journal*, *Theatre Survey*, *Journal of Dramatic Theory and Criticism*, and *Queer Dance: Meanings and Makings* (ed. Clare Croft; 2017). McKelvey's 2016 essay, "Ron Whyte's 'Disemployment'" (*Theatre Survey*), received three "best article" awards: from the American Society for Theatre Research, the American Theatre and Drama Society, and the Committee for LGBT History. McKelvey is currently completing his first book, *Disability Works: US Performance After Rehabilitation*.

CONTRIBUTORS

Jeff McMahon is a writer and performer and has performed in every iteration of Dixon Place since 1986. He has received support from the NEA, New York Foundation for the Arts, New York State Council on the Arts, and Arizona Commission on the Arts. He holds an MFA from the Writing Program at Columbia University and a BA in Interdisciplinary Art from SUNY/Empire State College. His essays have been published in *Hyperallergic* and the *Guardian* (among others). He is Professor Emeritus in the School of Music, Dance and Theatre at Arizona State University, where he taught 2001–2022. His *Six Monologues 1990–2007* was published in 2018. jeffmcmahonprojects.net.

Marci R. McMahon, Professor in the Literatures and Cultural Studies Department at The University of Texas Rio Grande Valley, is the author of *Domestic Negotiations: Gender, Nation, and Self-Fashioning in US Mexicana and Chicana Literature and Art* (2013). Some of her publications appear in *The Chicano Studies Reader: An Anthology of Aztlán* (3rd and 4th editions, 2016/2020); *Chicana/Latina Studies: Journal of MALCS*; *Frontiers: A Journal of Women's Studies*; and *Text & Performance Quarterly*. Her forthcoming book, *Sonic Cultural Ciizenship*, explores the relationship between music, aurality, and citizenship in Latinx theatre and performance.

Courtney Elkin Mohler is an Associate Professor of Theatre and the Associate Dean for Inclusion, Diversity, Equity, and Access for Jordan College of the Arts at Butler University. Her work in dramaturgy and directing focuses on new plays by Indigenous playwrights and works that advance social and reparative justice. She is the co-author (with Jaye T. Darby and Christy Stanlake) of *Critical Companion to Native American and First Nations Theatre and Performance: Indigenous Spaces* (2020) and has published articles in *Theatre Topics*, *Modern Drama*, and *Ecumenica*, among others.

Aviva Helena Neff is an artist-scholar-educator from Ypsilanti, Michigan, who studies mixed-Black representation throughout US literature, history, and performance. An honors graduate of the College of Wooster, Aviva received her MA with the highest distinction from Goldsmiths, University of London. She earned a PhD from The Ohio State University in 2021 (dissertation: "Blood Earth Water: The Tragic Mulatta in US Literature, History, and Performance"). She currently serves as Director for Youth and Community Learning at Columbus College of Art and Design.

Ariel Nereson is Assistant Professor of Dance Studies and Director of Graduate Dance at the University at Buffalo–SUNY. She is the author of *Democracy Moving: Bill T. Jones, Contemporary American Performance, and the Racial Past* (2022), as well as several essays appearing in journals and edited collections. Broadly, her research focuses on the intersection of racialization, embodiment, and movement-based performance. She serves on the Board of the American Theatre and Drama Society and is the book review editor for *Theatre History Studies*.

Charles I. Nero is a cultural critic and professor of rhetoric whose work sits at the intersection of communication studies, film and literary criticism, African American studies, and cultural studies. Notably, Nero's work also deeply engages the place of sexuality in African American studies and African American culture. His scholarly work has appeared in major academic journals and groundbreaking collections. Nero is currently the Benjamin E. Mays Distinguished Professor of Africana and Rhetoric, Film, and Screen Studies at Bates College.

Jimmy A. Noriega is Professor of Theatre at the College of Wooster and President of the American Society for Theatre Research. He is the co-editor of *Theatre and Cartographies of Power: Repositioning the Latina/o Americas* (with Analola Santana; 2018) and his research focuses on Latinx, Latin American, and queer theatre and performance. He has directed over 50 productions in English and Spanish, including invited performances at theatres and festivals in over a dozen countries. He is the founder of Teatro Travieso/Troublemaker Theatre (www.teatrotravieso.org).

David Román is Professor of English and American Studies at the University of Southern California. He serves on the Board of Directors of Labyrinth Theater and has written and edited books about AIDS and the arts, Latinx studies, and contemporary US culture and performance. His current projects include a book on the racial politics of American theatre in the 1940s, a study of the memoirs of pre-Stonewall gay and lesbian activists, and a historical project on AIDS and cultural production in the 1980s and early 1990s.

Bess Rowen is Assistant Professor in Theatre at Villanova University and author of *The Lines Between the Lines: How Stage Directions Affect Embodiment* (2021). She has published articles in *Modern Drama*, *Theatre Topics*, *Journal of Dramatic Theory and Criticism*, and *Theatre Topics*. She is currently working as a contributor and lead editor to an anthology on transfeminist work in theatre and performance.

Nick Salvato is Professor of Performing and Media Arts at Cornell University and the author of four books: *Uncloseting Drama: American Modernism and Queer Performance* (2010), *Knots Landing* (2015), *Obstruction* (2016), and *Television Scales* (2019). His writing has appeared in such venues as *Closet Drama: History, Theory, and Genre* (Routledge, 2018), *Imagined Theatres: Writing for a Theoretical Stage* (Routledge, 2017), *Modern Drama*, *TDR*, *Theater*, *Theatre Journal*, and *Theatre Survey*.

Analola Santana is Associate Professor of Theatre at Dartmouth College. She is the author of *Teatro y Cultura de Masas: Encuentros y Debates* (2010) and *Freak Performances: Dissidence in Latin American Theatre* (2018). She is also the co-editor of *Theatre and Cartographies of Power: Repositioning the Latina/o Americas* (with Jimmy Noriega; 2018). She works as a professional dramaturg and is a company member of Mexico's famed Teatro de Ciertos Habitantes.

Jordan Schildcrout is Professor of Theatre & Performance at SUNY Purchase and author of *In the Long Run: A Cultural History of Broadway's Hit Plays* (Routledge, 2020) and *Murder Most Queer: The Homicidal Homosexual in the American Theater* (2014). His work as an editor includes the première publication of the gay liberation era erotic comedy *Tubstrip* by Jerry Douglas. Other scholarly articles on theatre and performance have focused on subjects such as the Stonewall Riots, the apocalypse, spinster detectives, and the Muppets.

Lisa Sloan is a lesbian feminist scholar, nonprofit professional, and practicing dramaturg. She is currently the Deputy Director at the Pride Center of Staten Island, an LGBTQ+ community center. She earned her PhD in Theater and Performance Studies from UCLA. She is a member of the Women & Theatre Program. As a dramaturg, she has worked on Gina Young's *sSISTERSs*, the LA LGBT Center's production of Ike Holter's *Hit the Wall*, and Center Theatre Group's production of Martin Sherman's *Bent*.

Christy Stanlake is a Professor of English at the United States Naval Academy. Her publications include *Native American Drama: A Critical Perspective* (2009) and *Critical Companion to Native American and First Nations Theatre: Indigenous Spaces* (with Jaye Darby and Courtney Elkin Mohler; 2020). Christy has used Native theatrical theories to direct Lynn Riggs's *Green Grow the Lilacs* and JudyLee Oliva's *Te Ata*; both plays toured to the National Museum of the American Indian, Washington, DC.

CONTRIBUTORS

Sara Warner is Director of LGBT Studies and Associate Professor in the Department of Performing and Media Arts at Cornell University. She studies the art of activism, paying particular attention to the role joy, laughter, and pleasure play in creating social change. Her work takes many forms, from academic tomes and mainstream journalism to community-based plays and the staging of "patriot acts"—political performances on national holidays. Her book *Acts of Gaiety: LGBT Performance and the Politics of Pleasure* received the Outstanding Book Award from ATHE, an Honorable Mention for the Barnard Hewitt Award from ASTR, and was named a Lambda Literary Award finalist.

James F. Wilson is Professor of English at LaGuardia Community College, CUNY, and a member of the Theatre and Performance faculty at CUNY Graduate Center. Research and teaching interests include African American theatre and performance, gender and sexuality studies, and musical theatre history. He is the author of *Bulldaggers, Pansies, and Chocolate Babies: Performance, Race and Sexuality in the Harlem Renaissance* (2010), and his essays have appeared in numerous academic journals and chapter anthologies. He is co-editor of the *Journal of American Drama and Theatre* (*JADT*) and is a voting member of the Drama Desk.

Stacy Wolf is Professor of Theater and American Studies, and Director of the Program in Music Theater at Princeton University. She is the author of *A Problem Like Maria: Gender and Sexuality in the American Musical* (2002), *Changed for Good: A Feminist History of the Broadway Musical* (2011), and *Beyond Broadway: The Pleasure and Promise of Musical Theatre Across America* (2019).

Isaiah Matthew Wooden is a director-dramaturg, critic, and Assistant Professor of Theater at Swarthmore College. A scholar of African American art, drama, and performance, he has contributed articles and essays to *The Black Scholar*, the *Journal of American Drama and Theatre*, *Journal of Dramatic Theory and Criticism*, *Modern Drama*, *PAJ: A Journal of Performance and Art*, *Theatre Journal*, and *Theatre Topics*, among other scholarly and popular publications. He is the co-editor of *Tarell Alvin McCraney: Theater, Performance, and Collaboration* (2020) and is currently at work on a monograph that explores the interplay of race and time in post-civil rights Black expressive culture.

Patricia Ybarra is Professor in the Department of Theatre Arts and Performance Studies at Brown University. She is the author of *Performing Conquest: Five Centuries of Theatre, History and Identity in Tlaxcala, Mexico* (2009), co-editor with Lara Nielsen of *Neoliberalism and Global Theatres: Performance Permutations* (2012; paperback 2015), and *Latinx Theatre in Times of Neoliberalism* (2018). She is currently working on projects on Reza Abdoh's *Father Was a Peculiar Man* and the hemispheric history of theatre and debt. She is the former president of ATHE.

ACKNOWLEDGMENTS

The editors wish to thank Ben Piggott, Zoe Forbes, Steph Hines, Ronnie Morgan, Nikky Twyman, and the rest of the team at Routledge for their invaluable support and guidance on this collection from conception to publication. We're also grateful to the anonymous peer reviewers whose insights helped to shape the project. This book would not be complete without the amazing cover art from Chitra Ganesh, and we extend thanks to everyone at Chitra Ganesh Studio for their support.

Collaboration on *Fifty Key Figures in Queer US Theatre* began in November 2020, and the entire process has been conducted during a global pandemic. Contributors have written their entries while managing their health and the health of loved ones, teaching theatre on screens rather than in classrooms, creating shows on video rather than in a theatre, getting vaccinated, wearing masks, and moving forward into an uncertain future. We thank all of our contributors for their time, knowledge, and generosity through these many challenges. In this same period, many of the theatre makers named in this book were deprived of their livelihoods as theatres around the world closed, and one of our figures, Terrence McNally, was among the first to lose his life in a pandemic that has claimed millions.

This book is dedicated to the queer artists, scholars, and audiences who have kept the ghostlight glowing through dark times. We look forward to a future with many opportunities to gather and celebrate queer theatre in all its forms.

INTRODUCTION
Jimmy A. Noriega and Jordan Schildcrout

Fifty Key Figures in Queer US Theatre provides an overview of 50 artists working in the queer theatre that emerged in the United States following the 1969 Stonewall Riots. Whether creating Broadway musicals, experimental dramas, or outrageous comedies, these queer artists have contributed to the representation of LGBTQ lives and culture in a variety of theatrical venues, both within the queer community and across the US theatrical landscape. Their works span the spectrum of the field—award-winning and lesser-known, mainstream and subversive, canonical and new—and speak to the multiple ways that theatre can make a significant impact on culture and society. The essays, written by notable scholars, bring these artists into conversation with each other and offer an illuminating portrait of their works, aesthetics, philosophies, and lives. It is our hope that this collection not only celebrates, but also elevates, the field of queer theatre and prompts discussion on the many other artists and theatrical productions that comprise its past, present, and future.

Without a doubt, compiling a list of 50 key figures is both a daunting and seemingly impossible task. It only takes a moment to begin to identify the many theatre artists that were not included in the final table of contents of this volume. And, perhaps, that is the point. The number of queer artists—playwrights, performers, directors, choreographers, lyricists, designers, producers, and technicians—that have contributed to the US theatrical landscape over the past 50 years is immeasurable. Their impact is not only felt on the grand stages of Broadway and the playhouses of major cities, but in smaller communities and alternative spaces across the nation. In thinking through the many ways that we could present a portrait of the field, we were driven by a desire to challenge the traditional qualifications and expectations that guide these types of projects. Rather than generate a list of the "greatest" or "most important" theatre artists who also

DOI: 10.4324/9781003203896-1

happen to be queer, this book identifies 50 figures who have made unique and valuable contributions to queer theatre and amplified the visibility of queer subject matter in significant ways. The range of artists represented and the many genres in which they work—musical theatre, plays, solo performance, alternative theatre, community-based theatre—demonstrate the myriad ways that artists can have an impact on our understanding of queer theatre, as well as theatre more broadly. Many of the figures here have contributed their talents to the creation of major works of art that are considered milestones in US theatre, while other artists' works may not be as recognizable to the larger public because of the limitations placed on them by geography and resources. This intentional questioning of the "key"—to what door and where does that door lead?—guided our work at every turn. From the very beginning, our main goal has been to expand the scholarship in the field of queer theatre to more accurately represent the diversity of artists and audiences that inhabit performance spaces across the US. By doing so, this project aims to subvert the exclusionary practices that have dominated the field in the past, which often resulted in a "canon" of predominantly white, cis-male theatre artists who worked primarily in New York City. Instead, we offer a broader and more inclusive list of theatre makers whose works and cultural perspectives speak to the diversity of queer theatre across race, gender, physical ability, national origin, religion, and class.

We also made the decision to look forward with optimism and enthusiasm. Rather than only include those figures that have already created an impact, we have also pointed to the future by identifying individuals who are positioned to continue making significant contributions to US theatre if given the opportunity. This includes cutting-edge and contemporary works being created by and about trans, nonbinary, Black, Indigenous, Latinx, Asian American, and Muslim artists, as well as those of differing physical abilities. Much of what we try to accomplish in this project is a purposeful and radical response to the continued marginalization and erasure of BIPOC (Black, Indigenous, and People of Color) and other individuals who have historically been denied access to institutions of power and other forms of cultural capital. For these reasons, we hope our collection inspires students, educators, producers, researchers, and audiences to seek out these artists, as well as the many more like them, who are laboring to create a more inclusive and justice-driven world through their art.

50 YEARS OF QUEER CULTURE AND POLITICS

We position the Stonewall Riots of 1969 as our starting point, in part because this queer uprising against police harassment is widely regarded as a crucial turning point in the fight for liberation and in the formation of queer identities and communities. Playwright Doric Wilson, who had been part of the first wave of gay plays in the 1960s at the Caffe Cino, participated in the riots and later went on to found the seminal queer theatre company TOSOS in 1974. His play *Street Theater* (1982), a satirical depiction of queer life on the eve of the Stonewall Riots, asserted that this queer rebellion was, in fact, a form of theatre: it involved openly and collectively performing queer identities in public space and actively resisting the forces that criminalized and stigmatized those identities. For many, the theatre became and has continued to be an "anti-closet," a place where queer voices could be heard, queer stories told, queer aesthetics celebrated, and queer artists and audiences brought together as a community. Queer theatre, therefore, has been simultaneously deeply personal and inherently political.

Indeed, queer politics and queer theatre have often been intertwined in the decades following Stonewall, perhaps most fabulously realized in the figure of Marsha P. Johnson. A participant in the riots and a life-long activist, particularly for trans people and people of color, she was also a theatrical performer. She appeared regularly in shows with Jimmy Camicia's multi-gender drag troupe Hot Peaches for nearly two decades, beginning in 1972. In 1991, the year before her untimely death, Miss Marsha performed in *The Heat*, singing a song called "Love" while wearing a mirrored head wrap, glitter makeup, and a "Silence = Death" badge on her pastel-colored blouse. While her theatre work might not be the most significant aspect of her legacy, a strain of theatricality is evident in her activism, just as a strain of activism can be seen in her performances on stage. At the time, mass media generally erased or belittled queer lives, presenting LGBTQ characters within a narrow set of stereotypes, but the theatre became a thriving venue for diverse queer representations and performers, including the gloriously singular Marsha P. Johnson.

In the 50 years since Stonewall, several key events have impacted queer history, politics, and lives at the national level. Immediately following the riots, several activist organizations formed as part of the gay liberation movement, including the Gay Liberation Front (GLF), Gay Activists Alliance (GAA), and Street Transvestite Action Revolutionaries (STAR), which was founded in 1970 by Johnson and

Sylvia Rivera. These groups' legacies are felt in other organizations that emerged in the following decades, including the Gay & Lesbian Alliance Against Defamation (GLAAD), Parents and Friends of Lesbians and Gays (PFLAG), the Human Rights Campaign (HRC), Queer Nation, the Lesbian Avengers, and Gay, Lesbian & Straight Education Network (GLSEN). These national organizations, along with many operating at the grassroots and local levels, have worked across the social and political spectra to raise awareness about queer issues and make demands for the advancement of LGBTQ equality.

Like most movements, progress has not always been linear—steps forward are often followed by backlash, revealing the nation's ongoing battle over queer lives. For example, in the area of healthcare, in 1973 the American Psychiatric Association removed homosexuality from its list of official mental illnesses, which for many opened up new possibilities for thinking about LGBTQ health and wellbeing. Then, beginning in 1981, the HIV/AIDS epidemic, which disproportionately affected queer men in its early years, circulated through major cities and claimed the lives of countless individuals. The disease was infamously ignored at all levels of the US government because of its association with the gay community. As a response, activist groups like Gay Men's Health Crisis (GMHC) and AIDS Coalition to Unleash Power (ACT UP) began to form around the country, creating a network of support for the community and employing street theatre and other acts of performance to draw the public's attention to the epidemic. One of the most visible stagings was the AIDS Memorial Quilt, which was displayed for the first time on the National Mall in Washington, DC, on October 11, 1987, during the National March on Washington for Lesbian and Gay Rights. As scientists looked for treatments and sought to educate people on prevention, pop culture and celebrity also played a role in the public battle against AIDS. Figures like Rock Hudson, Freddie Mercury, Pedro Zamora, and Magic Johnson put a face to those living with HIV/AIDS, while people like Princess Diana, Elizabeth Taylor, Elton John, and Liza Minnelli popularized advocacy and support. The theatre community was deeply affected and especially quick to respond to the disease, founding Broadway Cares/Equity Fights AIDS and creating plays and performances that conveyed the personal and political dimensions of the crisis.

This rise in LGBTQ support and advocacy was paralleled by a right-wing, conservative movement beginning in the late 1970s that explicitly used homophobia to rise to power. Figures like Anita Bryant, Jerry Falwell, Jesse Helms, and Ronald Reagan demonized

LGBTQ populations and campaigned against their rights. Queer artists and their works were often targeted as part of these "culture wars," which questioned the role that art should play in public life. Robert Chesley's *Jerker* (1986) and Terrence McNally's *Corpus Christi* (1997) are two of the more prominent examples of theatre productions that generated widespread controversy because of their queer subject matter. Perhaps the most public and contentious battle over queer performance played out against the NEA Four—Karen Finley, John Fleck, Holly Hughes, and Tim Miller—whose case against the National Endowment for the Arts made its way to the Supreme Court in 1998.

Throughout the past 50 years, violence, harassment, and discrimination continued to impact queer lives and propelled the need for hate crimes legislation at the local and state levels. The October 1998 beating, torture, and murder of Matthew Shepard in Laramie, Wyoming, garnered unprecedented national attention and put a spotlight on hate crimes against the queer community, yet it was not until 2009 that President Obama would sign into law the Matthew Shepard and James Byrd Jr. Hate Crimes Prevention Act. Despite the narrative of progress, queer communities of color are erased from media representation that tends to center white queer lives. Sakia Gunn embodies this disparity—the fifteen-year-old lesbian and African American woman was murdered on May 11, 2003, when she and her friends rejected the advances of two men in Newark, New Jersey; her murder investigation and the subsequent media reporting paled in comparison to the Shepard reaction. In fact, queer people of color, and in particular trans people of color, are disproportionally the targets of hate crimes against LGBTQ people. The June 12, 2016, mass shooting at Pulse, an Orlando gay nightclub, once again propelled violence against queer bodies into the national spotlight. The fact that the attack occurred on "Latin Night," and that most of those murdered were people of color, speaks to the heightened vulnerability of queer communities of color.

The pendulum of US federal law has continuously swung in both directions, from the "don't ask, don't tell" policy against openly gay people serving in the military (1993) and the Defense of Marriage Act (1996), to the eventual repealing of the military ban (2011) and the Supreme Court decision to legalize same-sex marriage (2015). Through it all, pop culture and entertainment have brought attention to the debates on LGBTQ equality, with celebrities like Ellen DeGeneres, RuPaul, Neil Patrick Harris, Lea DeLaria, and Ricky Martin contributing to the dialogue on queer identity and visibility.

More recently, celebrities like Elliot Page, Laverne Cox, Lil Nas X, Sara Ramirez, Haaz Sleiman, and Hayley Kiyoko have generated needed attention for trans and intersectional identities in these discussions. These public figures, like their counterparts in the theatre, recognize the important role that performance plays in the advancement of LGBTQ equality. As you will see throughout this collection, queer theatre artists have actively engaged in the social and political spheres, offering their work and advocacy as part of the dialogue and push for progressive change. The entries offer a more detailed and focused discussion of the intersections of queer theatre, history, politics, and culture as they relate to each of the 50 key figures, as well as further readings to learn more about their work and lives.

CREATING QUEER THEATRE

The Stonewall Riots also coincide with a turning point in systems of theatre production in the US. The number of nonprofit off-Broadway and regional theatres exploded in the 1960s and 1970s, creating theatre spaces that, compared to Broadway, could afford to take more risks. Financially supported by subscription audiences and grants, these theatres were also smaller, and therefore could cater to more niche audiences. Nonprofit theatres such as The Public Theater in New York City and Victory Gardens Theater in Chicago became creative homes for queer theatre artists. Alternative venues, such as P.S. 122 in New York and Highways Performance Space in Santa Monica, California—both co-founded by queer performance artist Tim Miller—also regularly presented bold and boundary-pushing queer theatre.

In addition, following the example created by the Black theatre movement, gay and lesbian theatres sprouted up around the country, forming what became known as a "Purple Circuit" that produced LGBTQ-themed plays for LGBTQ audiences. Even with the acceptance of some queer theatre within the so-called mainstream, queer venues such as Theatre Rhinoceros in San Francisco, founded in 1977, have continued to thrive. Other queer venues still producing today include Chicago's About Face Theatre, Los Angeles's Celebration Theatre, San Diego's Diversionary Theatre, Omaha's Snap! Productions, Boston's Theatre Offensive, Portland's Triangle Productions, Minneapolis's 20% Theatre, Memphis's Emerald Theatre, Richmond's Triangle Players, Atlanta's Out Front Theatre, Madison's StageQ, and New York's TOSOS.

Some nonprofit and Purple Circuit theatres, although much more inclusive today, tended to focus primarily on plays representing the cis-gender gay white men who had the cultural capital to create and fill theatres. This disparity in resources and critical attention meant that women and BIPOC artists had to create homes in alternate venues. Lesbian and feminist theatre makers created companies like New York's WOW Café, founded in 1981, and San Francisco's Brava! for Women in the Arts, started in 1987. Other community-based theatres have also long served as locations for representations existing at the intersection of queerness, race, and ethnicity. These include the Asian American companies East West Players and Ma-Yi Theater Company, the Latinx companies INTAR and Borderlands Theatre, and the African American companies National Black Theatre, Penumbra Theatre, and The Fire This Time Festival. With the rise of queer studies, universities also served as host institutions to queer artists who spoke with voices not often heard in mainstream theatres.

IDENTIFYING 50 KEY FIGURES

The guiding criteria we've used to identify the 50 key figures for this collection are *identity*, *representation*, and *impact*. We selected theatre makers who publicly identify as LGBTQ; who create theatre that represents queer people, relationships, history, and/or social issues; and whose work contributes in a meaningful or innovative way to queer theatrical culture. To create a truly diverse group portrait, we selected some artists who will be well-known to most readers, taking a deeper look at the impact of their work, but we've also included some figures who may not be as familiar. In this vein, we introduce readers to exciting new artists who have begun to generate critical attention and are positioned to keep doing so for future generations. We also intentionally bring together artists from different periods, including those whose work emerged in the 1970s and those with more recent careers in the twenty-first century, which allows the entries in this volume to speak across generations and to shed light on historic practices and cultural shifts within the industry. For example, the entries on Muriel Miguel and Ty Defoe offer generational perspectives into Indigenous representation and artistic practice, while the essays on Sharon Bridgforth and Chisa Hutchinson provide insight into the ways queer Black women create theatre in different moments in time. Our selections also include artists working in different geographical regions and urban centers of the nation, including Chicago, Houston, Los Angeles, Phoenix, San Francisco, and St. Louis, illuminating the different approaches that queer artists take to creating theatre in their communities.

Any list of 50 key figures is by definition incomplete, since there are countless individuals involved in the creation of queer theatre. Therefore, we have encouraged our contributors to acknowledge the deeply collective nature of theatrical art, highlighting each figure's collaborators, influences, fellow travelers, and inheritors, positioning the artist within the larger field of queer theatre and acknowledging queer collectivities and genealogies. In order to ensure greater cultural diversity and inclusivity, we have in many cases selected a key figure as representative of a subgenre or field of production. For example, it would be impossible to include all the significant artists who created theatre that responded to the AIDS crisis, such as Victor Bumbalo, Robert Chesley, William Hoffman, Michael Kearns, Craig Lucas, Rebecca Ransom, Paul Rudnick, Pomo Afro Homos, and Nicky Silver. But within the entry on Tony Kushner, the reader will find him "in conversation" with Larry Kramer, and the entry on Terrence McNally includes a tribute from his protégé Matthew López. Similarly, the entry on Ana María Simo acknowledges the collaborative nature of her endeavors in lesbian-feminist theatre, which included playwright Sarah Schulman and producer Linda Chapman, both extraordinary theatre makers and activists in their own right.

We've also assembled a collection of contributors as diverse and inclusive as our 50 key figures, including theatre scholars and practitioners who approach the art from a variety of perspectives, working with varied aesthetic, cultural, and political investments. We asked the contributors to bring their individual and distinctive critical lenses through which to view the following questions: What unique contribution or impact has this artist made in the realm of queer theatre, in the broader theatre world, and within US culture? How do they engage with their particular time and place, especially in relation to movements in queer culture and politics? What are their innovations and interventions, and how has their work impacted artists and audiences?

Within the commercial realm of mainstream Broadway theatre, this book includes artists like Harvey Fierstein, William Finn, Nathan Lane, Joe Mantello, Terrence McNally, Billy Porter, and George C. Wolfe. But this list is admittedly highly selective and hardly exhaustive, and a book with twice as many pages might have added figures like Tennessee Williams and Edward Albee, theatrical giants who impacted the US theatre both pre- and post-Stonewall, but who have already received copious scholarly attention. Other key figures could have included Michael Bennett and Nicholas Dante, who created groundbreaking queer representation in *A Chorus Line* (1975);

Lanford Wilson, who created gay plays at the Caffe Cino in the 1960s and took his play *Fifth of July* to Broadway in 1980; or Jordan Roth, who has served as producer on numerous Broadway shows with queer content, including the 2018 revival of *Torch Song* and the musicals *Head Over Heels* (2018) and *Jagged Little Pill* (2019). Recent years have also seen a slew of out performers playing LGBTQ roles, including Jenn Colella, Ariana DeBose, Jesse Tyler Ferguson, Jonathan Groff, Beth Malone, Jeremy Pope, and Michael Urie, to name but a few. Additionally, there are plenty of stellar theatre artists, such as Eva Le Gallienne, Lorraine Hansberry, and Stephen Sondheim, who, while not necessarily hiding their own queerness, did not substantially focus their theatrical work on LGBTQ representation.

But we have intentionally limited the number of Broadway notables to make space for theatre artists working in other systems of production, including nonprofit regional and off-Broadway theatres, experimental and off-off-Broadway performance venues, the queer theatres of the Purple Circuit, and spaces dedicated to women and people of color. We have especially featured figures who established their own theatre companies or theatre spaces in order to create the queer representation that was lacking in the dominant culture. From producers like John Glines (The Glines) and Ellie Covan (Dixon Place) to artists like Charles Ludlam (Ridiculous Theatrical Company), Ana María Simo (Medusa's Revenge), Joan Lipkin (That Uppity Theatre Company), Moisés Kaufman (Tectonic Theatre), Sharon Bridgforth (root wy'mn theatre company), and Haruna Lee (harunalee theater company), numerous queer theatre makers built their own stages, changing the way queer theatre could be made and seen. We've also included artistic leaders who have used their positions to nurture and support the work of other queer artists, such as George C. Wolfe at the Public Theatre, Chay Yew at Victory Gardens, Guillermo Reyes at Teatro Bravo, and Snehal Desai at East West Players. There are also teachers like María Irene Fornés and Paula Vogel who have profoundly influenced whole generations of theatre artists.

The entries in this collection also shed light onto artists and works that respond to and interrogate the role of the body in performance. In the area of queer disability, the book includes an early pioneer (Ron Whyte) as well as a current leader (Joan Lipkin) as key figures in a field that includes John Belluso, Josh Castille, Terry Galloway, Ryan J. Haddad, Antoine Hunter, Nomy Lamm, Chella Man, Maria Palacios, and Kelsy Schoenhaar. Similarly, you will find trans, two-spirit, non-binary, and gender-nonconforming (GNC) artists, including those actively engaged in challenging dominant representations of gender within the theatre. We position theatre makers like Kate Bornstein, Will Davis, Ty Defoe, Haruna Lee, and Taylor Mac as key figures within a larger field of trans and GNC artists, which also includes playwrights Preston Max Allen, MJ Kaufman, Basil Kreimendahl, Azure D. Osborne-Lee, Sylvan Oswald, and Kit Yan, as well as performers like Becca Blackwell, Jess Barbagallo, Alexandra Billings, Justin Vivian Bond, Theo Germaine, Pooya Mohseni, L Morgan Lee, Shakina Nayack, Peppermint, and TL Thompson. Many of these artists are associated with organizations like Trans Lab, which was founded in 2018. As its website states,

> Plays by trans and gender nonconforming (TGNC) writers are a rarity in American theater. As transgender stories are co-opted, commercialized, and misrepresented by cisgender writers, Trans Lab fellowship supports the creation of a critical mass of TGNC plays by TGNC writers.[1]

It is important to note that, although our title indicates that the book focuses on figures who are making theatre within the United States, we queer hegemonic notions of nationhood with artists working from indigenous perspectives (Muriel Miguel, Cherríe Moraga, Ty Defoe), as well as artists with origins in the Commonwealth of Puerto Rico (Miguel Piñero and Edwin Sánchez) and outside of the US: Reza Abdoh (Iran), María Irene Fornés (Cuba), Moisés Kaufman (Venezuela), Haruna Lee (Hong Kong), Clint Ramos (Philippines), Guillermo Reyes (Chile), Ana María Simo (Cuba), and Chay Yew (Singapore). Theatre is normally rooted in the specific location of live performance, but it also has the ability to circulate across national boundaries. While this book has limited itself to artists working primarily in the US, we recognize the impact of queer artists from around the globe. The most visible of these are perhaps the actors, including several from the UK who have found success on Broadway, such as Ian McKellen, Stephen Fry, Rupert Everett, and Miriam Margolyes, though it is important to note that performers like Lindsay Kemp, Jackie Kay, and Mika Onyx Johnson have also influenced alternative spaces and artists. Indigenous (Cree) queer playwright Tomson Highway has written about issues affecting First Nations peoples in Canada and is most known for his plays *The Rez Sisters* (1986) and *Dry Lips Oughta Move to Kapuskasing* (1989). In 2000, Mexican lesbian theatre director and cabaret performer Jesusa Rodríguez won an Obie Award for *Las Horas de Belén: A Book of Hours*, her collaboration with Mabou Mines, which was performed at P.S. 122.

Additionally, Raphael Khouri, a trans Jordanian theatre artist, is credited with writing the first Arab transgender play, *She He Me* (2019), presented in the US in the National Queer Theatre's internationally focused Criminal Queerness Festival. In fact, one can find representation in queer theatre festivals around the globe, from Dublin to Delhi.

Like so many of the artists in the collection, we too would like to acknowledge our predecessors who made our work possible. Scholars and critics writing in the 1970s and 1980s helped to shape the understanding of queer theatre as a distinct form of cultural production and representation, including: Stefan Brecht's seminal *Queer Theatre* (1978); William M. Hoffman's introduction to *Gay Plays: The First Collection* (1979); Kaier Curtin's *"We Can Always Call Them Bulgarians": The Emergence of Lesbians and Gay Men on the American Stage* (1987); Sue-Ellen Case's *Feminism and Theatre* (1988); and Jill Dolan's *Feminist Spectator as Critic* (1988). The rise of queer studies within academia brought about much more scholarship on queer theatre, including book-length works offering an inclusive historical overview, such as John Clum's *Acting Gay* (1992); Alan Sinfield's *Out on Stage* (1999); and *The Gay & Lesbian Theatrical Legacy: A Biographical Dictionary of Major Figures in American Stage History in the Pre-Stonewall Era* (2005), edited by Billy J. Harbin, Kim Marra, and Robert Schanke.

Queer theatre and performance studies have become so expansive that it is impossible to name every example of significant scholarship. However, some of the groundbreaking studies that highlight diverse queer artists and historical perspectives are: José Esteban Muñoz's *Disidentifications: Queers of Color and the Performance of Politics* (1999); *The Queerest Art: Essays on Lesbian and Gay Theater* (2002), edited by Alisa Solomon and Framji Minwalla; *Cast Out: Queer Lives in Theater* (2006), edited by Robin Bernstein; Jill Dolan's *Theatre & Sexuality* (2010); and Kate Davy's *Lady Dicks and Lesbian Brothers: Staging the Unimaginable at the WOW Café Theatre* (2011). Books that expanded the field by integrating performance texts and scholarship include: *O Solo Homo: The New Queer Performance* (1998), edited by Holly Hughes and David Román; *Blacktino Queer Performance* (2016), edited by E. Patrick Johnson and Ramón Rivera-Servera; and *The Methuen Drama Book of Trans Plays* (2021) edited by Leanna Keyes, Lindsey Mantoan, and Angela Farr Schiller. Queer theatre scholarship is a rich and ever-expanding field, and we encourage readers to explore works beyond this initial list, including the many examples found in the further readings at the end of each entry.

A note on numbers: although, in keeping with the title of this book, this introduction has consistently referred to "50 key figures," the careful reader will notice that some entries feature more than one "figure," with collectives such as the NEA Four and the Five Lesbian Brothers. Those fond of counting may even find more than 50 entries. We hope that such readers will find it possible to forgive this very queer failure to stay within the expected parameters. We simply couldn't contain ourselves.

TOWARDS A QUEERER AND MORE INCLUSIVE FUTURE

We began this introduction by acknowledging the role that Marsha P. Johnson played in queer history—as well as queer theatre history—to highlight the intersections of politics and performance in the United States. More than 50 years later, queer artists of color are still fighting for greater visibility, opportunities, and equity in the theatre. And, once again, the social and political are influencing and pushing artists to rethink the role that theatre can play in movements for social justice.

The murder of George Floyd by Minneapolis police on May 25, 2020, sparked national protests and outrage against police brutality and the racial disparity in fatal police shootings. As video of Floyd's arrest and murder circulated online, people filled the streets in support of Black Lives Matter (BLM). The BLM movement was founded in 2013 by three Black women—Alicia Garza, Patrisse Cullors, and Opal Tometi—as a response to the acquittal of Trayvon Martin's murderer in a Florida court. The shooting death of Martin, a seventeen-year-old African American, is one of many instances where Black lives have been lost to the hands of police or where the judicial system failed to enact justice, including the murders of Ahmaud Arbery, Michael Brown, Philando Castile, Stephon Clark, Samuel DuBose, Eric Garner, Freddie Gray, Akai Gurley, Botham Jean, Atatiana Jefferson, Tamir Rice, and Breonna Taylor, as well as Tony McDade, a transgender man shot by police in Tallahassee, Florida, on May 27, 2020. It is important to note that, from its inception, BLM has put LGBTQ lives and voices at the center of its activist work and mission—in fact, Garza and Cullors both identify as queer. In an August 2020 interview with *The Advocate,* Garza says, "I'm young enough and old enough to remember the fight around same-sex marriage and really all of the cultural and policy shifts that had to lead to the highest court in the land saying that love is love." She continues, "With that being said, there have been critiques over a long period of time that within LGBTQ communities that largely communities of color and Black communities have been pushed out of that fold."[2]

As a response to BLM, different segments of society, including the political, economic, and cultural arenas, were forced to reflect on the ways their structures contribute to ongoing systemic racism. The critique against theatrical institutions and practices followed, shedding light onto issues that have plagued the industry for decades. One of the most significant of these endeavors was We See You, White American Theater (WSYWAT), which launched on June 8, 2020. The group's website explains,

> In reaction to civil unrest in our country, we—Black, Indigenous and People of Color (BIPOC) theatre makers—formed a collective of multi-generational, multi-disciplinary, early career, emerging and established artists, theater managers, executives, students, administrators, dramaturges and producers, to address the scope and pervasiveness of anti-Blackness and racism in the American theater.[3]

On July 8, WSYWAT released its 29-page manifesto and list of demands, which fall under the following categories: cultural competency; working conditions and hiring practices; artistic and curatorial practices; transparency; compensation; accountability and boards; funding and resource demands from BIPOC theatre organizations; commercial theatre and Broadway; unions; press; and academic and professional training programs.[4] Many of the signatories to the document are queer theatre artists and many of them are included in this collection.

Unfortunately, the rise in hate crimes over the past few years has meant that theatres and artistic organizations have needed to make public statements against violence at an increasing rate. On March 23, 2021, as a response to the murders of eight people in Atlanta—six of them Asian women—the Consortium of Asian American Theaters & Artists (CAATA) announced that it would develop programs to combat anti-Asian hate and violence; three weeks later, a second statement outlined its four-part initiative that included a social media campaign and webinar series.[5] Signatories to the anti-Asian hate statement include affinity groups like the Asian American Arts Alliance, the Asian American Performers Action Coalition (AAPAC), and Contemporary Asian Theatre Scene (CATS), as well as individual artists, including queer theatre makers Snehal Desai, Chay Yew, and Clint Ramos.

The Trans March on Broadway, which occurred on September 6, 2021, is yet another example of activism within the queer theatre community. Organized by Black trans theatre performer Sis, the march made demands for greater trans representation in casting and a recognition of trans issues in the industry. This was followed by the October 5, 2021, Jeremy O. Harris announcement that he would halt plans for the Center Theatre Group production of his critically acclaimed *Slave Play* in protest against the lack of women playwrights in their season. The move drew renewed attention to the continuing struggle being fought by longstanding groups like League of Professional Theatre Women and newer collectives like the Gender Parity Task Force and The Kilroys, which advocate for female, transgender, and nonbinary theatre artists. Collectively, these instances of activism illustrate the intersectionality of race, gender, and sexuality in the US theatre, as well as the ongoing need for collective action in order to create change.

Indeed, we recognize that we are facing an uncertain future. Fifty years post-Stonewall, and with the BLM movement and other social justice movements transforming our country and theatre industry, queer theatre must ask: What comes next? Who will be a part of it? And what will we stand for? The artists that create the next 50 years of queer theatre will build upon the legacies of the past while also offering new and exciting interpretations of the social and political realities of queer lives. What new forms and aesthetics will emerge? What will the next milestones be? What processes of collective and communal theatre making will enable these works? What will our audiences look like and how will artists continue to challenge them? If anything, the past 50 years have shown us that the queer community is brilliant and creative, defiant and resilient, and the next 50 years promise to do the same.

It is perhaps fitting to end this introduction with a shout-out to Chitra Ganesh, the queer Indian American visual artist whose work *Cadre* graces the cover of this book. *Cadre* is a site-specific mural commissioned by Contemporary Arts Museum Houston as part of its 2019 special exhibition "Stonewall 50," which brought together a diverse range of artists to reflect on and celebrate the Stonewall Riots' enduring legacy. Her piece is an assemblage of mixed media, composed of acrylic, beads, textiles, ink, marbles, hair extensions, wire, spray paint, clay, jewelry, sequins, chalk, glitter, and many other materials. As Ganesh explains,

> *Cadre* invokes the politicized underpinnings of collective formation, imagining an alternate family portrait of queer superheroes. The heterogeneity of materials points to the makeshift,

INTRODUCTION

improvisational modes harnessed in acts of queer performance and resistance of marginalized queer and trans subjects who conjured glamorous avatar transformations with a surprising economy of materials and means.[6]

The figures in Ganesh's mural evoke a spirited theatricality that is communicated through vibrant colors and an assortment of lines and forms that convey power, expressive freedom, conviviality, and solidarity. Her queer superheroes—like the 50 queer theatre superheroes of our book—form a diverse collective that occupies and reflects the artistic space of queer history. The celebratory and playful nature of the work is a testament to the queer joy that can be generated through collaboration and creativity. It is our hope that this book inspires the same kind of joy, pride, and celebration for the field of queer theatre and the many figures whose efforts have made it—and will continue to make it—thrive.

NOTES

1 Trans Lab, www.transtheaterlab.org
2 Michelle Garcia, "BLM Co-Founder Alicia Garza is Bringing Black Queer Folks to the Polls," *The Advocate*, August 11, 2020, www.advocate.com/exclusives/2020/8/11/blm-co-founder-alicia-garza-bringing-black-queer-folks-polls
3 "About," *We See You, White American Theater*, www.weseeyouwat.com/about
4 "BIPOC Demands for White American Theatre," *We See You, White American Theater*, July 8, 2020, www.weseeyouwat.com/demands
5 "CAATA Condemns Anti-Asian Hate and Violence in Second Statement," *Consortium of Asian American Theaters & Artists*, April 16, 2021, www.caata.net/caata-condemns-anti-asian-hate-and-violence
6 Personal interview with Jimmy A. Noriega, January 31, 2022.

REZA ABDOH
(Tehran, Iran, 1963–1995)
Joseph Cermatori

In the span of just a few short years, playwright and director Reza Abdoh produced a body of work that transformed queer theatre at the end of the twentieth century. He specialized in massive performance pieces, often staged environmentally or in site-specific locations, that addressed themes of violence, oppression, corruption, sexual desire, transgression, spirituality, grief, and transcendence. Abdoh created his most important works with Dar A Luz, the theatre company he founded in 1991 whose name means "to give birth" or "to bring to light" in Spanish. He led this company of regular collaborators for four years until his death from AIDS-related complications on May 11, 1995.

The early details of Abdoh's life are not always certain, partly because of his tendency to mythologize parts of his biography in public accounts. He was born to a prominent Iranian family on February 23, 1963, and moved to the United Kingdom as a youth. In 1970, he attended a performance of Peter Brook's *A Midsummer Night's Dream*, which he later counted among his earliest artistic influences. His family relocated in the aftermath of the Iranian Revolution to West Covina, California, and the young Abdoh completed a single semester at the University of Southern California in nearby Los Angeles. Shortly thereafter, he began working as a director in a number of small LA venues, staging plays from 1983 to 1985 by Howard Brenton, William Shakespeare, Franz Xaver Kroetz, and David Henry Hwang. Starting with *A Medea: Requiem for a Boy with a White White Toy* (1986), an adaptation of Euripides' tragedy, he began developing original projects of his own for both the stage and the emerging medium of video. Having established himself on the West Coast, Abdoh leaped to nationwide prominence in 1989 on receiving the Princess Grace Foundation's US Theater Fellowship Award.

Abdoh's fame rests on a handful of mature works created between 1990 and 1994 that unleashed the explosive energies of the theatre to an unparalleled degree. In the first of these, *Father Was a Peculiar Man* (1990, produced by En Garde Arts), a deconstruction of Dostoevsky's *Brothers Karamazov*, Abdoh's cast of 60 performers took over the sprawling streets of Manhattan's Meatpacking District at a time when it still housed actual slaughterhouses and queer cruising grounds. The production involved multiple, simultaneous plots, played at a frenetic pace, with grotesque and violent imagery, including simulated acts of sexual violence and the assassination of John F. Kennedy. In Abdoh's words, the script (co-written with Mira-Lani Oglesby) sought to capture certain "themes from the book, the disintegration of the family, killing the authority figure and our perpetual and futile efforts to regain lost innocence."[1]

That same year, in *The Hip-Hop Waltz of Eurydice* (1990, Los Angeles Theatre Center), he adapted the Greek myth of Orpheus into "a parable of the repression of homosexuality," with Orpheus and Eurydice's genders swapped.[2] A similar interrogation of repressive homophobia animates his massive spectacle *Bogeyman* (1991, Los Angeles Theatre Center), whose three-story set allowed for constant, simultaneous action across nine separate rooms. In 1991, he relocated on a full-time basis to New York to produce his last three major works, all site-specific productions. These include *The Law of Remains* (1992, at the abandoned Hotel Diplomat), discussed below; *Tight Right White* (1993), an immersive denunciation of racism in America based on the blaxploitation film *Mandingo* (1975); and *Quotations from a Ruined City* (1994, co-written with Salar Abdoh), an elegy for the devastations wrought by Western imperialism and militarism.

The Law of Remains is arguably Abdoh's most representative work. Staged in a ruined hotel ballroom, it "depicts" Andy Warhol making a film about the queer American serial killer and cannibal Jeffrey Dahmer (named Jeffrey Snarling in *Remains*). Any semblance of a coherent plot or psychological characters is continually interrupted in Abdoh's staging by fragments of spoken text, musical dance breaks, frequent and decontextualized sound effects, slapstick humor, graphic descriptions of pornographic sex, and bloody Grand Guignol images. The piece allegorizes the banal violence and homophobia of mainstream society, particularly in the face of an epidemic that disproportionately killed queers of color, who were also Dahmer's victims. It ends in a space described as "Heaven" that visually suggests both a hospital and a graveyard, where Snarling is among the dead and "God is a Puerto Rican drag queen."[3]

Abdoh's will stipulates that "no future performances of Reza Abdoh productions will ever be permitted."[4] Although his large-scale works toured the international festival circuit during his lifetime—including Canada, Spain, France, the Netherlands, Austria, and Germany—he intended that they would never be remounted posthumously. He conceived works not just for specific locations, but also for a specific ensemble of actors, Dar A Luz stalwarts like Tom Pearl, Juliana Francis, Tom Fitzpatrick, Tony Torn, and his romantic partner Brenden Doyle. In one of his printed scripts, he inserts the following note:

> In my written texts for the theatre I replace characters' names with the names of the people who are performing the roles. In my view, this creates a more objective context. I am not so interested in how the actors "play act" their roles but rather how they live them onstage.[5]

His works thus refuse reenactment. His most significant creations survive today only as remnants: printed performance texts and archival videos filmed by his frequent collaborator Adam Soch.

For this reason, Abdoh's output approaches Antonin Artaud's vision of a theatre no longer oriented around dramatic texts capable of being restaged. As Artaud wrote, "The theatre is the only place in the world where a gesture, once made, can never be made in the same way twice."[6] And indeed, Artaud is regularly cited as a major influence over Abdoh's artistic methods. Both men sought contact with what Abdoh called "Dionysian forces," dealing in dark, nightmarish, and sometimes graphic imagery.[7] In keeping with Artaud's manifesto for "The Theatre of Cruelty," Abdoh sought total control over the performance conditions of his pieces, creating a physical and spiritual trial for actors and viewers alike. In *Tight Right White* and *Law of Remains*, for example, spectators were effectively engulfed on all sides by a pandemonium of frenzied performance activity. In one review, *Village Voice* critic Michael Feingold described *Tight Right White* as

> a piece of intense and revolting accomplishment, executed with enormous skill, that assaults audiences with a near-two-hour barrage of obscenely racist images, for purgative purposes: a psychological enema, shoved up the id of liberal theatregoers to expel the unhealthy imprints a racist society has deposited there.[8]

This Artaudian language of assault and barrage could similarly be applied to Abdoh's other works.

Beyond the Theatre of Cruelty, Abdoh's influences and networks of artistic affiliation extend in a number of other directions, both classical and modern. Clear debts can be traced to the political theatre of Bertolt Brecht and John Vaccaro's Play-House of the Ridiculous. He also claimed to have acted as an extra in Robert Wilson's 1972 performance "KA MOUNTAIN AND GUARDenia TERRACE" in Shiraz, Iran, and to have studied Kathakali performance in India in 1979, although these claims are disputed and might best be considered declarations of artistic kinship. His interests in the arts and culture were wide-ranging: his performances juxtaposed elements of traditional Iranian mourning drama (*Ta'ziyeh*), Latin American *telenovelas*, the infernal landscapes of Dante and Brueghel, the visual imagery of sadomasochistic sex, punk subcultures, hip-hop and classical music, drag performance, and many other sources.

During his brief career, Abdoh was widely seen as a torchbearer for the next wave of radical theatre artists, following the generation of experimental theatre directors that had emerged between 1976 and 1990 to include Robert Wilson, Elizabeth LeCompte, and Richard Foreman. A wide range of contemporary American directors and playwrights, including Michael Counts, Caden Manson, Jim Findlay, Peter Sellars, and Jeremy O. Harris, cite him as a source of artistic inspiration. Outside the theatre, his work bears a further pronounced resemblance to a younger generation of queer performance makers in the contemporary visual arts, including Ryan Trecartin and Jacolby Satterwhite. Writing in *Artforum* in the wake of a MoMA PS1 retrospective of Abdoh's work, Jennifer Krasiniski asserted: "It is not an overstatement to say that had Reza Abdoh lived even one more year, had he created even one more production, American theatre would look very different now."[9]

NOTES

1 Quoted in Stephen Holden, "Review/Theater; A Carnival of Satire and Savagery, with a Karamazov as Ringmaster," *New York Times,* July 11, 1990.
2 Daniel Mufson, ed., *Reza Abdoh*. Baltimore, MD: Johns Hopkins University Press, 1999, 3.
3 Reza Abdoh, *The Law of Remains*, in *Plays for the End of the Century*, edited by Bonnie Marranca. Baltimore, MD: Johns Hopkins University Press, 1991, 91.
4 New York Public Library, Archives and Manuscripts. n.d. "Reza Abdoh Collections of Papers: Collection Overview." Accessed June 1, 2021. http://archives.nypl.org/the/21508

5 Abdoh, *Law of Remains*, 11.
6 Antonin Artaud, "No More Masterpieces," in *The Theater and its Double*, translated by Mary Caroline Richards. New York: Grove Press, 1958, 75.
7 Mufson, *Reza Abdoh*, 28.
8 Ibid., 104.
9 Jennifer Krasinski, "Loosed Threads." *Artforum*, vol. 57, no. 2 (October 2018). www.artforum.com/print/201808/jennifer-krasinski-on-the-art-of-reza-abdoh-76730

FURTHER READING

Cermatori, Joseph. "Reza Abdoh Today: Posthumous Reflections Fifty-Five Years After His Birth." *PAJ: A Journal of Performance and Art*, vol. 40, no. 3 (September 2018): 1–15.

Soch, Adam, dir. *Reza Abdoh: Theater Visionary*. Cultures on Film. New York, 2015. https://vimeo.com/ondemand/rezaabdoh/93815467?autoplay=1

LUIS ALFARO
(Los Angeles, California, 1963–)
Patricia Ybarra

A child of activist farmworker parents who were members of the United Farm Workers in Delano, Luis Alfaro was born and raised in the Pico Union district of Los Angeles, one of the poorest areas of L.A. From a young age, Alfaro was a storyteller who never shied away from the beauty and terror of his experiences. As he explained in a 2016 LAMDA keynote, his first story, about a man who stumbled onto his lawn after being run through with a pool cue, got him expelled from school, but convinced him to be a writer. As Alfaro suggests, "My desire is memory and yet I know it is not enough to just remember. I am learning that writing is the only way to pray."[1]

The link between spirituality, memory, and writing—largely in the voice of queer, femme, and feminist personae—lays at the crux of Alfaro's body of work, which includes poetry, prose, performance, and plays. Alfaro began his writing career as a poet, then as a performance artist. He worked alongside other queer Latinx artists such as Monica Palacios and Nao Bustamante. This was not surprising given the ways in which venues such as Highways and Teatro Viva! nurtured solo artists such as Palacios, Alfaro, Tim Miller, and Holly Hughes. Alfaro was also an activist with ACT UP/LA and other Latinx HIV organizations. His participation in protests at the height of the HIV/AIDS crisis in the 1980s and 1990s landed him a fair share of arrests before he won a 1997 MacArthur Genius Grant, awarded in recognition of pieces such as *Downtown* (1994) and *Cuerpo Politizado* (1994), which explore the complexities of gay Latinx identity. A well-known passage that was a part of both works exemplifies his deeply poignant formulation of intersectional identity:

> I am a queer Chicano
> A native in no land
> An orphan of Aztlán
> The pocho son of farmworker parents

> The Mexicans only want me
> when they want me to
> talk about Mexico
> But what about
> Mexican queers in L.A.?
>
> The Queers only want me
> when they need
> to add color
> add spice
> like *salsa picante*
> on the side.[2]

Alfaro credits his move into playwriting primarily to María Irene Fornés, who, while infamously resistant to being categorized as queer and/or Latina, arguably influenced Latinx playwriting more than any other figure of the twentieth and twenty-first centuries. Perhaps it is Fornés's influence that led Alfaro to bring the rich inner life of working-class women and queers onto the stage. While many of his characters share his Latinx Los Angelenx background, he also writes working-class Anglo characters, of varying genders and serostatuses. *Straight as a Line* (2000), which chronicles the end of life of a British HIV+ man and his Las Vegas hostess mother is but one example. It is telling that some of this text is found in his earlier prose work, *Bitter Homes and Gardens* (1995), in the mouth of a child of Latinx working-class parents. While these experiences are not interchangeable, they do speak to some of the shared sentiments of working-class queers and femmes who are stumbling towards a feminism that Cherríe Moraga would call "theory in the flesh."[3]

Alfaro is an artist of great generosity who makes work within and from his experience of community. Two clear examples are *Body of Faith* (2003), created with Cornerstone Theater in Los Angeles, and his more recent Greek Trilogy of plays (2003–2012): *Electricidad*, *Oedipus El Rey*, and *Mojada*. *Body of Faith* was created as an exploration of the spiritual practices of gay, queer, and trans believers. A key line from that play reveals Alfaro's spiritual poeticism: "The *trans* in transgender is also the *trans* of translation is also the *trans* of transformation is also the *trans* of transcendence is also the *trans* of transgression is also the *trans* of transubstantiation."[4] His award-winning Greek Trilogy, meanwhile, links the violence that Latinx people face at the border and the prison industrial system to the epic struggles of Greek heroes. As Rosa Andújar describes them, Electra, Oedipus, and Medea are "the daughter of a gang leader who vows revenge, a young man newly released from prison and an undocumented seamstress who toils endlessly to ensure the future of her son."[5] While Alfaro is not the first queer Latinx artist to play with the Greeks—Cherríe Moraga's *Mexican Medea (The Hungry Woman)* comes to mind—he is the one who has most intensely engaged with the idea of using Greek drama to talk about the difference between fate and destiny as part of life in Latinx LA. Each of his plays incorporates stories about people he has met doing work in prisons and other community centers. While Alfaro's Greek plays have fewer openly gay characters than his previous works, all of them continue his critique of heteromasculinity by exploring the desires of women and femmes, implicitly linking homophobia and misogyny in contemporary culture. His other short works, such as the *Gardens of Aztlan* (2010) and the theatre for youth play *Black Butterfly, Jaguar Girl, Piñata Woman and Other Superhero Girls Like Me* (2010), continue this commitment.

Perhaps this is why Alfaro has been so important for the development of queer theory in the Americas. It is not an accident that both David Román and José Muñoz developed their thinking watching Alfaro's performances. In *Acts of Intervention*, Román states, "In *Federal Building*, Alfaro demonstrates how AIDS issues for people of color cannot be understood without an analysis of race and class."[6] Muñoz, in an essay which became part of *Sense of Brown*, theorizes his critique of the anti-relational thesis and the rejection of family through Alfaro's work. He writes:

> Family has been criticized in contemporary queer theory as an oppressive totality. But such a characterization from the perspective of queers of color is deeply reductive. On one hand it is true that not all families of color affirm their queer children. On the other hand, the generalized gay community often feels like a sea of whiteness to queers of color, and thus the imagined family is often a refuge. The family is a space where all those elements of the self that are fetishized, ignored or rejected in the larger queer world are suddenly revalorized. Alfaro's memory performance attunes us to those enabling characteristics.[7]

Alfaro is also an important producer and mentor to the next generation of artists. As a producer/dramaturg, alongside Diane Rodriguez, he led the Latino Theatre Initiative at the Mark Taper Forum, launching and/or supporting the careers of many Latinx playwrights: Monica Palacios, Marga Gomez, Alina Troyano, and Eduardo Machado, among them.⁸ As a resident playwright, he worked to make small systemic changes—such as advocating for the hiring of Spanish-speaking box office employees—in all the places he goes and stays. Unlike most playwrights, Alfaro is really in residence, staying with theatre companies for years rather than months so as to build true community. The transformation of the theatres in which he worked as resident artist or playwright—Oregon Shakespeare Festival, Victory Gardens, and Hartford Stage—attest to his success. He is once again putting on the producer hat as Associate Producer at Center Theatre Group. Alongside his mentoring of students, as Associate Professor of Playwriting at USC, Alfaro will undoubtedly continue to change US theatre for the better. Alfaro is justly lauded for his creative work and vision; it is also important to lift up his ethic of service, which was incubated by his activist family and the communities of faith in which he was raised. Alfaro's quotation of Rabindranath Tagore in an interview underscores his commitment: "I slept and dreamt that life was joy. I awoke and saw that life was service. I acted and behold, service was joy."⁹

NOTES

1 "Biographical Statement," in *His: Brilliant New Fiction by Gay Writers*, edited by Robert Drake with Terry Wolverton. London: Faber & Faber, 1995, 233.
2 Luis Alfaro, *Downtown*, in *O Solo Homo*, edited by David Román and Holly Hughes. New York: Grove, 1998, 343.
3 Cherríe Moraga and Gloria Anzaldúa, *This Bridge Called My Back: Writings by Radical Women of Color*, 4th edition. Albany, NY: SUNY Press, 2015, 19.
4 Luis Alfaro, *Body of Faith*. New York: Dramatists Play Service, 2007, 87.
5 Rosa Andújar, "Introduction," in Luis Alfaro, *The Greek Trilogy of Luis Alfaro Electricidad, Oedipus El Rey and Mojada*, edited by Rosa Andújar. London: Methuen, 2021, 1.
6 David Román, *Acts of Intervention*, Bloomington, IN: Indiana University Press, 1998, 194.
7 José Muñoz, *A Sense of Brown*, edited by Tavia Nyong'o and Joshua Chamber-Letson. Durham, NC: Duke University Press, 2021, 72. This essay was originally published in Alisa Solomon and Framji Minwalla's *The Queerest Art* in 2002 and in a different format in Coco Fusco's *Corpus Delecti* in 2000.
8 For more on this initiative, see Chantal Rodriguez, *The Latino Theatre Initiative/Center Theatre Group Papers, 1980–2005*. Los Angeles, CA: University of California Chicano Research Center, 2011.
9 Luis Alfaro, interview with Trevor Boffone, 50 Playwrights Project, April 22, 2016. https://50playwrights.org/2016/04/22/luis-alfaro/

FURTHER READING

Alfaro, Luis. *The Greek Trilogy of Luis Alfaro*, edited by Rosa Andújar. London: Methuen, 2021.
Muñoz, José. "Queer Theatre, Queer Theory: Luis Alfaro's Cuerpo Politizado." In *A Sense of Brown*, edited by Tavia N'yongo and Joshua Chambers-Letson. Durham, NC: Duke University Press, 2021, 59–77.

KATE BORNSTEIN
(Asbury Park, New Jersey, 1948–)
Rye Gentleman

Attempting a succinct description of Kate Bornstein and their work feels at odds with who Bornstein is, how she understands herself, and how their work has helped many of us better understand ourselves. (I alternate between she/her and they/them pronouns for Bornstein, as those are the pronouns she uses.) In the self-written biography that accompanies her contribution to Holly Hughes and David Román's *O Solo Homo* (1998), Bornstein describes themself as "an author, playwright, and performance artist" but also as "an ex-Scientology cult member" and "a reluctant spokesperson for the world's fledgling transgender movement."[1] She goes on to describe herself as "a nice Jewish boy who grew up to be the girl of his dreams." Many trans people for whom she is an elder refer to her as "Auntie Kate." Toward the end of their bio in *O Solo Homo*, Bornstein writes that she is someone who is "more comfortable transitioning than she is arriving at some resting place called an identity."

As Susan Stryker writes in *Transgender History*, Bornstein "helped to define the transgender style in the 1990s."[2] That decade marked a shift in the way gender nonconformity was understood, moving from a disparate set of personal identities (transsexual, transvestite, etc.) to a collective category of gender nonconformity under the umbrella term "transgender." The public internet made it possible for trans people to communicate and share information regardless of geographic location. These shifts created the conditions for increased transgender activism in the US as well as more nuanced explorations of gender nonconformity by scholars, artists, and activists. Bornstein's work was an influential cultural force during this time because, whether on stage or on the page, it foregrounded performance. Trans theorist Sandy Stone writes that Bornstein "sees the purpose of the transgendered performance as disruption of the smooth and tightly knit surface of identity discourse, thereby creating an opening for transformation."[3] Although transgender representation existed in theatre prior to Bornstein's emergence as a performance artist, it was exceedingly rare and the few explicitly transgender characters that did exist were nearly all caricatures written by nontrans people. Bornstein's work created a disruption in that it featured complex trans characters who, rather than serving as caricatures of transness, troubled the very notion of gender identity.

Just as Bornstein herself refuses to arrive at a stable identity, their work uses performance as a strategy to continually question and disrupt identity discourse. Bornstein's work refuses easy categorization, spanning several decades, traveling across a number of mediums. In addition to her theatrical work, she has written books including *My Gender Workbook: How to Become a Real Man, a Real Woman, the Real You, or Something Else Entirely* (1998) and *Hello Cruel World: 101 Alternatives to Suicide for Teens, Freaks and Other Outlaws* (2006). Bornstein's books function as something akin to event scores. *My Gender Workbook*, for example, is not content to let the reader learn in disembodied silence but rather asks them to conduct exercises such as trying on a piece of clothing for the "wrong" gender and tracing the source of any feelings that arise while wearing it.[4]

Bornstein's theatrical works, like those of many queer and trans performance artists of the 1990s, are grounded in autobiographical experiences. However, Bornstein harnesses these experiences in order to destabilize the sense of self-identity many autobiographical works attempt to capture. A good example is Bornstein's earliest play, and arguably one of their best known, *Hidden: A Gender*. The play debuted at San Francisco's Theatre Rhinoceros in 1989 and has since been produced by a number of other theatres, including the Trumpet Vine Theatre Company in Washington, DC, in 2005. It contrasts the struggles against social gender expectations experienced by Herculine Barbin, an intersex person who lived in nineteenth-century France (originally played by future cabaret star and Tony Award nominee Justin Vivian Bond), and by Herman Amberstone, a character generally understood as an autobiographical proxy for Bornstein (originally played by Sydney Erskine). The play begins by positioning the audience as onlookers at a carnival sideshow under the direction of ringmaster Doc Grinder (originally played by Bornstein), who lectures the audience about the importance of maintaining "good gender standing" and warns that, in the course of the show, they will hear the tales of "two pitiful persons of doubtful and dubious gender identity."[5] Herman and Herculine share their stories in turn, revealing both commonalities and differences in their experiences of gender nonconformity in their respective societies. Although Herman acknowledges that, in the twentieth century, they have more choices than Herculine did, they also share that, after gender confirmation surgery, they feel no more comfortable in their gender identity than Herculine did. By the play's end, the notion of a stable gender identity is itself positioned as a sideshow freak rather than the characters who refused to maintain such an identity.

This destabilization of identity is an enduring feature of Bornstein's performance work. In *The Opposite Sex is Neither* (1993), for example, Bornstein plays Maggie, a goddess in training called upon to channel the souls of seven people who have transcended their identity. Bornstein plays each of these seven characters in the play, including jazz pioneer Billy Tipton. In this moment in the show, Bornstein, a nonbinary person who medically transitioned from male to female, plays a male-identified person who was once assigned female. During their solo performance piece, *Virtually Yours* (1994), Bornstein plays a "virtual reality game" during which they assume the identity of several avatars—modeled after both famous women and women they have had a personal relationship with. As Bornstein tries on each of these identities, the video game, with its ability to understand the world only in terms of stable binaries, crashes.

Just as the characters in these shows eschew a stable identity, so too are audiences called upon to question and destabilize their own identities. Throughout *Hidden: A Gender*, Doc Grinder interacts with the audience, attempting to "sell" them gender to relieve the "nagging feeling" that none among them is quite a man or quite a woman. Bornstein also offers workshops to youth and college students that provide space for them to confront their own identities. In one such workshop, "The Language of Paradox" (LOP), Bornstein works with attendees to create their own solo performance works over the course of a week-long intensive, culminating in a public showing. A number of LOP participants have carried their work with the ensemble forward into their own creative practice, including performance artist Kestryl Cael Lowrey and writer Sassafras Lowrey, who considers Bornstein a mentor and refers to LOP as "one of the best writing lessons I've received."[6]

Bornstein has built a decades-long, multidimensional creative practice on working through her own discomfort with the confines of identity and helping others do the same. In recent years, Bornstein has reached even broader audiences and worked with numerous collaborators, appearing in Young Jean Lee's *Straight White Men* (2018) at the Hayes Theatre, making them one of only a handful of trans performers to have ever appeared on Broadway. In this role, Bornstein performed alongside Ty Defoe, a two-spirit Ojibwe and Oneida performer, as Persons in Charge who introduce the play and discuss its themes with the audience. Bornstein has also appeared in the reality TV series *I Am Cait* (2015) alongside activists Chandi Moore, Angelica Ross, and Jen Richards; the feature film *Saturday Church* (2017) with Mj Rodriguez and Indya Moore; and Sam Feder's documentary *Kate Bornstein is a Queer & Pleasant Danger* (2014). Attempting to pin Bornstein down as a particular kind of artist who makes a particular kind of work, then, is to risk reimposing the very identity constraints their work aims to disrupt. Perhaps, then, it would be best to leave the final description to Bornstein themself, when they write that the best bio for them would read simply: "KATE BORNSTEIN: traveling."[7]

NOTES

1 Kate Bornstein, "About Kate Bornstein," in *O Solo Homo: The New Queer Performance*, edited by Holly Hughes and David Román. New York: Grove Press, 1998, 232–235.
2 Susan Stryker, *Transgender History*. Berkeley: Seal Press, 2008, 144.
3 Allucquére Rosanne Stone, "Kate Bornstein's *Gender Outlaw*." *Artforum International*, vol. 33, no. 8: 31.
4 Kate Bornstein, *My Gender Workbook: How to Become a Real Man, a Real Woman, the Real You, or Something Else Entirely*. New York: Routledge, 1998, 196.
5 Kate Bornstein, *Gender Outlaw: On Men, Women, and the Rest of Us*. New York: Vintage, 2016, 218.
6 Scott Dagostino, "Sassafras Lowrey's New Take on Peter Pan is the Queerest Yet." *Xtra**, April 15, 2015. https://xtramagazine.com/culture/second-streetlight-to-the-right-67039
7 Bornstein, "About Kate Bornstein," 235.

FURTHER READING

Bornstein, Kate. *A Queer and Pleasant Danger: The True Story of a Nice Jewish Boy Who Joins the Church of Scientology, and Leaves Twelve Years Later to Become the Lovely Lady She is Today*. Boston: Beacon Press, 2012.
Bornstein, Kate. "Interview with Kate Bornstein." Digital Transgender Archive, November 4, 2019, audio, 1:31:15. www.digitaltransgenderarchive.net/files/xd07gs899

SHARON BRIDGFORTH
(Chicago, Illinois, 1958–)

T. Chester

Sharon Bridgforth's first experience seeing a play was Ntozake Shange's *for colored girls who have considered suicide/when the rainbow is enuf* (1976), and she describes seeing this pioneering choreopoem in the Bay Area as the event that changed her life and affirmed what was possible for Black theatrical artists. Her move from Santa Monica, California, to Austin, Texas, marked the beginnings of her career as an artist. There she transitioned from her work as a sexually transmitted disease interventionist, HIV/AIDS outreach specialist, and community organizer to a full-time artist who began performing her work publicly in the early 1990s.[1] From 1993 to 1998, she served as the founder, writer, and artistic director of Austin's root wy'mn theatre company, which toured the United States performing work that centered the experiences of Black American women.

Although Bridgforth grew up in Los Angeles, she identifies as Southern. Both her father and mother are from Southern cities, where she spent a lot of time as a child. Connecting the voices and the history of the people in the South as part of her blood memories, Bridgforth reminds us that, despite the migration of Black people to Western and Northern cities, they carry with them the traditions and ways of being of Southern communities.[2] This perspective is evident in Bridgforth's first poetic novel, *the bull-jean stories*, published in 1998 by RedBone Press, a Black lesbian and gay independent publisher. Winner of a Lambda Literary Award for Best Book by a Small Press and a nominee for Best Lesbian Fiction, *the bull-jean stories* is set in the 1920s rural South and "uses traditional storytelling and nontraditional verse to chronicle the course of love returning in the lifetimes of one woman-loving-woman named bull-dog-jean."[3] Bridgforth has performed pieces featured in *the bull-jean-stories* around the country since 1993, including the poetic performance drama *blood pudding*. First produced in Austin at the Hyde Park Theatre in 1998, *blood pudding* would later kick off New York City's 25th SummerStage Season in 2010. The piece celebrates the history of New Orleans and was hailed as an "innovative piece that blurs the lines between theater, song and dance."[4]

In Austin, Bridgforth came to know her partner in both the theatrical jazz aesthetic and in life, Dr. Omi Osun Joni L. Jones, now a Professor Emerita of African & African Diaspora Studies at the University of Texas at Austin. Bridgforth credits the intensive workshops she did with Jones in 1991 as helping her to flesh out her initial ideas as well as providing language that gave her context for what she was doing in her artistic practice. Through their partnership they formed the foundations of the theatrical jazz aesthetic, which incorporates the jazz principles of improvisation and the ensemble, releasing performers from the strict Western confines of performing the script verbatim, making each performance different. As performance scholar Matt Richardson describes it, "Jazz aesthetics rely on the ability to imagine more than one event, sound, or idea at a time in order to tell stories that have not been told."[5] Bridgforth served as the anchor artist for the Austin Project led by Dr. Jones from 2002 to 2009, and they've documented their work in the book *Experiments in a Jazz Aesthetic: Art, Activism, Academia and the Austin Project*, published by University of Texas Press in 2010, and the article "Black Desire, Theatrical Jazz, and *River See*," published in *TDR: The Drama Review* in 2014.

Bridgforth's second poetic novel, *love conjure/blues*, was published by RedBone Press in October 2004 and served as the basis for a performance piece called *The love conjure/blues Text Installation*. The term "text installation" is used "because the written text is layered throughout the performance and because the live performer reads directly from the script onstage."[6] The piece was directed/composed by Helga Davis and workshopped at the John L. Warfield Center for African American Studies, University of Texas at Austin, in both March and September of 2004.[7] After the workshop production, Bridgforth created an "altar film," shot in black and white, featuring the voices of Laurie Carlos and Annelize Machado, and showing the process of Omi Osun Joni L. Jones creating an outside altar. Next she produced a text installation film, a series of ten shorts created with filmmaker Jen Simmons, as a way to invoke "the text as a LIVING body of work."[8] During performances, the shorts are projected on three large screens, "creating a circular environment for celluloid cast members, the performer and the audience to co-exist in."[9] From June 2007 to April 2008, *The love conjure/blues Text Installation* was presented in Austin (performed by Bridgforth), Dallas (performed by

Bridgforth and Florinda Bryant), and at Northwestern University's Blacktino Queer Performance Festival (performed by Omi Osun Joni L. Jones). In these performances, Bridgforth maintains her tradition of centering rural working-class Black folk through the depiction of a range of possibilities of gender expression and sexuality, reimagining the traditional role of griots and asserting that Black queer histories and rituals are sacred.

Bridgforth weaves together Black communities past, present, and future throughout her artistic work. In *con flama*, which debuted in Austin in 2000 under the direction of Laurie Carlos, she draws on her memories "traveling from her working-class, South Central Los Angeles home to her high school in Echo Park, and places in between, ... cross[ing] borders between cultures and classes."[10] In other notable works, like *delta dandi* (2007) and *River See* (2013), Bridgforth continues to integrate jazz improvisation and audience engagement. According to Bridgforth, *delta dandi* "asks how does collective grief and trauma inform the Black-American experience and what must a Soul do to heal," and the *Austin Chronicle* describes how the performance "builds to a frenzy and crescendos in a love ritual chant, in which all the various elements and characters are embraced and integrated into one."[11] Rev. Irene Monroe describes *River See* as the story of "a young queer sister heading North to the Promised Land from the Mississippi Delta" and notes how Bridgforth

> infuses movement, singing, dance, ritual, storytelling, and audience participation as she stands in the midst of all the action while directing it. Her technique helps to illustrate there is structure and form in the telling of the narrative as well as focus and intentionality in See's seemingly noisy, chaotic and peripatetic journey North.[12]

Bridgforth celebrates the rich cultural tradition and stories of Black queer and gender expansive people through *dat Black Mermaid Man Lady/The Show*, which was produced in 2018 by the Pillsbury House Theatre in Minneapolis and streamed via Twin Cities PBS.[13] Bridgforth also developed a companion oracle deck, which features the nine oracles or characters from the performance and the text on the cards are from *dat Black Mermaid Man Lady*.[14] She's currently the host and executive producer of the "Who Yo People Is" podcast, which serves to give space to artists "whose work and artistic practices are rooted in serving our communities through healing/spiritual and cultural traditions centered in love."[15] Her podcast highlights the work of many in her artistic community, including Sonja Parks, who was an original member of root wy'myn (season 3); artist and energy worker Daniel Alexander Jones, who often performs as their alter ego, Jomama Jones (season 2); founder and editor of RedBone Press Lisa C. Moore (season 2); and Black queer performance studies scholar E. Patrick Johnson (season 2). As an artist, her work continues to develop and incorporate a variety of mediums to imagine and create Black Queer Southern possibilities.

NOTES

1 NBJC (National Black Justice Coalition), "Sharon Bridgforth," NBJC Ubuntu, February 24, 2021, accessed January 7, 2022. https://beenhere.org/2018/05/15/sharon-bridgforth/
2 Anita Gonzalez, "Interview with Sharon Bridgforth," in *Solo/Black/Woman: Scripts, Interviews, and Essays*, edited by E. Patrick Johnson and Ramón H. Rivera-Servera. Evanston, IL: Northwestern University Press, 2014, 227–237.
3 Sharon Bridgforth, *the bull-jean stories*. Austin, TX: RedBone Press, 1998.
4 Gabrielle Sierra, "City Parks Summerstage Season Continues With BLOOD PUDDING, Kicks off 7/23," BroadwayWorld.com, July 19, 2010, accessed May 24, 2022. www.broadwayworld.com/off-broadway/article/City-Parks-Summerstage-Season-Continues-With-BLOOD-PUDDING-Kicks-Off-723-20100719
5 Matt Richardson, "Reinventing the Black Southern Community in Sharon Bridgforth's *The love conjure/blues Text Installation*," in *Blacktino Queer Performance*, edited by E. Patrick Johnson and Ramón H. Rivera-Servera. Durham, NC: Duke University Press, 2016, 65.
6 Ibid., 74.
7 Sharon Bridgforth, *The love conjure/blues Text Installation*, in *Blacktino Queer Performance*, edited by E. Patrick Johnson and Ramón H. Rivera-Servera. Durham, NC: Duke University Press, 2016, 21.
8 Sharon Bridgforth, "Our Gurl, from *The love conjure/blues Text installation*," accessed January 4, 2022. https://vimeo.com/37003005
9 Sharon Bridgforth, *The love conjure/blues Text Installation*, accessed January 4, 2022. https://vimeo.com/37002888
10 Belinda Acosta, "On the Bus: The 'Con Flama' Experience." *Austin Chronicle*, September 22, 2000, accessed May 24, 2022. www.austinchronicle.com/arts/2000-09-22/78630/
11 Abe Louise Young, "A Revolution of Spirit." *Austin Chronicle*, January 9, 2009, accessed January 7, 2022. www.austinchronicle.com/arts/2009-01-09/724122/

12 Irene Monroe, "Qu(e)erying the Black Migration." *Bay Windows*, November 20, 2014, accessed January 7, 2022. www.baywindows.com/Queerying-the-black-migration
13 "Stage: *dat Black Mermaid Man Lady/ The Show*," Twin Cities Public Television, accessed January 7, 2022. www.tpt.org/tpt-stage/video/dat-black-mermaid-man-ladythe-show-38818/
14 "Oracle Deck," *dat Black Mermaid Man Lady*, accessed September 26, 2021. www.datblackmermaidmanlady.com/oracle-deck
15 "About," Sharon Bridgforth, accessed September 26, 2021. www.sharonbridgforth.com/about

FURTHER READING

Anderson, Lisa M. "Signifying Black Lesbians: Dramatic Speculations." In *Black Feminism in Contemporary Drama*. Urbana, IL: University of Illinois Press, 2008, 95–114.

Richardson, Matt. *The Queer Limit of Black Memory: Black Lesbian Literature and Irresolution*. Columbus, OH: Ohio State University Press, 2013.

CHARLES BUSCH
(Hartsdale, New York, 1954–)
Sean F. Edgecomb

Charles Busch is an American playwright, drag performer, and cabaret chanteuse based in New York City. With a career spanning almost 40 years, Busch is a doyenne of New York City's queer theatre scene, having found critical acclaim and popular success downtown, on Broadway, and in Hollywood cinema. This achievement reflects Busch's adaptability and his commitment to generating a contemporary queer theatre that revels in satire while elevating theatrical traditions, drag, and American culture as filtered through a camp lens. Busch's personal interpretation of camp is "an affectionate celebration of the outrageous and sentimental elements of popular culture of the past, as handed down through generations of gay people."[1]

Busch first moved to Manhattan as a young boy, following the tragic death of his mother. Fostered by his Aunt Lil, whom Busch likens to gay icon Auntie Mame, he was exposed to the world of professional theatre. This foundational experience would not only encourage Busch to pursue a performance degree at Northwestern University, but also shaped the drag roles that he would write and embody, primarily *femmes fatales* drawn from classic plays, novels, and Old Hollywood, all filtered through an adoring homage to French actress Sarah Bernhardt and a pinch of Aunt Lil. Additionally, Busch credits self-proclaimed female impersonators Charles Pierce and Lynne Carter as virtuosic role models for the development of his craft.[2]

Prior to college, Busch fortuitously attended two plays at Charles Ludlam's Ridiculous Theatrical Company in the West Village, *Eunuchs of the Forbidden City* (1971) and *Camille* (1973). Ludlam had carved out a space for a queer contemporary American theatre through a genre deemed "Ridiculous" during the period of gay liberation. Ludlam's Ridiculous relied on a pastiche of high and low pop culture, a celebration of theatrical traditions like clowning and *commedia dell'arte*, and a commitment to ridiculing heteronormative culture through camp performance. Of Ludlam's performances, Busch remarked, "it was a wonderful tightrope walk between sincerity and outrageous, burlesque comedy," and this balancing act between the sublime and the absurd would become a hallmark of Busch's oeuvre while making him a legatee of Ludlam's Ridiculous.[3]

While a student, Busch reconnected with Ludlam and his company on tour in Chicago, and this led to a future opportunity for the young actor to perform his solo show entitled *Hollywood Confidential* (1979) at Ludlam's theatre at Sheridan Square and a brief stint as the character of Hecate in Ludlam's repertory production of *Bluebeard* the same year. During this period Busch began to tour several moderately successful original solo shows: *Vagabond Vignettes* (1979), *A Theatrical Party* (1980), and *After You've Gone* (1983). These early shows relied heavily on Busch's affinity for impressions of female stars drawn from the Golden Age of Hollywood, but performed *sans* drag.

In 1984, Busch became acquainted with the performance artist Bina Sharif, who regularly performed at a down-at-heels, queer club in Manhattan's East Village named the Limbo Lounge. With Sharif's encouragement, in three short weeks Busch composed an original script, *Vampire Lesbians of Sodom*, and cobbled together a cast with his roommate Kenneth Elliott, to be performed at the Limbo Lounge on a summer night. Though largely ignored by the press, the performance would prove a cult triumph and the following year transferred off-Broadway to the Provincetown Playhouse, where it remained open for a record-breaking five years. The play, a spoof about rival, immortal, lesbian vampires that moves epically from the Ancient Dead Sea to 1920s Hollywood to contemporary Las Vegas, solidified not only a style, but a repertory company including Busch as the star and featuring Tom Aulino, Arnie Kolodner, Robert Carey, Andy Halliday, Theresa Marlowe, Meghan Robinson, and eventually Julie Halston (who would become Busch's muse) and Elliott, who would go on to direct a majority of the plays. Beyond its spirit of queer decadence, *Vampire Lesbians* offered escapism and kinship to a gay urban audience that was being ravaged by HIV/AIDS and the fear surrounding the disease.

With the newfound success of *Vampire Lesbians*, Busch's company, reverentially named Theatre-in-Limbo, commenced a prolific period of successful productions, penned by Busch, running from 1984 to 1991, primarily at Limbo Lounge and WPA Theatre. These included *Theodora She-Bitch of Byzantium* (1984), *Times Square Angel* (1985), *Sleeping Beauty or Coma* (1985), *Gidget Goes Psycho* (1986), *Pardon My Inquisition* (1986), *Psycho Beach Party* (1987),

The Lady in Question (1988), and *Red Scare on Sunset* (1991). The shows followed a similar formula, employing drag, encoded queer satire, historical spoof, and cinematic reference, filtered through the fantasy that Theatre-in-Limbo was a depraved, touring theatre company from the nineteenth century. This ruse was elevated when Busch closed each performance with a divaesque "curtain speech," which thereafter became a hallmark of all of his performances to date. The company disbanded in 1991, in part due to the tragic deaths of Carey and Robinson from AIDS-related complications.

Even without the troupe, Busch generated new work, including *You Should Be So Lucky* (1994), a Cinderella tale about a young New York electrologist that featured him out of drag. During its brief run at Primary Stages, the play received lukewarm reviews and the experience convinced Busch to return to drag roles in three new productions written in the style of Theatre-in-Limbo, including a USO satire titled *Swingtime Canteen* (1995), a nineteenth-century-style melodrama, *Queen Amarantha* (1997), and *Shanghai Moon* (1999), an Art Deco fantasy set in 1930s China featuring BD Wong. This period also set in motion Busch's ongoing relationship with Carl Andress as his primary director.

Busch credits his comic approach to his intersectional identity as gay and Jewish. Just as Ludlam's Roman Catholic boyhood had been a key reference point in his plays, Manhattan's urban Jewish culture has been afflatus for Busch. The joyful apotheosis of his viewpoint took shape in *The Tale of the Allergist's Wife* (2000), opening at Manhattan Theatre Club (MTC) before transferring to Broadway. The play tells the story of Miriam Passman (played by Linda Lavin), a "raging Jewish Lady" living on the Upper West Side and wallowing in midlife crisis.[4] The play, inspired in part by Kaufman and Hart's *The Man Who Came to Dinner* (1939), garnered Best Play nominations from the Tony and Drama Desk committees and won the John Gassner Award from the Outer Critics Circle. Furthermore, the play introduced the Ridiculous style to Broadway audiences (a feat Ludlam had not achieved) by folding it within the trappings of a one-set, five-character comic realism that was often associated with mainstream Broadway. Busch's success also created opportunities for the next generation of queer, Ridiculous-inspired, Tony-nominated performances like *Kiki and Herb: Alive on Broadway* (2007), featuring Justin Vivian Bond and Kenny Mellman, and *Gary* (2019), written by Taylor Mac and starring Nathan Lane.

Because Busch had become an established part of New York City's queer theatre scene in the 1980s and 1990s, his writing attracted attention and he was commissioned to originate books for several musicals including Broadway's *Taboo* (2003), based on queer, gender-fluid, pop sensation Boy George and produced by Rosie O'Donnell. All of the books Busch crafted maintained his trademark witty repartee, spirited dialogue, and his distinct queer, camp perspective while simultaneously introducing his work to a mainstream audience.

Busch's success on Broadway led to opportunities in Hollywood including starring roles in the films *Psycho Beach Party* (2000) and *Die, Mommie, Die!* (2003), which followed as a stage production, but it was back in New York City that Busch continued to find his inspiration and core audience in theatre. Combined with Busch's prolific, two-decade career, the success of *The Tale of the Allergist's Wife* led to a Drama Desk Award in Career Achievement (2003) and an invitation by MTC to write a new play, *Our Leading Lady* (2007), a queer reframing of Abraham Lincoln's assassination.

In addition to an active career in cabaret, since 2009 Busch has returned to writing and starring in a second phase of queer plays, reuniting earlier cast members, like the stalwart Halston, and reinstating Busch as the repertory ingenue turned diva. These productions, which attracted a younger audience, were *The Divine Sister* (2010), *Cleopatra* (2016), and *The Confession of Lily Dare* (2018), all at Theater for the New City. *Lily Dare* sends up "weepies," or 1930s melodramatic films about women who overcome the challenges of a cruel world. As with all of his drag roles, Lily Dare becomes a metaphor for Busch himself, equal parts "camp and compassion," transforming American pop culture into a site for queer diversion while building community across generations.[5]

NOTES

1 Email with the author, June 8, 2021.
2 Josh Ferri, "Five Burning Questions with the One and Only Charles Busch," *The Daily Scoop*, February 5, 2014, www.broadwaybox.com/daily-scoop/five-burning-questions-with-the-one-and-only-charles-busch/
3 "Charles Busch on Charles Ludlam in *Camille*," *Backstage*, March 22, 2012, www.backstage.com/magazine/article/charles-busch-charles-ludlam-camille-52512/
4 Busch quoted in the author's *Charles Ludlam Lives!* (Ann Arbor, MI: University of Michigan Press, 2017), 79.
5 Jesse Green, "Review: Camp and Compassion in 'The Confession of Lily Dare'." *New York Times*, January 29, 2020, www.nytimes.com/2020/01/29/theater/confession-of-lily-dare-review-charles-busch.html

FURTHER READING

Busch, Charles. *Whores of Lost Atlantis*. Westport, CT: Hyperion, 1993.
Edgecomb, Sean F. *Charles Ludlam Lives! Charles Busch, Bradford Louryk, Taylor Mac and the Queer Legacy of the Ridiculous Theatrical Company.* Ann Arbor, MI: University of Michigan Press, 2017.

JANE CHAMBERS
(Columbia, South Carolina, 1937–1983)
Sara Warner

One of the first out lesbian dramatists to depict the love between women as happy and healthy (as well as complicated and querulous), Jane Chambers revolutionized American theatre with unapologetically Sapphic plays informed by her participation in second-wave feminism and the nascent gay and lesbian movement. An actress by training, Chambers studied at Rollins College and the Pasadena Playhouse (neither of which allowed females to take writing or directing classes in the 1950s), then moved to New York's Greenwich Village, where she starred in several queer-themed, off-Broadway shows, including The Actors Mobile Theatre production of Robert Anderson's *Tea and Sympathy* (1956). Chambers landed a feature role in the star-studded, but ill-fated, *Single Man at a Party* (1959), which *New York Times* reviewer Brooks Atkinson deemed an "anxious tour of the abominations" featuring "homosexuality, blackmail, death by abortion, and other evidences of bad taste."[1] In the early 1960s, Chambers, lured by a charismatic high school teacher, moved to rural Maine, where she dedicated herself to writing.

A prolific author who created work for the stage, screen, and a variety of print media, including homophile publications *ONE* and *The Ladder*, Chambers' reputation rests largely on six plays she penned about lesbian life in remote locations along the Eastern Seaboard, utopian outposts where dykes, free from the pathologizing gaze of straight society, could be themselves. These largely autobiographical dramedies feature characters and plots inspired by the amorous antics of her friends and lovers. *A Late Snow* (1970) finds Ellie, an English professor, confined by a blizzard in a cabin with her current partner, her former girlfriend, and her college crush. Ellie fears her paramours will out themselves to Margo, a visiting artist she's invited to campus. As the cocktails flow, Margo reveals that she too is a lesbian, one who remains strategically closeted, like the author Tally in Chambers' *Eye of the Gull* (written 1971/premiered 1991), to protect her livelihood. Produced by Playwrights Horizons at the Clark Center for the Performing Arts in 1974, *A Late Snow* garnered critical and commercial success, but its graphic lesbian content resulted in Chambers being sacked from the soap opera *Search for Tomorrow*, despite winning a Writers Guild Award for her work on the series.

Blacklisted in Hollywood, Chambers saw her television and film projects fizzle. Her unproduced scripts—*Here Comes the Iceman,* one of the first situation comedies to feature an African American family; *Batt'lin Bertha: The Senator from Waterloo*, an homage to Shirley Chisholm; and *Rosie Love Apple*, about a Puerto Rican family in Spanish Harlem—reflect Chambers' deep and abiding commitment to racial justice, a position catalyzed by her upbringing in the Jim Crow South and the artist's attempts to reckon with her family's slaveholding legacy.

Stigmatized as a queer degenerate by the entertainment industry, Chambers was abandoned by theatre producers, who were unwilling to risk an extended run of *A Late Snow* or mount new work. Undeterred, Chambers continued writing, eking out a living by penning erotica under different pseudonyms. She was rescued from obscurity by producer John Glines, who invited her to stage *A Late Snow* as part of the First Gay American Arts Festival in 1980. The play was optioned, so Chambers suggested *Last Summer at Bluefish Cove* (written in 1976), about a close-knit group of lesbians whose annual vacation is interrupted when an uninitiated stranger rents a cottage at their retreat. Starring Jean Smart as Lil, a rakish dyke who finds her soulmate just months before she dies of cancer, *Bluefish Cove* was the runaway hit of the festival. Dubbed "The Girls in the Sand," a reference to Mart Crowley's trailblazing drama *The Boys in the Band* (1968), the play enjoyed an extended New York run before moving to Los Angeles and San Francisco, racking up awards, and queer community productions, along the way.

As a headliner (along with Harvey Fierstein) for the Second Gay American Theatre Festival (1981), Chambers premiered *My Blue Heaven*, one of the earliest examples of a same-sex wedding in American drama. This comedy of manners follows a lesbian couple who leave Manhattan for country life after writer Molly loses her job for authoring a gay book. Mirth and merriment ensue when her weekly column about rural living, written to disguise her identity and the gender of her lover, attracts the interest of a Christian publishing firm.

Chambers was in rehearsals for *Kudzu* at Playwrights Horizons when she was diagnosed with cancer. Her brain tumor proliferated even quicker than the malignant vine of the play's title. The planned Broadway run was canceled when Chambers lost the ability to write and make necessary edits to the script. This Southern Gothic dramedy about four elderly people, two gay and two straight, would have been the first lesbian play by an out lesbian author to grace the Great White Way. Audiences would have to wait decades for alternatives to those goddamned sick and dirty dykes whose sexual desire for other women resulted in their condemnation (*The God of Vengeance*), suicide (*The Children's Hour*), or antisocial urges (*The Killing of Sister George*).

Glines paid tribute to Chambers in his history-making Tony Award speech (for *Torch Song Trilogy*, 1983) and with a one act play about her life, *In Her Own Words,* staged at Town Hall in 1985 on a double bill with *The Quintessential Image* (which he had produced in 1982). Originally titled *The Quintessential Dyke*, this, the sixth of Chambers' "lesbian plays," takes place at a television studio where host Margaret Foy interviews her idol, a reclusive photographer Lacey Lanier, who comes out on camera, revealing that her success stems from an obsessive desire to document her unrequited love. Lesbian-feminist theatre scholars Jill Dolan and Sue-Ellen Case applauded the play's experimental form and use of multimedia to comment on the misogyny and homophobia of representational regimes. These critics bristled at Chambers' earlier lesbian plays, which employed realism, a genre they denounced as perniciously reinforcing a tragic view of lesbian life and love.

Stylistically, *The Quintessential Image* resembles Chambers' lesser-known plays inspired by the epic theatre of her mentor Erwin Piscator. *Tales of the Revolution and Other American Fables* (1969), a dystopian expressionistic drama about the warping effects of sexism, homophobia, and racism, takes place in a Greenwich Village bar on Halloween night. It opens with a stage full of mannequins that come to life, engaging in lewd banter with a perverse cast of characters, two of whom are named Dyke and Faggot. If *Tales of the Revolution* is "ever produced," Chambers told her thesis adviser at Goddard College, "I'll be cell-mates with Angela [Davis]!"[2] The play earned her a 1972 fellowship to the O'Neill Playwriting Center, where it received its only production to date.

That same year, Chambers, who had transferred from Maine to New Jersey with Job Corps for Women, a cornerstone of Lyndon B. Johnson's War on Poverty, was elected Chairperson of the New Jersey Women's Political Caucus, agitating alongside Gloria Steinem and Bella Abzug. She also co-founded Women's Interart Theatre in New York City with Margot Lewitin, who directed four of Chambers' feminist, avant-garde plays. Two one-act plays, *Mine* and *The Wife*

(1973), examine the socioeconomic conditions that keep women oppressed, a theme shared by *Random Violence* (1973). Staged in the round, this consciousness-raising performance features a woman assaulted on all sides. The ambiguous ending of *Random Violence* leaves the audience to determine how best to address cultural misogyny. The fourth play, *The Common Garden Variety* (1974), follows Sari, a girl raised by her grandmother after her parents' divorce. The protagonist shares many attributes with Chambers, who suffered sexual abuse from her father and uncle. Incest is a recurring topic in her journalism and erotica.

Chambers' plays, originally published by Terry Helbing's pioneering JH Press, another gay arts venture funded by John Glines, are included in the anthologies *Gay Plays: The First Collection* (1979) and *Amazon All-Stars: 13 Lesbian Plays* (1996). Sadly, these works are all out of print. Chambers' legacy lives on in the Women & Theatre Program's annual Jane Chambers Playwriting Award, founded in 1983. A second prize in her name, given by the Gay Theatre Alliance, ended when the organization disbanded. Chambers is celebrated with an annual playreading series at TOSOS (The Other Side of Silence), the Chesley/Chambers Reading Series, which also honors dramatist, critic, and composer Robert Chesley.

Last Summer at Bluefish Cove remains Chambers' most popular work. In 2014, Venezuelan director Fina Torres released a film adaptation, *Liz en Septiembre*, and in 2020 Cynthia Nixon was slated to direct a 40th-anniversary revival, which was postponed due to the COVID-19 pandemic. The star-studded production team (Ellen DeGeneres, Portia de Rossi, Lily Tomlin, Jane Wagner, and Harriet Newman Leve) hoped for a 2022 opening, but the show's fate remains uncertain.

NOTES

1 Brooks Atkinson, "Theatre: Seamy Side; 'Single Man at a Party' Opens Off-Broadway," *New York Times*, April 22, 1959.
2 Jane Chambers, "Letters to Paul," Preface to her Goddard College Thesis (1971), 41.

FURTHER READING

Case, Sue-Ellen. *Feminism and Theatre*. New York: Routledge, 1988.
Dolan, Jill. *Presence and Desire: Essays on Gender, Sexuality, Performance*. Ann Arbor, MI: University of Michigan Press, 1993.
Roth, Maya E., and Mobley, Jennifer-Scott, eds. *Lesbian & Queer Plays from the Jane Chambers Prize*. Morrisville, NC: Lulu, 2019.

ELLIE COVAN
(Corpus Christi, Texas, 1955–)
Jeff McMahon

Since moving to New York in the mid-1980s and founding her peripatetic performance space, Dixon Place, the Bessie and Obie award-winning producer Ellie Covan has remained dedicated to the presentation of new works and works-in-progress by theatre, dance, performance, and literary artists, queer and not. Presenting over 1,000 artists a year, budgets are modest, but artists, whether at the beginning of their career or well established, get paid.[1] Several have told her, "You gave me my first payment for a performance."[2]

Covan spent her childhood in Texas participating in community theatre, often produced by her parents. After studying at the Alley Theatre, this self-described "black sheep, nonconformist, when-you-gonna-get-a-real-job person" pursued an Associate's Degree in Animal Science, but soon returned to theatre, pursuing a BFA at the University of Texas at Austin. In her senior year, "all the women decided to be lesbians and the faculty freaked out. It was a movement, and it was great." Then Ellie's only aunt left her husband for a woman, further normalizing gayness for Ellie when she and her then-boyfriend visited the couple on their army base. She says, "There was never a closet for me," and she now considers herself, as a therapist deduced many years ago, "a textbook bisexual."

After her arrival in New York in 1978, Covan's former University of Texas classmate, Mark Russell, urged her to come to the weekly Open Movement event at Performance Space 122 (P.S. 122, founded in 1980 and renamed Performance Space New York in 2018), where she met a variety of artists, including the performer/director Tom Keegan. In 1982, they began a three-year collaboration, *Out in the World*, a solo piece for Covan focused on the bisexual writer Jane Bowles. Self-produced in a theatre on 22nd Street, "no one saw it. I was using it [the performance] therapeutically. But it didn't work." So, in 1985, she went to Paris for several months. In her apartment there, she hosted mostly visual and literary artists and historians,

DOI: 10.4324/9781003203896-8

becoming "an accidental doyenne; I was antisocial but ended up with a salon."

Out of money, she returned to New York and rented a minuscule storefront apartment. Thus began Dixon Place, presenting art shows and literary readings, soon branching out to theatre and performance, with Tom Murrin (aka The Alien Comic) the first performance/theatre artist to take the tiny stage in front of her kitchen. (Dixon Place would create the "Tommy," an annual residency and honorarium, following his death in 2012.) After a few months she remained open five nights a week, having decided "I'm gonna open my place, see what comes in, and only lock the door at night." During that time, there were many small club-like venues (Pyramid, 8BC, King Tut's Wah Wah Hut), but "I wanted people to sit down and pay attention." There was no "typical" at Dixon Place, but evenings developed a pattern: personal welcome by Covan (it was, after all, her home), performance, intermission, bingo, live band. Tuesdays were literary events. Starting her theatre in the era of Ronald Reagan and the AIDS epidemic, Covan established a safe haven, an incubator for artists to explore the range of their identity and aesthetics. Founded the year Mayor Ed Koch finally signed the law making discrimination due to sexual orientation illegal in housing and employment, Dixon Place asserted itself as an expansively queer space.

Five years in, with the rent rapidly rising, Covan moved herself and her theatre to a loft at 258 Bowery. As with the storefront location, the new space was not licensed as a public venue, and performers shoehorned themselves into the larger, but still modest, playing area. Anything was possible at Dixon Place, as long as you didn't mind having your audience a few inches away, sitting in a motley collection of chairs and sofas (memorialized in the Dixon Place logo). Backstage? There was a curtain a few inches from the wall. Maybe. As performer Susana Cook puts it, "Dixon was her house, we were using her bathroom, her towels, using her kitchen as the bar."[3] Another performer, Paul Zaloom, says, "The key difference between Ellie and other NYC presenters I've worked with is that she really *is* the space, not a transitory 'artistic director' on her way to bigger/better things." For solo performer Mike Albo, "Ellie and Dixon Place have kept the rough-edged quality of performance alive … giving people space to make work that doesn't necessarily lead to a Netflix deal."

In 1992, soon after moving to the loft, Covan started the Hot! Festival to celebrate queer culture. Not wanting to compete with June Pride events, she scheduled this annual fest for July, and it remains Dixon Place's most popular series. Covan's commitment to the "under-told story," and "surreal ethnography," in writer/director Kate Conroy's words, often falls outside the mainstream gay narrative. Past Hot! Festivals have included Marga Gomez teaming up with Carmelita Tropicana to "get dirty" in *Gomez and Tropicana Do Jan Brewer* (2012), Dan Fishback's surreal musical about Jewish and queer revolutionaries, *The Material World* (2012), the nonbinary performer Monstah Black (of The Illustrious Blacks) performing their *Hyperbolic (The Last Spectacle)* (2016), and trans performer D'Lo narrating his journey through testosterone in *To T, or Not to T* (2017). The festival's opening-night performance party, with each upcoming performer showing a brief excerpt, is a delicious introduction to the breadth of this theatre we call queer.

Dixon Place not only presents queer theatre, it has consistently queered the way that theatre is presented. Moe Angelos, a performer with both the Five Lesbian Brothers and the Builders Association, makes this clear:

> We keep changing, keep trying on new expressions of our "otherness," keep trying to say what has not yet been said or say something anew in our quirky, downtown, fabulous, wrong, silly, queer ways. Dixon Place has always welcomed us "others" and Ellie has egged us on.

According to Peggy Shaw, whose collaborations with Split Britches are iconic,

> Ellie Covan has always supported my queer work and Lois Weaver's for a good 30 years. She always found a space for us, and always trusted our new shows. Dixon Place is the best queer-friendly place I know of in New York City.

Dixon Place has premiered work by all four members of the "NEA Four," including John Fleck, who states,

> Ellie Covan has been in my corner of the boxing ring ever since the culture wars of the 90s when artists such as myself were fighting for freedom of expression. While other venues avoided controversy by canceling our performances, Ellie fought alongside us, never hesitating in offering us a platform to express ourselves.

This close identification of producer and venue can be seen in other performance spaces that became havens for queer artists, including

New York's La MaMa Experimental Theatre Club, identified for many decades with its founder, Ellen Stewart, and Santa Monica's Highways Performance Space, co-founded by Tim Miller and Linda Burnham.

After a few years of Dixon Place also presenting work in venues off-site, it came time for Covan to completely separate the theatre from her home. She built a theatre from the ground up, partnering with supporters and a developer to create a new venue at 161 Chrystie Street, which opened in 2008. Dixon Place now has a real lighting grid, fixed seats, a balcony, and a lot more room for performance. It also has a (for-profit) bar that makes money to support the (nonprofit) theatre. Dixon Place keeps its focus on new work, with expanded support to an artist-in-residence series, curated series, and intimate performances in the Lounge that run concurrently with the shows in the theatre.

Having witnessed and experienced segregation and discrimination in her Texas childhood, Covan recognized early on the necessity to bring other voices not only onto the stage, but into the selection process. She established curatorial positions focusing on artists of color, acknowledging the crossovers in multiple identities, yet Dixon Place remains the only venue of its kind with the founder intimately involved in its day-to-day operation. While being interviewed for this chapter, the conversation was frequently interrupted by texts from Dixon Place staff with issues ranging from plumbing problems to the reopening for the first week of live presentations since the COVID-19 pandemic hit in spring 2020 and forced theatres to close. Not that the crisis stopped Covan from presenting new performances: Dixon Place TV (DPTV) put new work into virtual space, so new ideas could find an outlet and the artists could keep developing. As with the artists it presents, Dixon Place keeps its queer heart beating.

NOTES

1 Dixon Place mission statement, accessed July 7, 2021. http://dixonplace.org/about-us/mission/
2 Interview with author, New York City, May 8, 2021. All direct quotes from Ellie Covan are from this interview.
3 All quotes from people other than Ellie Covan are from email correspondence with the author, between May 8 and July 11, 2021.

FURTHER READING

Carr, C. "Home is Where the Art is," *Village Voice*, September 21, 1999, 65.
Green, Penelope, "She's Made a Life in her Theater. She's Made a Theater in her Home," *New York Times*, September 26, 2004, RE4.

WILL DAVIS
(Santa Monica, California, 1983–)
Joshua Bastian Cole

Transgender artists are not new to the theatrical landscape but have recently received unprecedented attention, marking a significant shift in the broader American culture. Central to this shift is director and choreographer Will Davis, whose far-ranging career has included working at hot spots for new experimental plays and at incubators for avant-garde contemporary performance, like Brooklyn Arts Exchange and Wild Project. Working around the country in regional professional theatres such as Actors Theatre of Louisville, Shakespeare Theatre Company, and Long Wharf Theatre, Davis has garnered acclaim, including multiple nominations for Lucille Lortel and Helen Hayes awards. Davis has also worked off-Broadway at New York Theatre Workshop, Rattlestick Playwrights Theater, Soho Repertory Theatre, MCC Theater, Playwrights Horizons, and Manhattan Theatre Club. Davis's historic appointment as Artistic Director of Chicago's American Theater Company (ATC) is of particular importance: the first openly transgender person to lead a major nonprofit institution without a defined LGBTQ mission.

Growing up in Santa Cruz in the 1980s, with his mother and godmother both in the arts, Davis acknowledges his brother as an influential figure in what became an imaginative, collaborative directorial style. Building forts together as children in the northern California woods, he and his brother would "take the [same] three pieces of wood and make something new and wholly different," which Davis claims as "training in [making] something out of nothing and turning the finite into the infinite!"[1] Davis also devoted himself at an early age to classical ballet training. But, due to the rigidly gendered expectations of the form, his childhood was rife with body dysmorphia and gender dysphoria, later compounded by the toll puberty takes on young trans people.

Davis attended DePaul University to, at first, study acting. He further explored theatre making using the language of dance, largely influenced by the revolutionary dance theatre artist Pina Bausch, while pursuing an MFA in Directing at the University of Texas at Austin. In addition to Bausch, Davis readily points to an array of influences including choreographer Deborah Hay, site-specific installation artist Ai Weiwei, painter Marc Chagall, surrealist filmmaker David Lynch, singer-songwriters David Bowie, Bob Dylan, and Willie Nelson, and even ensemble comedy groups Monty Python and the Muppets. There is a hint of anarchic aesthetic mixed in, as well, as Davis feels his style of directing is profoundly influenced by the punk shows he attended in the Bay Area in the 1990s.

Though Davis is inspired by myriad artistic styles and forms, he is singularly fascinated with William Inge, a closeted gay mid-century American playwright who tragically ended his own life ten years prior to Davis's birth. A somewhat counterintuitive interest for Davis, Inge's plays demonstrate desperate and terrified sexual futility; queerness, for Inge, was not a livable option. In Davis's first encounter with Inge in 2006, assistant directing *The Dark at the Top of the Stairs* (1957) at ATC, he recognized within the writing something indefinable about "the unknown, uncharted land of want and desire and belonging and identity."[2] When Davis returned to ATC as Artistic Director and chose to revive Inge's 1953 Pulitzer Prize-winning *Picnic* in 2017, the production included a fully realized dream ballet, as well as casting that selected people right for the roles, regardless of assigned body, including Molly Brennan as Hal, the typical rugged drifter, and a young trans woman, Alexia Jasmene, as Millie, the sophomoric sister. Though the production received mixed reactions, many critics were impressed by Davis's move beyond the reductive implications of "gender-blind" casting, finding a genuine yearning for human connection and acceptance in the performances.[3]

Gender, for Davis, is choreography. He uses the stories bodies tell to help convey a play's intentions. While still students at University of Texas at Austin, Davis began collaborating with Andrew Hinderaker on *Colossal*, a play that fuses dance with the ultra-masculine sport of football. *Colossal*'s rolling world premiere from the National New Play Network allowed it to develop over several professional productions in 2014 and ultimately led Davis to a Helen Hayes Award for Outstanding Direction. Although development began before Davis's transition, he was already attached to this "testosterone-driven"[4] material that conceives of "being a man" *as* play—a game and a dance.

In a different kind of playfulness, Jaclyn Backhaus's highly acclaimed *Men on Boats*, first presented by Clubbed Thumb at the Wild Project in 2015, is an adventure about men, but with no cis-gender male actors involved. Clubbed Thumb's co-production with Playwrights Horizons in 2016 earned Davis a Lortel nomination for Outstanding Director, and he also brought it to ATC in 2017. Epic in scope, but minimal in scale, through meticulously rehearsed movement and dialogue, *Men on Boats* recounts the 1869 Powell expedition down the Colorado River. Davis's original cast included a pair of trans actors who are noted to revel in the silly surrealism of gender, Becca Blackwell and Jess Barbagallo, whom critics found "wonderfully odd and often deliriously funny."[5] Avoiding what could have been "a one-joke, evening-length bore,"[6] the play and the cast together interrogate American storytelling that privileges white male heroes.

Davis has been instrumental in promoting new work by queer, trans, and nonbinary playwrights. His working history with MJ Kaufman began in 2013 with the New Harmony Project's production of *Sagittarius Ponderosa* and more recently included Kaufman's *Galatea*, presented by the Women's Project in collaboration with Red Bull Theater. Loosely based on John Lyly's 1585 play *Gallathea*, *Galatea* is a modernized trans love story in which Davis cast trans, nonbinary, and two-spirit actors, including Ty Defoe, Pooya Mohseni, and TL Thompson. Davis has also directed the plays of longtime collaborator Basil Kreimendahl, including *Orange Julius* at San Diego's Moxie Theatre in 2015 and *We're Gonna Be Okay* at ATC in 2018. In these productions, Davis mined Kreimendahl's themes of masculinity and familial relationships, informed by pivotal moments in US history such as the Cuban Missile Crisis and the Vietnam War. Following a similar conceit, Daniel Alexander Jones's *Duat* also reimagines communal history. Directed by Davis at the Soho Rep in 2016, *Duat* combines queer Black identity with ancient Egyptian mysticism in a three-part extravagant spectacle that culminates in a musical pageant featuring the playwright's drag alter ego, Jomama Jones.

With a visibly trans take on theatrical convention, Davis removes the "right and wrong binary" to allow instead for an artistic process to "be wrong as long as possible, to cultivate a fierce love for imperfect things."[7] According to Davis, a director's greatest skill is the tolerance for "I don't know." Walking joyously into the unknown is not only a queer aesthetic, but a distinctly trans one. Davis follows an impulse that says

> I have no idea why or what will happen, but just do it and we'll sort it out on the other side. That was true when I changed my

name, it was true when I started making physical changes to my body, and it is true today.

Impacting both Davis's sense of identity and his direction, grappling with "I don't know" means that, if something does not "feel right," one must sit inside that ineffable feeling, and "if you're patient enough, eventually … you change your name to Will."[8] Davis gave himself a name that signals an act of volition: the power of self-determined decision-making. "'Will' is a verb, and it's a promise," he explains.[9] For Davis, naming, like theatre making, represents magic and bringing something to life. He sees a play as "a living document"[10] that moves and changes like a body, perhaps especially like the unanticipated trans body. His work is always informed by queerness, and vice versa. As Davis explains, "Queerness and Trans-ness in my life has been about mystery and complexity and never arriving … my trans identity is expressed through a queer song."[11] In all of his theatrical endeavors, he choreographs the story to that song.

NOTES

1 Will Davis, email to author, June 7, 2021.
2 Suzy Evans, "The Curiosity of Will Davis," *American Theatre*, May/June 2017. www.americantheatre.org/2017/04/20/the-curiosity-of-will-davis/
3 Rachel Weinberg, "Will Davis Casts an Imaginative, Modern Lens on William Inge's *Picnic*," *Rachel Weinberg Reviews*, March 27, 2017. https://rachelweinbergreviews.com/2017/03/27/picnic-american-theater-company-review/
4 Elizabeth Blair, "Play, Ball: A Theatrical Look at the 'Beauty and Brutality' of Football." *All Things Considered*, NPR podcast. October 9, 2014. www.npr.org/2014/10/09/354820407/play-ball-a-theatrical-look-at-the-beauty-and-brutality-of-football
5 Dan Dinero, "Men on Boats," *Theatre Is Easy*, June 29, 2015. www.theasy.com/Reviews/2015/M/menonboats.php
6 Tony Adler, "There's Not a Single WASP Penis in the Pants of *Men on Boats*," *Chicago Reader*, January 18, 2017. www.chicagoreader.com/chicago/american-theater-company-men-on-boats-will-davis/Content?oid=25133813
7 Will Davis, "Queering the Room: Some Beginning Notions for a Queer Directing Practice," *HowlRound Theatre Commons*, October 24, 2014. https://howlround.com/queering-room
8 Nelson Pressley, "Body of Work: Transgender Director Returns to Olney Theatre Center with *Evita*," *Washington Post*, June 24, 2016.

www.washingtonpost.com/entertainment/theater_dance/body-of-work-transgender-director-returns-to-olney-theater-center-with-evita/2016/06/23/3a24a982-36f7-11e6-8f7c-d4c723a2becb_story.html

9 Novid Parsi, "After a Life-Changing Transition, Will Davis Sets out to Transform a Chicago Theater," *Chicago Reader*, December 30, 2016. www.chicagoreader.com/chicago/will-davis-american-theater-company-gender-transition-men-on-boats/Content?oid=24844211

10 Will Davis, "Making Room for the New Work Director," *HowlRound Theatre Commons*, December 24, 2012. https://howlround.com/making-room-new-work-director

11 Davis, email to author, June 7, 2021.

FURTHER READING

Davis, Will. "Portfolio: Will Davis." www.willdavis.work/

Haas, Phil. "Investigating Inge with Will Davis." CSC (podcast). December 29, 2020. https://csc-podcast.castos.com/episodes/investigating-inge-with-will-davis-part-1

TY DEFOE (GIIZHIG)
(Oneida and Ojibwe, Northern Wisconsin)
Courtney Elkin Mohler

Ty Defoe—rooted in the stories, traditions, performances, and values of the Oneida and Ojibwe peoples—learned to hoop dance as soon as he could walk. By the time he was seven, he began the lifelong journey of studying the cultural and sacred arts of his ancestors. Recognizing Defoe's gifts in movement, presence, precision, and transformation, Lakota flute player and hoop dancer Kevin Locke began to mentor and perform with Defoe. This mentorship-apprenticeship opened the world to Defoe; the two toured internationally for years, embodying creative reciprocity through cultural and artistic exchange with communities across the globe. Defoe describes this kind of exchange as a "type of gift-giving" that "is essential for what I like to think of as art: the reciprocity of exchange or the reciprocity of teachings."[1] Defoe's praxis embodies this dynamic value of reciprocity—his contributions to queer and Indigenous performance transform both fields as he shares his lived experience through his work.

Defoe's artistry defies a tidy or succinct description, but he is described as a "two-spirit interdisciplinary shape-shifting artist."[2] In interviews, he makes clear that he does not separate his two-spirit (2S) or Indigiqueer identity from his artistic work, advocacy, and work as a healer:

> The concept of Two-Spirit, where the masculine and the feminine coexist in a person, has always been there among Native people; it's just that it has been shamed and oppressed ... for me, changing form and name was a process I undertook to make the flow a little bit easier and help others on the same path. Being a Two-Spirit person, it's not about a gender identity overpowering the other. The soul craves movement around these concepts of masculine and feminine we have created. Right now it's a time for healing for the Two-Spirited community ... there is tremendous creative potential and an amazing sense of fearlessness.[3]

DOI: 10.4324/9781003203896-10

As such, Defoe grounds his craft in the dedicated study of ancient performance traditions, Ojibwe and Oneida cosmology, and love of and concern for the four-legged and the two-legged, the rooted, and the winged. An animating purpose for Indigenous performers is not to show one individual's mastery over a form, but rather to identify what the community needs, and then to share a song, a dance, or a story that helps build a bridge between communities.[4]

In the twenty-first century, audiences of all kinds—from collegiate to Broadway and from Native communities to predominantly white spaces—*need* to see thriving 2S performers and hear their stories. Significantly, in Young Jean Lee's *Straight White Men* (2018), Defoe was the first 2S trans male Native American to originate a role for a Broadway play, and the first two-spirit actor to perform on Broadway. This is important, because Broadway, and indeed most commercial theatre, has been inhospitable to Indigenous theatre makers, with little to no representation of Indigenous identified actors.[5] Within the first few moments of the play, Defoe, who plays Person in Charge 2, states directly to the audience: "I'm from the Oneida and the Ojibwe Nations. My gender identity is niizhi manitouwug, which means 'transcending gender' in the Ojibwe language."[6] His ability to disarm through his own strength of character allowed audience members to confront, listen to, and meet him as a 2S actor, artist, and storyteller. As one reviewer noted, central to the success of *Straight White Men* is the way in which "Ms. [Kate] Borstein and Mr. Defoe hover near the action throughout," illustrating that the despair of the piece "affects people of all stripes." Their presence illuminates the key question the play asks not just of straight white men, but of us all: "how, in a world where worth is determined by economic output, good people can still be useful?"[7]

Defoe's theatrical work also transcends form, as he meshes artistic styles and media in the service of telling the story the community most needs to hear. Defoe has been prolific and often collaborates with others. Some of his works include: *Tick, Tick* and *Clouds Are Pillows for the Moon*, both written by Defoe, with music by Tidtaya Sinutoke (2014 and 2016); *In the Cards, CRANE: On Earth, in Sky*, co-created and co-written with Heather Henson (2017); *Before the Land Eroded, We Were Here Once* (2020); and *Firebird Tattoo* (2021).

In addition to his work in theatre, performance art, and traditional arts, Defoe is also an award-winning composer, choreographer, and multimedia artist. His 2011 album, *Come to Me Great Mystery: Native American Healing Songs*, won a Grammy Award. He also received awards, residencies, and fellowships from the Indigenous

Heritage Festival (2011), Johnny Mercer Foundation (2015), Robert Rauschenberg Foundation (2016), Jonathan Larson Award (2017), Trans Lab (2020), and the Helen Merrill Award (2021). He received the 2021 Cultural Capital Fellowship for his work in community outreach and cultural preservation.

Defoe has shared cultural arts at the Millennium celebration in Cairo, Egypt; Ankara International Music Festival in Turkey; and Festival of World Cultures in Dubai, UAE. Oregon Shakespeare Festival's 2021 Visual Sovereignty Project featured an excellent example of Defoe's multimedia performance style with his mediated poem "Strong Like Flower," which overlays original traditional flute and electronic music, with Defoe performing his choreography and poetry over video and still images. The poem describes an intimate connection, perhaps between Defoe and a non-Native lover, who asks him to keep his wampum belt on: "you liked how the buckskin ties slapped into the back of your shape, maybe because you felt guilty knowing that this colonized land is my home."[8] In 2020, the New York Public Theater produced *GIZHIBAA GIIZHIG | REVOLVING SKY*, a collaboration between Defoe and All My Relations Collective. Performed in English and Anishinaabemowin, *REVOLVING SKY* merged "immersive performance and interactive multimedia to explore the intersection of science and sacred knowledge" by creating "a lens to view Indigiqueerness and the current climate crisis."[9] Defoe explains Indigiqueerness by stating,

> I like to refer to it as having more of a gender spectrum, or that you're transcending gender ... So, I say that I'm Indigiqueer, which is an Indigenous person that likes to Indigenize spaces and also queer spaces at the same time.[10]

With Sicangu Lakota playwright Larissa Fasthorse, Defoe cofounded Indigenous Direction, a "consulting firm for companies and artists who want to create accurate work about, for and with Indigenous Peoples."[11] Defoe described their goals as they accepted the Association for Theatre in Higher Education's 2020 Award for Leadership in Community-Based Theatre:

> Every time we have a project and we work within the community, it is a mental, emotional, and physical dedication to protecting the sacred, creating narrative reparations, and creating community ... we developed various indigenous cultural protocols and ways of looking at theatre in the world and we wanted

to foster and facilitate equitable connections between institutions and our communities.[12]

This work speaks to Defoe's dedication to advocacy and activism. His ability to blur the boundaries between disciplines illustrates how twenty-first-century theatre and performance can present hybrid and emerging ways of thinking about hybrid and emerging identities. Defoe also models how nonbinary identities and dynamic worldviews are rooted in traditions that predate colonialism and white supremacist thinking. As theatre/performance/music/film/dance/storytelling/poetry defy strict definitions or boundary policing, the culture makers have a responsibility to put forth entirely different visions of what art can be and do. As Defoe says,

> I think about [improvising with seven generations in mind] so often, about dreaming seven generations ahead. It allows me to think about telling the story that I need to tell in this moment. If I were not here, or if we weren't here, what would be left? How can the future weave the story back together if it ever gets lost? I think about accuracy, about archiving, about giving as real a depiction as possible of what's happening in the moment of me as an Indigenous queer artist. It makes me think about time capsules and portals and things—I definitely dream a lot about Indigiqueer futurism ... There is something about the form of art, it creates a social impact. We are in the container of social impact.[13]

NOTES

1 Courtney Boddie, "Episode 20: Ty Defoe – Story Nurturer," Boddie interviews Ty Defoe, Teaching Artistry Podcast, July 11, 2019, https://soundcloud.com/user-4096609/tawcjb-ep-20-final
2 "Ty Defoe," Trans Lab, www.transtheaterlab.org/ty-defoe
3 Febna Reheem Caven, "The Shapeshifting Artist: Ty Defoe," *Cultural Survival Quarterly Magazine*, September 2015, www.culturalsurvival.org/publications/cultural-survival-quarterly/shapeshifting-artist-ty-defoe
4 For more on Indigenous theatre and performance as medicine, see: Jaye T. Darby, Courtney Elkin Mohler, and Christy Stanlake, *Critical Companion to Native American and First Nations Theatre and Performance: Indigenous Spaces*, London: Bloomsbury, 2020, 6–10, 42–61, 72–77, 131–152; and Yvette Nolan, *Medicine Shows: Indigenous Performance Culture*, Toronto: Playwrights Canada Press, 2015.

5 According to the 2018–2019 Asian American Performers Action Coalition report, Broadway theatres employed 0% Indigenous actors for its 2018–2019 season. This unfortunate trend is typical of commercial theatre.
6 Jean Young Lee, "Straight White Men," in *Straight White Men/Untitled Feminist Show*, New York: Theatre Communications Group, 2020, 77.
7 Jesse Green, "Review: 'Straight White Men,' Now Checking Their Privilege on Broadway," *New York Times*, July 3, 2018, www.nytimes.com/2018/07/23/theater/straight-white-men-review-armie-hammer-josh-charles.html
8 Ty Defoe, "Strong Like Flower," posted by OSF Video Department, June 7, 2021, https://vimeo.com/560124899/79815046ac
9 "All MY Relations Collective: GIZHIBAA GIIZHIG | REVOLVING SKY," The Public Theater, https://publictheater.org/productions/season/1920/utr/revolving-sky--gizhibaa-giizhig/
10 Nic Gareiss, "Indigiqueer the Space: An Interview with Ty Defoe," *Critical Studies in Improvisation/Études critiques en improvisation*, vol. 14, nos 2–3 (2021): 2, www.youtube.com/watch?v=amD0etbyX-4
11 www.indigenousdirection.com
12 Nic Gareiss, "Indigiqueer the Space," 2.
13 Ibid., 3–4.

FURTHER READING

Defoe, Ty. *Firebird Tattoo*. In *The Methuen Drama Book of Trans Plays*, edited by Leanna Keyes, Lindsay Mantoan, and Angela Farr Schiller. London: Bloomsbury Publishing, 202.

Reheem Caven, Febna. "The Shapeshifting Artist: Ty Defoe," *Cultural Survival Quarterly Magazine*, September 2015, www.culturalsurvival.org/publications/cultural-survival-quarterly/shapeshifting-artist-ty-defoe

SNEHAL DESAI
(Quakertown, Pennsylvania, 1980–)
Dan Bacalzo

Representations of queer South Asians in American theatre are relatively few. The New York City-based Asian American writing and performance collective Peeling the Banana spotlighted queer South Asian artists in several shows, most notably *Queer N'Asian* (1997). D'Lo, a transgender Sri Lankan American, created solo performances such as *Ramble-Ations: A One D'Lo Show* (2007) and *To T, or Not to T* (2017). Genderqueer artists Alok Vaid-Menon and Janani Balasubramanian toured as performance poetry duo DarkMatter from 2013 to 2017. One of the most prominent and influential theatre creators working at the intersection of South Asian and LGBTQ+ identity is playwright, performer, director, and artistic director Snehal Desai.

While studying for his MFA in Directing at Yale University, Desai began developing material that eventually became his first one-man show, *Finding Ways to Prove You're NOT an Al-Qaeda Terrorist When You're Brown (and Other Stories of the gIndian)*, which he premiered in 2008. The "gIndian" part of the title references the identity of an Indian American gay man, which Desai shares with the central character of his play, Akash. The rest of the title is a tongue-in-cheek reference to how many brown-skinned individuals (from a range of South Asian and Arab backgrounds) are looked upon with suspicion following the terrorist attacks of September 11, 2001.

The solo play offers a multi-perspective view of the intersection of Indian identity and homosexuality, particularly in regard to expectations surrounding marriage. Desai spent two years touring *Finding Ways* across the United States, including runs at New York City's HERE Arts Center and San Francisco's Theatre Rhinoceros. Commenting upon the experience, he observed that one of the rewards of doing this intersectional show was "attracting a good turnout among Indian theatergoers who were expecting a show about racial profiling, but not expecting a lot of talk about what it means to be gay and South Asian."[1]

The duality of Desai's ethnic and sexual identities has cropped up at various other points in his artistic career. For example, he participated in a 2013 autobiographical performance workshop led by performance artist Tim Miller—best known as one of the "NEA Four," whose work was controversially defunded by the National Endowment for the Arts in 1991. This culminated in a one-night-only performance entitled *Exhibit Q: Queer Bodies* at the New Museum.

Trials with Brownies—first performed at Queens Theatre in the Park in 2013—is another solo show, this one a mix of Indian American history and more personal anecdotes. Among the latter is a compelling story of the writer/performer's reaction to the trial of Dharun Ravi, an Indian American man who attempted to livestream a sexual encounter between his roommate, Tyler Clementi, and another man, without either's consent. At a dinner party at his parents' home, Desai found himself unable to join in the conversation about the crime. "I thought it was better to say nothing," he says in the piece. "I thought it was better to keep the idealized picture of who I am up."[2] The latter comment speaks to a desire to project a sanitized version of sexual and racial identification—particularly with family members—when the truth is that it can oftentimes be messy and contradictory. Desai finds himself unable to address a perceived disjuncture between his identities as Indian and gay. His silence at the dinner party is mitigated by his reflection on the event within his solo show, but there is no solution offered and the tension it engenders remains disquietingly unresolved.

In addition to his writing and performing, Desai has also brought his intersectional identifications into play as a director, most significantly with the world premiere of Madhuri Shekar's *A Nice Indian Boy* at East West Players (EWP) in 2014. This comedy centers around Naveen, an Indian American man whose interracial romance with Keshav—a white man adopted by Indian parents—results in some culture clashes as the two plan their wedding. A review in the *Los Angeles Times* called it "pleasantly funny" and "smartly directed."[3]

Desai's work with EWP is arguably where he has had the most impact. He began working with the company in 2013, as literary manager, before becoming the organization's artistic director in 2016. "East West Players felt like that welcoming inclusivity for my whole self in all of its different messiness," says Desai.

> That was something I had not necessarily recognized, and what I saw was that I often presented different aspects of myself that I thought would be most welcomed. If the connection was being

Asian, I would do that, or if the connection was child of immigrants, or being gay.[4]

At EWP, he no longer needed to bifurcate his identity; all aspects were welcome and nurtured. The Los Angeles-based theatrical organization was founded in 1965 as the first theatre company dedicated to work by Asian Americans, and it has maintained its influence in succeeding decades. This includes the presentation of work by queer Asian American theatre artists. In fact, EWP produced the world premiere of the first Asian American play featuring a gay protagonist, Soon Tek-Oh's *Tondemonai: Never Happened* (1970). The theatrical organization also featured work by other queer-identified Asian Americans, such as Denise Uyehara's *Hiro* (1994), Chay Yew's *Whitelands* trilogy (1996), and the 2010 revival of *Mysterious Skin* (2003), adapted by Prince Gomolvilas from Scott Heim's novel of the same name.

As artistic director, Desai has continued to present queer work at EWP, such as Nathan Ramos's *As We Babble On* (2018), a play centering on a gay Asian American comic book artist. A rave review in the prominent Asian American news and culture publication *Hyphen* noted that the play "asks honest questions about our own assumptions of race while avoiding platitudes and social sermonizing."[5] The production was presented in association with the Los Angeles LGBT Center, underscoring EWP's commitment to partnering with other organizations to further diversity in representation.

This same commitment led to one of the most significant actions taken by Desai, who penned an open letter to the Los Angeles Stage Alliance—producer of the Ovation Awards—that called out the organization's systemic racism. Despite EWP serving as a producing partner for two of the nominated productions at the 2021 Ovation Awards ceremony, they were not mentioned at all. "What the Ovation Awards cannot be bothered to do is understand that community and coalition building happens through these partnerships," he notes in his letter. "This is what erasure of our work and our community looks like."[6] Using the hashtag #LeavingLASA, East West Players led a mass exodus of the organization, with over 50 theatres—including large organizations such as Center Theatre Group and Pasadena Playhouse—revoking their membership, which soon resulted in the permanent disbanding of the Los Angeles Stage Alliance.

That was not Desai's intention when he wrote his letter, nor was his letter the only reason for LA Stage Alliance's collapse.[7] In fact,

Desai is much more interested in building coalitions and furthering representations that cover a large spectrum of identifications, including those of queer and Asian. In a 2017 interview he did for the *Los Angeles Times*, he stressed the importance of partnerships as a way of melding art with activism, partly spurred by the election of Donald Trump. "Suddenly, speaking up seemed very important," he said at the time.

> I was in the midst of planning our year and realized that if we made every show a collaboration we could have a larger impact. More than the individual works, the season as a whole is a statement of who we are.[8]

NOTES

1. Gail O'Neill. "Playwright Snehal Desai Brings Fresh Perspectives to Emory's Inaugural Global Voices Series." Arts ATL. January 26, 2015, www.artsatl.org/playwright-snehal-desai-emorys-inaugural-global-voices-series/
2. Snehal Desai, *Trials with Brownies*, unpublished manuscript, 2013, 17.
3. David C. Nichols. "Review: Rooting for *A Nice Indian Boy* at East West Players." *Los Angeles Times*. March 7, 2014, www.latimes.com/entertainment/arts/la-xpm-2014-mar-07-la-et-cm-review-a-nice-indian-boy-at-east-west-players-20140305-story.html
4. Natalie Bui. "Snehal Desai on Respectability Politics, Inclusivity and South Asians in Theatre." *The Slant*. Vol. 56. June 15, 2018. Republished on https://medium.com/the-baton/snehal-desai-on-respectability-politics-inclusivity-and-south-asians-in-theatre-b48591a1821b
5. Christian Ting. "As We Babble On – East West Players' Latest Kicks Off a Promising Summer Theater Season." July 5, 2018. https://hyphenmagazine.com/blog/2018/07/we-babble---east-west-players-latest-kicks-promising-summer-theater-season
6. Snehal Desai. Open letter to the LA Stage Alliance. March 31, 2021. https://eastwestplayers.org/leavinglasa/
7. A nuanced analysis of the situation is found in Howard Ho. "No, LA Stage Alliance Didn't Fold Over a Single Anti-Asian Blunder." *American Theatre*. April 7, 2021. www.americantheatre.org/2021/04/07/no-la-stage-alliance-didnt-fold-over-a-single-anti-asian-blunder/
8. Karen Wada. "The Future of Asian American Theater? East West Players' New Leader Charts a Course," *Los Angeles Times*. November 9, 2017, www.latimes.com/entertainment/arts/la-ca-cm-snehal-desai-east-west-players-20171109-story.html

FURTHER READING

Gray, Margaret. "Snehal Desai: Making a Statement." *SDC Journal*. Summer 2015: 13–17.

Kramer, Rob, and Pier Carlo Talenti. "Art Restart Podcast: Snehal Desai." Kenan Institute for the Arts. June 28, 2021. www.uncsa.edu/kenan/art-restart/snehal-desai.aspx

HARVEY FIERSTEIN
(Brooklyn, New York, 1954–)
Jordan Schildcrout

As a teenager growing up in Bensonhurst, Brooklyn, Harvey Fierstein performed in drag clubs, and he earned his first professional role in 1971 playing an asthmatic lesbian maid in Andy Warhol's *Pork*. He spent the next ten years creating queer theatre, performing, often in drag, in the plays of H.M. Koutoukas, Robert Patrick, Ronald Tavel, Megan Terry, and John Vaccaro, as well as writing his own camp vehicles with titles like *In Search of the Cobra Jewels* (1973), *Freaky Pussy* (1974), and *Flatbush Tosca* (1975). Ellen Stewart of the legendary La MaMa Experimental Theatre Club provided the initial home for the one-act plays that would become *Torch Song Trilogy*, Fierstein's semi-autobiographical comic drama about a New York Jewish drag performer looking for love and respect. John Glines premiered the full four-hour-long trilogy off-off-Broadway in 1981, with Fierstein playing drag queen Arnold Beckoff, Estelle Getty as his disapproving mother, and Matthew Broderick, in his professional debut, as his gay foster son. Queer critics such as Michael Feingold and Tish Dace had long championed Fierstein's work, and a rave review from Mel Gussow in the *New York Times* turned *Torch Song* into a mainstream hit that transferred to off-Broadway and then to Broadway, where it won Tony Awards in 1983 for Best Play and Best Actor, ultimately running 1,222 performances.

Torch Song Trilogy follows Arnold's relationship with Ed, a closeted bisexual schoolteacher who will leave Arnold in order to marry a woman, but then return to him when his marriage falls apart. By the final curtain, Arnold has created his own version of gay domesticity, cooking for his handsome lover and his adopted gay son, but moreover he has achieved dignity by fighting for the legitimacy of these relationships. In the era of Ronald Reagan and the Moral Majority, this is no mean accomplishment, and James Saslow, reporting on the opening night for *The Advocate*, stated, "The final curtain brought a moment I'd never thought I'd live to see in the very heart of American theater: a standing ovation for a drag queen."[1] But other gay critics saw a conservative and assimilationist worldview in the play's appeal to "family values." Reviewing the 1988 film version, the *Chicago Tribune* critic argued that *Torch Song* "doesn't ask its audience to alter its moral assumptions, but only to expand its existing prejudices just enough to allow Arnold to slip in."[2] This tension has followed Fierstein throughout his career, as he has continued to create queer representations for predominantly straight audiences.

Fierstein's star was further burnished by his third Tony Award, for writing the book of the Jerry Herman musical *La Cage aux Folles* (1983), which intertwined spectacular drag numbers with the story of a middle-aged gay male couple winning the acceptance of their straight adult son. He now found himself in the role of spokesperson for LGBTQ America, one of the first celebrities who never had to "come out" because he arrived *as a gay celebrity*, appearing on late-night talk shows and doing interviews with the likes of Barbara Walters, who naively asked, "What's it like to be a homosexual?" The AIDS crisis spurred Fierstein on to further activism, joining the boards of the AIDS Medical Foundation and the Gay Men's Health Crisis, while regional performances of *Torch Song Trilogy* functioned as fundraisers for AIDS organizations around the country.

Fierstein's trilogy of one-act plays *Safe Sex* (1987) received mixed reviews and quickly closed on Broadway, but it offers insight into Fierstein's ambivalence about bringing queer culture into the mainstream, with a character he plays ruefully noting that, due to the devastation of AIDS, "Now they know who we are ... The myths slowly peel away and the mysteries fade ... Now we have safe sex. (*Turning accusingly to the audience*) Safe for them!"[3] The third act of the trilogy became an ACE Award-winning HBO special, titled *Tidy Endings* (1988), starring Fierstein and Stockard Channing, and Fierstein revived the second act off-Broadway in 1991 and also performed a monologue from it in his cabaret act, *This is Not Going to Be Pretty* (1995).

The 1990s saw Fierstein's greatest success in film and television, often appearing as a gay supporting character, fluctuating between brassy and nurturing, flamboyant and wise, frequently aiding the main (heterosexual) character in their journey. In addition to an Emmy-nominated guest appearance on *Cheers* in 1992, his role in the short-lived sitcom *Daddy's Girl* (1994) was reported to be the first time an openly gay actor played a gay recurring character in a US television series. Film appearances included *Mrs. Doubtfire* (1993), *Bullets Over*

Broadway (1993), and *Independence Day* (1996), and Fierstein's distinctive voice, which had previously narrated the Academy Award-winning documentary *The Times of Harvey Milk* (1984), was also heard in animated characters, giving Homer an executive makeover on *The Simpsons* (1990) and befriending the cross-dressing heroine of Disney's *Mulan* (1998).

Fierstein returned to Broadway in 2002 in the musical *Hairspray*, playing the unglamorous housewife Edna Turnblad, a role originated by the drag queen Divine in John Waters' 1988 film. Once again, Fierstein infused a socially denigrated character with joy and dignity, belting out in the finale, "You can't stop my happiness, 'cause I like the way I am." The performance brought him his fourth Tony Award, making him the only person to win Broadway's highest honor for both writing and performing in both plays and musicals. A minor controversy erupted when Macy's invited Fierstein to appear as Edna dressed as Mrs. Claus in the 2003 Thanksgiving Day Parade. The day before his appearance, Fierstein published an op-ed in the *New York Times*, addressing the battle over marriage equality and asking, "What if Santa Claus really was gay?"[4] Despite homophobes decrying the "politicization" of the Macy's parade, the performance carried on as planned. Fierstein continued to use his celebrity to address political issues, penning opinion pieces in mainstream publications, but also speaking within the queer community in commentary segments filmed for the PBS LGBTQ news program *In the Life* between 2001 and 2005.

Some critics questioned the wisdom of having a famously gay actor take over the role of the Jewish patriarch Tevye in a revival of *Fiddler on the Roof*, but Fierstein successfully played the role on Broadway for a full year in 2005. In Fierstein's next major contribution to queer representation, he collaborated with pop singer (and ardent LGBTQ rights supporter) Cyndi Lauper on *Kinky Boots* (2013). This musical, which ran for six years, brought renown to Billy Porter for his Tony Award-winning performance as Lola, a drag queen whom Fierstein frequently stated was written as heterosexual. He further explored the complex intersections of gender, sexuality, and cross-dressing in his play *Casa Valentina* (2014), directed on Broadway by Joe Mantello. Based on true events, the play depicts an organization of "transvestites," many of them married men, some of whom by contemporary understandings might identify as transgender, gathering in the Catskills in 1962. The heterosexual members, hoping to achieve social legitimacy, propose ejecting the homosexuals, creating a lavender scare that rips apart the community.

Fierstein continued to appear on stage in the second decade of the twenty-first century, stepping into the role of Albin in the 2010 Broadway revival of *La Cage aux Folles*, reprising his role as Edna for television in *Hairspray Live* (2016), playing an older gay man in a relationship with a younger man in Martin Sherman's *Gently Down the Stream* (2017), and appearing without drag as feminist politician Bella Abzug in his one-person show, *Bella Bella* (2019). Fierstein also has an active presence on social media, regularly posting his takes on culture and politics, and he has now assumed the role of queer elder, often addressing his thousands of followers as "my children." Indeed, the roles he created in the era of gay liberation and the AIDS crisis are now performed by a new generation of queer theatre artists, such as Michael Urie in the role of Arnold in the widely praised 2017 revival of *Torch Song*. As Fierstein posted in 2020 when reflecting upon the passing of Larry Kramer, Mart Crowley, Terrence McNally, and Jerry Herman, "I wave the next generation forward. You've got some big heels to fill, children."[5]

NOTES

1 James Saslow, "But has the Rest of the 'Family' Been Disinvited?" *The Advocate*, July 22, 1982, 41.
2 Dave Kehr, "In 7-Year Journey to Film, *Torch Song* Loses Social Edge," *Chicago Tribune*, December 23, 1988.
3 Harvey Fierstein, *Safe Sex*, New York: Atheneum, 1987, 57–58.
4 Harvey Fierstein, "You Better Watch Out," *New York Times*, November 26, 2003, A25.
5 Harvey Fierstein, Facebook post, May 28, 2020, www.facebook.com/harvey.fierstein/posts/10222341429591663

FURTHER READING

Hart, Norman. "The Selling of *La Cage aux Folles*: How Audiences Were Helped to Read Broadway's First Gay Musical." *Theatre History Studies* 23 (June 2003): 5–24.
Schildcrout, Jordan. *In the Long Run: A Cultural History of Broadway's Hit Plays*, Abingdon: Routledge, 2020.

WILLIAM FINN
(Natick, Massachusetts, 1952–)
Ryan Donovan

Musical theatre writer William Finn's depictions of queer life—and queer family—shifted the paradigm of what musicals could do and whom they could represent. Finn consistently foregrounds queer characters in his musicals to an unmatched degree, centering the experiences of a generation marked by AIDS in *Falsettos* (1992), *A New Brain* (1998), and his song cycle *Elegies* (2003). Writing the words, the music, and often the spoken text, too, Finn creates profoundly personal works that demonstrate how an artist can respond to their historical circumstances. Finn explains, "What I was trying to do was make my mark, in a world that had absolutely no interest in welcoming me."[1] The representations of gay men in Finn's musicals chart a path from the time just before AIDS to the grieving communities of family, friends, and lovers left behind in its wake.

Finn's work resounds with Broadway songwriting traditions in its sophisticated lyrics that reveal a penchant for the wit of Cole Porter and Stephen Sondheim, but also the occasional flair for an unabashed show tune that recalls Jerry Herman's knack for building a song to an infectiously emotional climax. However, unlike these gay male Broadway songwriter predecessors, Finn did not need to be closeted in order to have his shows produced. He was out personally and professionally from the start of his career, with musicals that centered queer subjects.

Finn graduated in 1974 with a music degree from Williams College, which he chose to attend because Broadway composer-lyricist Stephen Sondheim was an alumnus.[2] He came of age during the peak of gay liberation and was nearing 30 when AIDS was discovered to be infecting gay men in 1981. He made the impact of AIDS on contemporary life clear in his "Marvin Trilogy," three one-act off-Broadway musicals—*In Trousers* (1979), *March of the Falsettos* (1981), and *Falsettoland* (1990)—that follow the character of Marvin and his lover, ex-wife, son, psychiatrist, and neighbors

DOI: 10.4324/9781003203896-13

through the late 1970s and early 1980s. If these works were not initially all well received (the *Times* critic referred to *In Trousers* as "a bare germ of an idea" that "is decidedly unwell"),[3] time has been on their side, and they are now vital portraits of a specific time and place. *In Trousers* stages Marvin's anxieties over coming out, while *March* and *Falsettoland* focus on his relationship with his son, now ex-wife, and his lover, Whizzer. Whizzer was the first character in a Broadway musical to die of AIDS when *March* and *Falsettoland* were combined into a new two-act musical under the name *Falsettos* in 1992.

That the "Marvin Trilogy" was about a gay father and, eventually, his lover as a co-parent, was revolutionary in ultra-conservative 1980s America, where the dominant rhetoric of "family values" vehemently excluded queer people. That *Falsettos* was produced on Broadway was doubly remarkable; it was the first Broadway musical to include AIDS and only the second to feature gay protagonists, following Jerry Herman and Harvey Fierstein's musical *La Cage aux Folles* (1983), whose gay leads were, not incidentally, also gay male co-parents. Like *La Cage*, *Falsettos* was a Broadway success in part because of its emphatic repurposing of "family values." Critic Frank Rich explained that *Falsettos*

> depicts homosexuals neither as abject victims of prejudice or disease nor campy figures of fun but as ... people no more or less extraordinary than the rest of us. In other words, gay people are just part of the family.[4]

Unlike *La Cage*, *Falsettos* was not desexed: whereas *La Cage*'s couple barely touched each other, Marvin and Whizzer went further. Writer Wayne Hoffman attended the original production and he recalls

> being moved to tears not by the specter of death that hangs over the end of the show, but by a simple love song earlier in the score called "What More Can I Say," which features two men in bed together—something I had never seen on stage before, and only very rarely since.[5]

The friendship between Marvin, Whizzer, and the "lesbians next door" in *Falsettos* also broke new ground on Broadway as examples of queer kinship; its depiction of a romantic lesbian couple was also revelatory in a Broadway musical and would be succeeded by *Rent*'s lesbian couple Joanne and Maureen in 1996.

Falsettos bore witness to HIV/AIDS on the US theatre's biggest stages at a time when HIV infection was the leading cause of death for men aged 25–44,[6] and the stigma attached to HIV/AIDS and homophobia was immense. Yet *Falsettos* proved a critical and commercial success, winning Finn Tony Awards for Best Book and Best Score. The show continues to appeal to twenty-first-century audiences, as seen in the Tony-nominated 2016 revival starring Christian Borle and Andrew Rannells.

Finn's work is often semi-autobiographical, which in his case means he foregrounds Jewish gay themes, as he does in the memorable opening number of *Falsettos*, "Four Jews in a Room Bitching." In describing his trajectory as an artist, he told *Playbill*, "It took me a long time to develop *my* voice, the voice of William Finn. The voice I use in all these songs in *Elegies* is a very distinct New York Jewish gay voice."[7] His next major musical, *A New Brain*, drew directly from his own brush with death and recovery from brain surgery—the main character was even a songwriter. Finn again openly drew from his own life in his song cycle *Elegies*, in which he made queer friendships sing in songs like "Monica and Mark" and "Mark's All-Male Thanksgiving," and in which he memorialized his relationship with his mother. *A New Brain* and *Elegies* both premiered off-Broadway at Lincoln Center Theater.

Finn's next Broadway musical foray was also his biggest commercial success and his first major musical not to center queer characters (though one main character has two dads who appear briefly). *The 25th Annual Putnam County Spelling Bee* (2005) came to Broadway after a successful run off-Broadway, and this move to the mainstream speaks to the ways that his work was able to be specific, idiosyncratic, and appealing to mainstream audiences. *Spelling Bee* was a departure for Finn in terms of content, yet his voice remained intact—and he found a way to include a queer family, yet not make them or their queerness the focus.

The sound of a William Finn song is distinctive and recognizable: intelligent and edgy, frequently hilarious in one turn, and romantic or heartbreaking in the next. Finn's music, with its wide range of influences from Sondheim to 1960s and 1970s folk, pop, and rock, and its emotional range running the gamut from anxious neuroses to joy has proven to be a powerful showcase for performers. His holistic focus on queer people as whole individuals, flaws and all, is one of his major contributions to queer representation. His characters are humans—as opposed to caricatures or stock figures—who have relationships with lovers, parents, children, and friends. Finn's characters are complicated, complex, and sometimes messy; his work moves beyond simple affirmation.

Finn's personal, idiosyncratic, and queer-centric musicals paved the way in both form and content for other shows focused on the self-searching of queer characters. *Fun Home* (2015), with its radical reinvention of musical theatre dramaturgy, is part of the same family tree as Finn's work, and Finn's queer parent-child relationships created possibilities realized in *A Strange Loop* (2019). One can also hear echoes of Finn's influence in the songs of the late Michael Friedman, in musicals such as *The Fortress of Solitude* (2012). Finn further impacts new generations of musical theatre writers by teaching in New York University's Graduate Musical Theatre program, in addition to his role as Artistic Producer of Barrington Stage Company's Musical Theatre Lab.

Finn's works provide a vital record of a generation of gay Jewish men in New York City from the late 1970s through to the 2000s. While much of Finn's oeuvre is self-reflexive, it is important to place his self-reflexivity in historical and cultural contexts, since he was one of but a handful of queer musical theatre makers who openly dared to approach their careers with such translucence. Finn's musicals like the "Marvin Trilogy" and *Elegies* offer future generations crucial documentation of what it was like not just to live through, but to survive, public and private crises from AIDS to 9/11 while still recognizing life's infinite joys—in song.

NOTES

1 Matthew Schneier, "An AIDS-Era Musical in an Age of Marriage Equality," *New York Times*, October 27, 2016, www.nytimes.com/2016/10/30/theater/falsettos-broadway.html
2 Mark Dundas Wood, "An Intimate Conversation with William Finn," *Backstage*, July 31, 2002, www.backstage.com/magazine/article/intimate-conversation-william-finn-41435/
3 Richard Eder, Review of *In Trousers*, Playwrights Horizons, *New York Times*, March 17, 1979, www.nytimes.com/1979/03/17/archives/in-trousers-is-fantasies-of-a-boy-14.html
4 Frank Rich, "Discovering Family Values at *Falsettos*," *New York Times*, July 12, 1992, www.nytimes.com/1992/07/12/theater/theater-discovering-family-values-at-falsettos.html
5 Wayne Hoffman, "The Man Behind Broadway's Big Jewish Musical," *Tablet*, October 26, 2016, www.tabletmag.com/sections/news/articles/the-man-behind-broadways-big-jewish-musical

6 Centers for Disease Control and Prevention, "Update: Mortality Attributable to HIV Infection Among Persons Aged 25–44 Years—United States, 1991 and 1992," November 19, 1993, www.cdc.gov/mmwr/preview/mmwrhtml/00022174.htm
7 William Finn, interview by Robert Viagas, *Playbill*, February 10, 2004, www.playbill.com/article/playbill-on-lines-brief-encounter-with-william-finn-com-329495

FURTHER READING

Anderson, Virginia. "'Something Bad [Was] Happening': *Falsettos* as an Historical Record of the AIDS Epidemic." *Studies in Musical Theatre* vol. 13, no. 3 (2019): 221–234.

Bádue, Alex. "Performing Gender, Sexuality, and Jewishness in the Songs of William Finn's Musical *Falsettoland* (1990)." *Studies in American Jewish Literature* vol. 38, no. 2 (2019): 159–178.

THE FIVE LESBIAN BROTHERS: MOE ANGELOS, BABS DAVY, DOMINIQUE DIBBELL, PEG HEALEY, AND LISA KRON (New York City, 1989–)

Lisa Sloan

The American stage has produced some incredible sibling acts: Vaudeville had the Watson Sisters, the circus had the Flying Karamazov Brothers, but the theatre has the queerest of them all—the Five Lesbian Brothers. This chosen theatrical family consisting of Maureen Angelos, Babs Davy, Dominique Dibbell, Peg Healey, and Lisa Kron emerged as the Five Lesbian Brothers in 1989 at the WOW Café, the now-celebrated feminist theatre collective in New York's East Village. Together, the Brothers have created five plays: *Voyage to Lesbos* (1990), *Brave Smiles ... Another Lesbian Tragedy* (1993), *The Secretaries* (1994), *Brides of the Moon* (1998), and *Oedipus at Palm Springs* (2005). In these plays, the Five Lesbian Brothers use camp and satire to send up patriarchal, homophobic, homonormative, and even feminist cultural norms. As Kate Davy (sister to Brother Babs Davy) writes, "In the edgy outrageousness of their work, the Brothers are both a product of feminism and a precursor of 'queer.' Indeed, [their work is] an instance of the 'new American queer theater'."[1] Just as they trade the 1970s emphasis on sisterhood for a queer brotherhood, the Five Lesbian Brothers discard some lesbian feminist ideas, but bring others into the 1990s with a queer sensibility.

Camp humor, cross-dressing, slapstick comedy, and pop culture references permeate the Brothers' plays, often directed in their original productions by Kate Stafford. The company's artistic style builds on a queer downtown New York theatre aesthetic exemplified by the Ridiculous Theatrical Company as well as Split Britches, Holly Hughes, Carmelita Tropicana, and other WOW Café performers. A hotbed of lesbian feminist performance in the 1980s and 1990s, the WOW Café Theatre also featured the talents of Alice Forrester, Jewish feminist organizer Cheryl Moch, lesbian comedian Reno, Jewish lesbian writer and activist Sarah Schulman, and costume designer Susan Young. Highlighting WOW's importance to the company's development, Brother Lisa Kron says, "The assumption was that the world was a lesbian world. It was an amazing place to really learn to be out in the world in a lesbian context."[2] Unlike most other WOW artists, the Five Lesbian Brothers' plays have been produced off-Broadway at more mainstream venues such as New York Theatre Workshop, the Public Theater, and Performance Space 122—although this necessitated revising their playscripts to be more legible to nonlesbian audiences. Outside of New York, the Five Lesbian Brothers have performed at queer theatres such as Theatre Rhinoceros (San Francisco), Highways (Los Angeles), Alice B. Theatre (Seattle), and The Drill Hall (London).

Like their WOW Café birthplace, the Five Lesbian Brothers' way of working is built on a lesbian feminist model that eschews notions of individual ownership in favor of collective creation. The Brothers create work by writing in shared notebooks, doing group improvisations, and riffing on source material. An individual Brother sometimes organizes the resulting material into a playscript, but the Brothers share writing credit for nearly all of their plays. Their work has received praise from critics in mainstream publications, but the commercial successes and Broadway transfers enjoyed by Terrence McNally, Harvey Fierstein, and other gay male contemporaries eluded the Five Lesbian Brothers. As Jill Dolan writes,

> Their working methods and the politics of their plays' content seemed to keep them outside more lucrative production venues. Their collaborative lesbian feminist working methods, too, both empowered and financially constrained them. Despite their success, they hit a lavender ceiling.[3]

Instead, the company's tremendous work has been recognized by their peers with several awards, including a Bessie (1993), an Obie (1995), and a Lambda Literary Award (2010).

Just as lesbian feminist ideas inform the Brothers' artistic process, they also inform the content of the Brothers' plays—but these ideas are often queerly enacted. The plays carry patriarchal and homophobic notions to extremes, performing them to humorous heights to reveal their limits. But the Brothers also engage in queer disidentification, reveling in negative representations that some lesbian feminists would cast off. As Brother Peg Healey explains, "A lot of …

lesbian theatre is aimed specifically at providing a support for lesbians, at reflecting positive role models and ... positive images of our life ... but I think the Brothers also want to challenge."[4] In *The Secretaries*, the most widely produced of the Brothers' plays, they enact a feminist critique of sexism in the workplace, but also take down radical feminist ideals of women as inherently nurturing and supportive, demonstrating how women participate in the enforcement of patriarchal gender norms. When receptionist Patty is promoted, she finds herself in a cult of murderous secretaries who regulate each other's appearance, eating habits, and even sexual behavior. In the quest for physical perfection, the secretaries obsessively exchange information about workout classes and forgo food in favor of slurping SlimFast® shakes. To cement their sexist sorority, the secretaries murder a lumberjack every 28 days. Contrary to 1970s lesbian separatist ideals, women are not inherently less violent or more peaceful, loving, and nurturing than men. *The Secretaries* has developed a cult following, staged by regional theatres across the United States and frequently included in university theatre seasons because of the performance opportunities it provides for women.

While the Five Lesbian Brothers do not accept all lesbian feminist ideas at face value, they do celebrate lesbian subcultural production. The play *Brave Smiles ... Another Lesbian Tragedy* lovingly restages tragic cultural representations of lesbians to expose and poke fun at the lesbian death trope. Classics of lesbian representation such as the films *Mädchen in Uniform* (1931) and *The Children's Hour* (1961) and the play *Last Summer at Bluefish Cove* (1980) become funny fodder for *Brave Smiles*. When a group of orphan schoolgirls reunite as adults, they are quick to act on their desires for one another. Every time the promise of a lesbian "happily ever after" looks as if it will be fulfilled, this narrative possibility is abruptly foreclosed by the farcical death of one of the lovers. The death toll is visualized with a "necklace of tears" that increases in size every time it appears on stage. The play skillfully balances the women's tragic ends with disidentificatory humor.

In addition to her work with the Five Lesbian Brothers, each member of the company has pursued an artistic career in her own right. Peg Healey has written for film and television, while Dominique Dibbell wrote and performed the short film *LADY* (dir. Ira Sachs, 1994) and gave an Obie-winning performance in the Builders Association's *Jet Lag* (2000). Babs Davy has created several shows in the tradition of queer solo performance, *Women and Children First: Outstanding Perk or Tool of Oppression?* (1992), *How I Drank My Way through*

Heterosexuality (1999), *Blest Like Me: Psycho Pharmacology and Salvation* (2015), and *The Best Medicine* (2017). She has also appeared in several lesbian films, including fellow WOW alumna Madeline Olnek's *The Foxy Merkins* (2013). Moe Angelos has collaborated with the performance company The Builders Association as a performer and writer since 1999. In 2013, she adapted the writings of Susan Sontag into a performance called *Sontag: Reborn*, and in 2019, in association with the arts organization Queer|Art, Angelos led a walking tour focused on the changing East Village called "This Used to Be Gay!" Lisa Kron has gained the most recognition as an individual theatre artist. She wrote the book and lyrics for *Fun Home* (2013), a musical adaptation of Alison Bechdel's graphic memoir, which garnered her two Tony Awards in 2015. Other theatrical works of Kron's include the solo *2.5 Minute Ride* (1999) and the ensemble plays *Well* (2004) and *In the Wake* (2010). Most recently, the Brothers reunited for a one-night-only digital livestream of *Brave Smiles ... Another Lesbian Tragedy* (dir. Leigh Silverman) as part of Pride Plays 2020, a theatre festival that celebrates LGBTQ+ Pride Month.

NOTES

1 Kate Davy. *Lady Dicks and Lesbian Brothers: Staging the Unimaginable at the WOW Café Theatre*. Ann Arbor: University of Michigan Press, 2010, 10.
2 "A Roundtable with the Five Lesbian Brothers." *Playbill*. Accessed June 26, 2021. www.playbill.com/video/a-roundtable-with-the-five-lesbian-brothers. 3:50–4:00.
3 Holly Hughes, Carmelita Tropicana, and Jill Dolan, eds. *Memories of the Revolution: The First Ten Years of the WOW Café Theatre*. Ann Arbor: University of Michigan Press, 2015, 67.
4 Jean Carlomusto, Catherine Saalfield, Dolores Perez, and Polly Thistlethwaite. "Not Just Passing Through." 1994. Accessed May 24, 2022. http://archive.org/details/NotJustPassingThrough. 38:40–39:01.

FURTHER READING

Five Lesbian Brothers. *Four Plays*. New York: Theatre Communications Group, 2000.
Warner, Sara. "Rage Slaves: The Commodification of Affect in The Five Lesbian Brothers' 'The Secretaries'." *Journal of Dramatic Theory and Criticism* vol. 23, no. 1 (2008): 21–46.

MARÍA IRENE FORNÉS
(Havana, Cuba, 1930–2018)
Gwendolyn Alker

María Irene Fornés,[1] playwright, director and teacher, was one of the most important and enduring, yet simultaneously under-acknowledged theatre practitioners to come out of the off-off-Broadway movement of the 1960s. Despite little formal theatre training, Fornés wrote prolifically beginning in the early 1960s. Her first well-known play, *Tango Palace* (1963), was directed by Herbert Blau, signaling her entry into the downtown theatre scene of New York City and her burgeoning relationship with Judson Poets' Theater. She remains most well-known for the plays of her middle period, including *Fefu and Her Friends* (1977), *Mud* (1983), and *Conduct of Life* (1985). Her later work, including sprawling plays such as *Abingdon Square* (1987) and *What of the Night?* (then called *And What of the Night?*, short-listed for a Pulitzer Prize in 1990),[2] remain underproduced and undervalued. Beginning with *Fefu*, Fornés insisted on directing her own work, and subsequently directed the first production of all her plays from that point forward. She also directed her students' plays, including Caridad Svich's *Any Place But Here* (1995), as well as productions such as Chekhov's *Uncle Vanya* (1987) and Ibsen's *Hedda Gabler* (1987). She earned nine Obie Awards, including one for sustained achievement, and her plays were the focus of the 1999–2000 Signature Theatre season.

Many labels have been applied to Fornés' work through the years—Latina, feminist, lesbian—but these were neither descriptions that Fornés cultivated nor labels that she consistently denied.[3] Instead, she primarily identified as an artist, playwright, and *maestra*, or teacher, to many Latinx artists with whom she worked at the INTAR Hispanic Playwrights Lab, which she ran from 1981 to 1992. Through this work, she mentored a generation of queer-identifying playwrights, including many in this volume, such as Cherríe Moraga, Ana María Simo, and Luis Alfaro. She is also cited by Paula Vogel and Tony Kushner as a central influence. While hugely influential within queer theatre, Fornés was hesitant to engage in identity politics, or to place her own experiences as a gay Latina directly in her work. Therefore, the lens of queerness can be applied to Fornés' life and aesthetic, but should also be problematized as a way of understanding her body of work.

The urban legend of how Fornés began to write came from Ross Wetzsteon, who described Irene (as she was usually called) and her then "roommate" Susan (as in Sontag), who was struggling with writer's block. They sat in a café in the West Village; it was spring of 1961. Irene decided that she would show Susan how easy it was. "[S]he almost feels like she's babysitting," said Wetzsteon in a damning description of Fornés' relationship with Sontag.[4] Fornés subsequently wrote a short story by pulling cookbooks off the shelves and using the first word as the beginning of each sentence—foreshadowing her subsequent use of found objects for inspiration. Then Sontag began her first novel. This story is set against a backdrop of queerness—the two women were in a romantic relationship. In the documentary on Fornés, *The Rest I Make Up* (2018), by Michelle Memran, Fornés admits that Sontag was the love of her life. She also remains steadfast in her choice not to discuss her sexual identity with her family in Cuba.

Three years later, Sontag published "Notes on Camp," an influential essay on gay life in pre-Stonewall New York City. A year after that, Fornés wrote *Promenade*, with music by Al Carmines, which ran at Judson Church and later moved uptown to the newly named Promenade Theatre, for her longest commercial run of 259 performances. This musical, an absurd, carnivalesque critique of class and the Vietnam War, centers on two escaped convicts, 105 and 106. While there are no explicitly gay characters, this musical is exemplary of Carmines' camp style, developed while he was a minister at Judson: full of genre-bending music, with a stripper jumping out of a huge cake, and ladies battling to "be naked too."[5] Many years later, Fornés noted to her students at INTAR that she should have been credited as co-author of Sontag's seminal essay on the development of the camp aesthetic.[6]

What is intriguing about this genealogy is an expansion of Fornés' queer aesthetic; with *Promenade*, queerness was not centralized through characters or storylines, but was present in a Fornesian style and in the roots of a play's development. And, by witnessing the birth of this musical in the roots of Sontag and Fornés' relationship in the early 1960s, camp is expanded from the domain of white male homosexuals, living and loving in Greenwich Village in New York City, to one inscribed and theatricalized by two lesbians in a cross-cultural relationship, who began their love affair in Paris.

In Fornés' over 40 plays, there are only three instances of gay characters in her work: in *Fefu and Her Friends* (1977), *Springtime* (1989), and *Enter the Night* (1993). Perhaps with the exception of *Enter the Night,* what is most remarkable about these gay characters is how Fornés writes them with the care, empathy, and focus on the tribulations of romantic love that she devotes to all of her scripted romances—they do not differ from her heterosexual ones.

Fefu and Her Friends, by far her most often-staged and well-known work, was first produced at the Relativity Media Lab in New York City's SoHo district in 1977. Constructed environmentally, this was also her breakout moment as a multidisciplinary artist. The intimacies of the relationships of the eight characters are what animate this play.[7] One such relationship emerges between Paula and Cecilia, who, in Part II, "In the Kitchen," are revealed to be ex-lovers. Their dialogue focuses on the all-too-human challenges of becoming a stranger to someone whom you still love. It is almost as if Fornés' choice to cast only female characters in the play necessitated that the one on-stage romance occurs between two women.

Springtime, an intimate one-act which Fornés later embedded as the second act of *What of the Night?*, revolves around a romance between Rainbow and Greta. In a frequent plot device used by Fornés, this romantic bliss is corrupted by Ray, the protagonist of the larger four-act cycle. The play chronicles the abandonment of Rainbow by Greta. Along the way, Rainbow defends her lesbian relationship to Ray, with words that sound somewhat similar to Fornés' own beliefs: "Why should it be important whether I like men or women? Does it make any difference to anyone? … Why should I try to love someone I don't love when I already love someone I love?"[8]

Enter the Night details another bizarre love triangle—here, between two women and a gay man, Jack. The sex described in the play includes an extremely brutal description of Jack being group-fucked without protection, and his horror and pleasure at that moment. The play ultimately circles around Jack's fear that he has HIV, Paula and Tressa's insistence that he does not, and the intimacies in their caretaking relationship. As such, this can be seen as Fornés' AIDS play, but in characteristic fashion she turns it into a work about illness, violence, and an empathetic portrayal of those who dwell at the margins of society.

In his posthumously published book *The Sense of Brown*, José Muñoz includes Fornés' play *Mud* as exemplar of his notion of "brownness" through her "strangely minimalist and excessive language."[9] Muñoz describes his "brown commons" as "not about the production of the individual but instead about a movement, a flow, and an impulse to move beyond ... individualized subjectivities."[10] This description provides a useful way to understand Fornés' complex relationship with her identity. Her queerest aesthetic can be found in *Promenade* or in *Tango Palace*,[11] an absurdist play about an otherworldly relationship between an older, androgynous Isidore and a young Leopold stuck together in an intimate dance that eventually leads to their destruction. Technically, however, neither of these two plays includes gay characters. Instead, Fornés' artistry was about creating a unique aesthetic shaped by and connected to her own complex self, but not reducible to it. Her legacy remains in the inspiration and mentorship she provided to a generation of Latinx and off-Broadway playwrights, as well as a body of work that remains uncompromising in its originality.

NOTES

1 This chapter both includes diacritics on Fornés' name and not, if they were not included in the original publication. During her lifetime, Fornés chose not to include accents on her published work.
2 *And What of the Night?* premiered in Milwaukee in March of 1989, but Fornés later published the play in 2008 with the "And" dropped from the title.
3 As discussed in more detail in Gwendolyn Alker's "Fornesian Animality: María Irene Fornés' Challenge to a Politics of Identity," *Journal of Dramatic Theory and Criticism* 35:1 (Fall, 2020), 9–28.
4 Wetzsteon, Ross, "Irene Fornes: The Elements of Style," in *The Theater of Maria Irene Fornes*, ed. Marc Robinson (Baltimore, MD: Johns Hopkins University Press, 1999), 25.
5 Fornés, Maria Irene, *Promenade and Other Plays* (New York: PAJ Press, 1987), 14.
6 Caridad Svich, email message to the author, October 21, 2021.
7 In a recent production of *Fefu* at the Theatre for a New Audience (2019), the director added lesbian overtones to Fefu and Emma's friendship. This is a less common interpretation.
8 Fornés, María Irene, *What of the Night? Selected Plays* (New York: PAJ Press, 2008), 123.
9 Muñoz, José Esteban, *The Sense of Brown*, eds Joshua Chambers-Letson and Tavia Nyong'o (Durham, NC: Duke University Press, 2020), 126.
10 Ibid., 2.
11 Thanks to Scott Cummings for his suggestion of *Tango Palace* as Fornés' "queerest" play.

FURTHER READING

Alker, Gwendolyn. "Teaching Fornes: Preserving Fornes in Critical Context," *Theatre Topics* 19:1 (September, 2009), 207–219.

Cummings, Scott T. *Maria Irene Fornes* (Abingdon and New York: Routledge, 2013).

Delgado, Maria M. and Svich, Caridad, eds. *Conducting a Life: Reflections on the Theatre of Maria Irene Fornes* (Lyme, NH: Smith and Kraus, 1999).

JOHN GLINES
(Santa Maria, California, 1933–2018)
Jordan Schildcrout

John Glines, who founded the pioneering gay and lesbian arts organization The Glines in 1976 in partnership with Barry Laine and Jerry Tobin, became one of the preeminent producers of queer theatre, supporting the work of LGBTQ+ theatre artists and bringing queer representation into the mainstream. Glines grew up in the Bay Area, graduated from Yale, and then attempted a theatre career in New York, first as an actor and then as a playwright and director. Deciding he would be more successful if he produced his own plays, he set out to learn the business of theatre by serving as the administrative director for TOSOS (The Other Side of Silence), the first professional gay theatre company, founded by playwright Doric Wilson. Wilson had begun his own career at the legendary Caffe Cino and later became a participant in the Stonewall Riots. With the creation of TOSOS in 1974, Wilson successfully merged the adventurous ethos of off-off-Broadway with the community politics of the burgeoning gay liberation movement. Glines adapted this approach for his own company, and he would repay his mentor by providing the artistic home for many of Wilson's later plays.

Opening in April 1976, the stated mission of The Glines was "the creation and presentation of work which deals with the gay experience in meaningful and artistic ways in order to create positive self-images and dispel negative stereotyping."[1] Operating their own performance space at 260 West Broadway, The Glines produced plays and musicals, screened films, displayed the work of visual artists, and hosted special events with queer poets, authors, comedians, drag troupes, dance troupes, musicians, cabaret artists, and scholars.

Their first commercial success was the musical *Gulp!* (1977), co-written and directed by Glines, which combined gay romance and farce on the beach of Coney Island on Gay Liberation Day. While the characters—including a twink pining for a closeted lifeguard, a drag queen fighting with her blue-collar lover, and a priest-turned-hitman-turned-activist—were ridiculously stereotypical, this zany musical addressed gay desire and coming out with sincerity, leading *The Advocate* to praise *Gulp!* and opine that "expressing serious thoughts in humorous form is a new stage for gay theatre, which until now has oscillated between propaganda and camp."[2] The *New York Times* refused to print an advertisement for the show with the word "gay" in it, but Glines ran *Gulp!* for 94 performances in 1977, revived it the following summer, and published its complete script in the softcore gay magazine *Blueboy*.[3] Nevertheless, by September 1978, the company could no longer afford to maintain its own performance space, and Glines, who had previously spent seven years writing for the children's television program *Captain Kangaroo*, took a job as a writer for *Sesame Street* to make ends meet.

In its next major endeavor, The Glines, supported by a grant from the National Endowment for the Arts, produced the First Gay American Arts Festival for six weeks in the summer of 1980, featuring new plays by playwrights Glines consistently championed: Jane Chambers (*Last Summer at Bluefish Cover*, starring Jean Smart), Doric Wilson (*Forever After*, starring Casey Wayne), and Robert Patrick (*T-Shirts*, starring Jack Wrangler). Along with film screenings and readings by authors like Edmund White, John Rechy, and Audre Lorde, the festival also imported productions from San Francisco's Theatre Rhinoceros and Minneapolis's Out and About Theatre. The Second Gay American Arts Festival, in 1981, increased the diversity of representation, showcasing more works by lesbians, including *My Blue Heaven* by Jane Chambers, Pat Bond in *Gerty, Gerty, Gerty Stein is Back, Back, Back*, and the Radical Lesbian Feminist Terrorist Comedy Group, as well as Assotto Saint's choreopoem of Black gay experience, *Risin' to the Love We Need*.

The festival also featured readings of scenes from three plays by the downtown drag performer Harvey Fierstien. John Glines proposed trimming the plays and producing them in a single evening, and in 1981 The Glines mounted the off-off-Broadway premiere of *Torch Song Trilogy*, a four-hour comic drama about the life and loves of a New York Jewish drag queen, played by Fierstein. The production struggled to attract an audience, and Glines considered closing the show after four weeks, but a rave review from the *New York Times* turned the play into a hit. After transferring to a larger off-Broadway venue, Glines eventually convinced Fierstein to take *Torch Song Trilogy* to Broadway, where it won the Tony Award for Best Play.

When accepting the award, Glines thanked "my partner and my lover, Lawrence Lane," and this groundbreaking acknowledgment of a same-sex mate on a nationally televised awards show was condemned by most of the press and brought death threats against Glines. Astute analysis of the brouhaha came from theatre critic Jack Viertel, who noted:

> The challenge that Glines was throwing out by publicly thanking his male companion was simply this: You have accepted us overwhelmingly as long as we stay behind the proscenium arch ... Now, act with your hearts as you have with your box-office dollars—accept us in the real world.[4]

Glines claimed, "From the beginning, our purpose has been to get into the mainstream, to prove that a gay theme is viable."[5] He continued this mission by using the profits from *Torch Song Trilogy* to transfer *As Is* (1985) by William M. Hoffman, directed by Marshall W. Mason, from the Circle Repertory Company to Broadway, where it ran for 285 performances and became the first Tony-nominated play to deal with the AIDS crisis. Along with donating a portion of each ticket to AIDS organizations, Glines also founded the fundraising campaign Stamp Out AIDS and became a founding trustee of Broadway Cares/Equity Fights AIDS.

Reflecting on how his theatre existed to challenge the homophobia of mainstream culture, Glines said, "One of the purposes of The Glines was to succeed and put itself out of business."[6] But, as plays with queer content became more frequently produced by mainstream theatres, Glines returned to his off-off-Broadway roots, most notably with *Untold Decades* (1988) by Robert Patrick and *The Quintessential Image* (1989) by Jane Chambers. Increasingly, Glines pursued his own playwriting, creating what he called "second generation AIDS plays, which deal with how a gay person gets along after the death of a loved one."[7] His plays, such as *On Tina Tuna Walk* (1988), *Men of Manhattan* (1990), and *Body and Soul* (1991), continued to mix comedy and romance, often advertised with images of handsome actors embracing, and proved financially successful for the company.

In 1993, The Glines co-produced Howard Crabtree's camp musical *Whoop-Dee-Doo*, which won the Drama Desk Award for Outstanding Revue, and Glines defended producing a frothy extravaganza at the height of the AIDS crisis by asserting the importance of "entertaining the troops in wartime."[8] The Glines continued producing two or three plays a season through the 1990s, culminating in the critically and commercially successful *An Evening with Quentin Crisp* (1998), featuring the witty and wise 90-year-old British raconteur. In 2005,

Glines went into retirement and moved to Bangkok, where he focused his creative energies on photography until his death in 2018 at the age of 84.

When asked about the name of his company, Glines stated, "One reason I called the organization The Glines was to be personally out and open, because at the time many actors and playwrights didn't want to use their real names when working in the gay arts."[9] Over three decades, Glines broke down closet doors in the theatre, establishing viable models for producing theatre by, for, and about the queer community, as well as building bridges for queer theatre artists into the mainstream of US culture. His life's work also demonstrated that, even with a degree of mainstream acceptance and success, LGBTQ+ artists and audiences benefited from the communal visibility and engagement created within a theatre dedicated to queer experience and expression.

NOTES

1 The Glines, "Theatre Program: *A Perfect Relationship*," 1979.
2 James M. Saslow, "New York," *The Advocate*, June 29, 1977, 20.
3 John Glines, *Gulp!* in *Blueboy*, Act I, January/February 1979, 40; Act II, March 1979, 85.
4 Jack Viertel, "Kudos, Not Gossip, for Gay Producer," *Los Angeles Herald Examiner*, June 9, 1983, n.p.
5 John Corry, "Broadway," *New York Times*, April 2, 1982, C2.
6 Gary Stern, "John Glines: There's a Place for Daring Theatre on Broadway," *Backstage*, July 22, 1983, 73.
7 Terry Helbing, "Fighting All the Odds," *New York Native*, August 14, 1989, 28.
8 Michael Portantiere, "And the Boys in the Band Play On," *Backstage*, June 28, 1996, 3, 37.
9 Natalie Hope McDonald, "John Glines: Engine and Booster of GLBT Theatre," *Gay & Lesbian Review Worldwide*, Nov/Dec 2008, 42–43.

FURTHER READING

Glines, John. "The Glines: Photo Gallery," https://pbase.com/johnglines/the_glines/
Saslow, James M. "A Glimpse of The Glines," *The Advocate*, May 31, 1978.

DAVID GREENSPAN
(Los Angeles, California, 1956–)
Nick Salvato

As a celebrated writer, performer, and director, David Greenspan uses antirealistic formal experimentation in the service of queerly contesting norms of gender and sexuality. Three phases of his work explore the confessional, the fantastical, and the theatre-historical, respectively. His influences include not only explicitly queer playwrights like Gertrude Stein and Oscar Wilde but also playwrights and theatre theorists whom he comprehends queerly, ranging from Aristotle and Plato to Shakespeare and beyond. An Obie Award-winning actor participating in the projects of his queer contemporaries, he is especially regarded by critics for his performances in his own work, including his marathon solo performances.

Writing about elements of David Greenspan's collaboration on the musical adaptation of *Coraline* (2009), Tanya Dean could just as easily be describing the defining characteristics of the theatre at the heart of his career: singly authored plays in which Greenspan acts, either solo or as part of an ensemble, and sometimes directs—and that create "a reality that eschew[s] realism, bordered by ... fantastical realm[s] fashioned without special effects."[1] Indeed, over the course of 30-plus years of making professional work, mostly produced in New York City and regularly Obie Award-winning, Greenspan has conceived an "antirealistic project," rooted in a queerly nonnormative vision of the stage and the world to which it gestures and beckons.[2] In some of Greenspan's early plays, such as *Jack* (1987), *The HOME Show Pieces* (1988), and *2 Samuel 11, Etc.* (1989), the realities of coming out, masturbating, having sex, and coping with AIDS-related loss—enacted through putatively stammering (though carefully calibrated) repetitions and various forms of rehearsal—are juxtaposed with explicitly queer sexual fantasies. The next phase of Greenspan's work, including plays like *Son of an Engineer* (1994) and *The Myopia* (1993–2003), moves the fantasies into mythical, cosmological, and otherwise otherworldly dimensions, juxtaposed with satirical depictions of straight, straitened, and straitening realities. However, more recent work, including *The Argument* (2007) and *Plays* (2010), collides the fantasy of vivifying texts in—and ghosts of—theatre theory and theatre history with the reality of Greenspan's chameleonic, kaleidoscopic approach to embodied performance.

Calling Greenspan's work *queer* rather than *gay* aligns with the critical orientation of Marc Robinson, who argues for such an approach to Greenspan's corpus in the introduction with which he frames his edited collection of five representative, pioneering works by Greenspan, *The Myopia and OtherPlays* (2011). There, Robinson finds his way into this issue of rhetoric—and politics—through a consideration of two characters who act as surrogates for Greenspan in his plays: one who says in *The HOME Show Pieces*, "I really don't consider myself a ... gay playwright";[3] and another, Simon Lanquish in *She Stoops to Comedy* (2003), who "joins him in disdaining obvious categories"[4] when he quips, "who needs a play about a gay man who ... ?" and then rattles off a series of clichéd ways to fill the ellipsis.[5] For Robinson, the takeaway from such metatheatrical moments, not merely comic, is that

> to call these "gay plays" is to miss their point and duck their challenge. A more accurate tag would reflect an approach to playwriting that, as David Savran puts it in a discussion of queer drama in general, "represents not a stabilization but a disarticulation of identity."[6]

Or, to put the problematic at stake in a slightly different way, Greenspan is engaged in an ongoing "interrogation of norms, conventions, and coherences of gender and sexuality as well as the pleasure that comes from such an interrogation."[7]

This interrogation manifests for Greenspan not just in writing but in a number of ways in live performance, including his many vivid turns on stage as women—turns in which he famously eschews drag and related exaggerations (or even less cartoonish approximations) of femininity. With reference to this aspect of his work, Steven Drukman muses, in an interview with Greenspan, "It's not drag, what you do, ever. It's more like what used to be called gender-fuck."[8] Perhaps nowhere has the "gender-fuck" been so memorable and charming than in *She Stoops to Comedy*. In its first production at Playwrights Horizons, Greenspan played an actress who is at times impersonating a man in the play that she is rehearsing (and otherwise): in other words, he appeared on stage simply—that is to say, complexly—as a pants-wearing man, in what he calls a "disguiseless disguise" of multiple, palimpsestic layers, pointedly referential to *As You Like It*.[9]

Of course, as an actor for hire, Greenspan *has* been costumed in drag—or at least semi-drag—most indelibly in his performance as Queen Elizabeth I in the Classic Stage Company production of Sarah Ruhl's *Orlando* (2010). Thinking about a performance such as that one alongside Greenspan's citations and allusions in pieces like *She Stoops to Comedy* prompts an invocation of the title of one of his earliest plays, *The Horizontal and the Vertical* (1986), as a rubric through which to comprehend both the queer genealogies (vertical) in which Greenspan knowingly, often winkingly, inserts himself and the equally queer networks (horizontal) in which he collaborates with his contemporaries. Where the former is concerned, Greenspan tends to operate in two modes: either he invokes or figures historical forebears who are explicitly queer (for example, Gertrude Stein in *The Myopia* and *Plays*, Oscar Wilde in 1997's *Only Beauty*), or he serves up a queer take on such forebears (Shakespeare in *She Stoops to Comedy*, Aristotle and Plato in *The Argument*)—not so much "refer[ring] and defer[ring] to theatre history," as Drukman would have it, but reforming and deforming theatre's histories and theories for the intellective, often heady, pleasures that can result from such transubstantiations.[10] As for the ecologies and assemblages in which Greenspan serves the visions of other queer writers and directors, they include performances in a 1996 revival of Mart Crowley's *Boys in the Band*, in a 2007 production of Terrence McNally's *Some Men*, and—also in 2007—in Linda Chapman and Kate Moira Ryan's adaptation of the fabulously pulpy, campy *Beebo Brinker Chronicles*.

Laudable, and lauded, as these performances are, critics writing admiringly about Greenspan tend to gravitate to his acting in his own plays—and not surprisingly so, given just how herculean become the challenges Greenspan sets for himself in this work and just how virtuosically he meets those challenges. Take, for instance, *The Myopia*, in which Greenspan plays 21 different roles over the course of two hours, all while sitting in an armchair. One might think the result would be boring or airless, but Greenspan transforms that chair into everywhere and nowhere as he uses a complex suite of vocalizations, facial expressions, gestures, and poses to animate his pageant of characters. Helen Shaw has dubbed this kind of excessive, bravura solo performance "Impossible Theatre," and that coinage resonates precisely because it *should* be impossible to pull off the energetic, multifaceted (non-)self-presentation, at times crisply comic and at others unsentimentally poignant, that emerges in pieces like *The Myopia*.[11]

With Shaw's language in mind, one may find it difficult—though not, exactly, "impossible"—to imagine anyone besides Greenspan himself bringing a piece like *The Myopia* (or *Son of an Engineer*, or *The Argument*) to life. This putative limitation might at first blush seem to diminish what could be variously called the influence, impact, and importance of Greenspan's work, but in fact what it invites, even forces, is a queer reckoning with the narrow view that would privilege the site of the play-text above the enchanted, darkened rooms in which Greenspan's pieces *move* (in both senses of that word). Yet not merely moving, Greenspan's plays also provoke profound, eminently philosophical questions. For Shaw, they include, "How do we know what is imagination and what is experience? How do we know the limits of our minds? Why is it that we can feel a thing and know a thing at two different times?"[12] For Robinson, Greenspan "ask[s] how the primal instinct for telling has been able to survive a sophisticated understanding of the tale's inadequacy. Other questions pile up around stories that failed to deliver or that delivered too simplistically."[13] A crucial one of those "other questions" must be: What shifts and eruptions come from queer experimentation with theatrical form and delivery, and who do we become on the other side of encountering them?

NOTES

1 Tanya Dean, "Piano Guts and Other Mothers: Staging Fantasy in David Greenspan and Stephen Merritt's Musical Adaptation of Neil Gaiman's *Coraline*." *Journal of the Fantastic in the Arts* 24:2 (2003), 264.
2 Nick Salvato, "A Horse's Husband: David Greenspan's Queer Temporalities and the Politics of Same-Sex Marriage." *Theatre Survey* 52:1 (2010), 19.
3 David Greenspan, *The HOME Show Pieces*. In *The Myopia and Other Plays*. Ed. Marc Robinson. Ann Arbor: University of Michigan Press, 2011, 59.
4 Marc Robinson, "Introduction." In *The Myopia and Other Plays*, 7.
5 David Greenspan, *She Stoops to Comedy*. In *The Myopia and Other Plays*, 176.
6 Robinson, "Introduction," 7; see David Savran, "Queer Theater and the Disarticulation of Identity." In *The Queerest Art: Essays on Lesbian and Gay Theater*. Eds Alisa Solomon and Framji Minwalla. New York: New York University Press, 2002, 161.
7 Salvato, 8.
8 Steven Drukman, "David Greenspan." *BOMB* 83 (2003), 40.
9 Greenspan, quoted in Drukman, 40.
10 Drukman, 38.

11 Helen Shaw, "David Greenspan and Sybil Kempson Breathe New Life into Impossible Theatre." *TheatreForum* 38 (2010), 61.
12 Ibid., 64.
13 Marc Robinson, "Running Lines: Narratives of Twenty-First-Century American Theatre." In *The Oxford Handbook of American Drama*. Eds Jeffrey H. Richards and Heather S. Nathans. New York: Oxford University Press, 2014, 507.

FURTHER READING

Robinson, Marc. "An Interview with David Greenspan." In David Greenspan, *The Myopia and Other Plays*. Ann Arbor: University of Michigan Press, 2011, 263–275.

Sellar, Tom. "Near and Far: David Greenspan's Dramatic Vision." *Theater* 29:2 (1999), 57–59.

JEREMY O. HARRIS
(Danville, Virginia, 1989–)
David Román

Jeremy O. Harris is a playwright who has revitalized US theatre through his provocative plays on race and sexuality, his outspoken and media-savvy advocacy for the performing arts, and his behind-the-scenes philanthropy for theatre artists. Harris has become one of the most recognizable figures in US theatre, largely due to the sensational impact of *Slave Play*, his first produced play, which he wrote while a student in Yale University's MFA Playwriting Program under the tutelage of Tarell Alvin McCraney. *Slave Play* had its off-Broadway debut in fall 2018 at New York Theatre Workshop, the celebrated East Village theatre, which under the direction of James Nicola, NYTW's out artistic director, has championed new plays by queer writers such as Paula Vogel, Five Lesbian Brothers, and Tony Kushner, and new musicals such as *Rent* (1996) and *Hadestown* (2016) that later moved to Broadway. *Slave Play* follows this trajectory into the commercial mainstream. The Broadway production surpassed Tony Kushner's *Angels in America* as the most nominated play in Tony history, with 12 individual nominations, including Best Play.

Slave Play addresses with intelligence, wit, and insight the complex history of race relations in the United States. The play focuses on racial fetishization through a series of seemingly independent scenes featuring various sets of young interracial couples; each couple includes a Black partner sexually withdrawn from the relationship, suffering a form of anhedonia, or the inability to feel pleasure. Initially, audiences are introduced to the couples as they enact sexual power dynamics informed and structured by slavery and racial oppression. The first scene—featuring a white slave master and a Black female slave—is degrading and uncomfortable, although something seems immediately off in the performance. The music is contemporary, the costume is period, the dialect is ambiguous, and Rihanna's song "Work" frames the scene, calling into question the historical period we are witnessing. It's only later that we learn that each of the couples—which also include an interracial gay cisgender couple and a heterosexual cisgender couple—are playing out racial fantasies as a form of trauma therapy led by a queer interracial female couple (one is Black, the other Latinx). The couples are enrolled in "Antebellum Sexual Performance Therapy" and participate in sessions where they role-play predetermined scenes of interracial power.

The play is divided into three separate acts. Act 1, "Work," introduces the role-play scenes. Act 2, "Process," includes a symposium where each of the characters ruminates on their sexual history and racial identity, forcing the white characters to deal with their "whiteness." Led by the two women of color, the main couples sit in a group therapy setting to think through the implications of their sessions and how they might learn to reconnect sexually. Act 3, "Exorcise," returns to the couple that introduced the play and confronts the issue of "white privilege" and its impact on both parties. The play's explicit focus on queer sexuality links pleasure and desire to racial trauma and the legacy of slavery.

Harris is among the first queer playwrights of color to address the psychological and political consequences of interracial desire. *Slave Play* doesn't take an overt position on interracial desire; rather the play interrogates the topic from multiple angles of inquiry. The production was directed by Robert O'Hara and featured a cast of relatively unknown actors. When the play moved to the John Golden Theatre in 2019, it made history as the first play to be staged on Broadway featuring a Black gay playwright and a Black gay director. Nearly the entire off-Broadway cast moved with the production to Broadway, making it one of the few new plays featuring young and relatively unknown actors on Broadway. Several cast members were nominated for Tony Awards, including: Joaquina Kalukango for Best Actress in a Leading Role; Ato Blankson-Wood and James Cusati-Moyer for Best Performance by an Actor in a Featured Role; and Chalia La Tour and Annie McNamara for Best Performance by an Actress in a Featured Role. Harris also used print journalism, social media, and late-night television to promote the play and guide its reception by framing his intentions in various interviews. As a result, the play became a national sensation, generating tremendous buzz within the theatre world and among queer communities and communities of color. When he learned of *Slave Play*'s historic multiple Tony Award nominations, Harris, who has over 50,000 followers on Twitter, posted the following:

> Obviously my first response is to say "insane", make a "Thanks Amy Cooper" joke, or just remind everyone all the people these

awards generally ignore, but i can't do that. / Im lit crying. / In Shock. A play about Black inferiority, psychic death, & chattel slavery. Most ever?[1]

The video accompanying this text was seen by over 100,000 people. His next play, *Daddy: A Melodrama*, opened off-Broadway in spring 2019 and featured a cast of nine, including Alan Cumming, who won a Tony for his role as the MC in the 1998 revival of *Cabaret*. *Daddy*, too, addresses interracial desire, but introduces intergenerational desire into the mix. Cumming's character is an affluent middle-aged white art collector involved with a young Black gay artist. The play details the dynamics between them, which include not only differences in race and age, but also class. As in *Slave Play*, Harris creates opportunities for his characters to discuss in great detail and with much success the issues at hand. In *Daddy*, the characters address the nature of art and the art market with a deep and sophisticated knowledge of the scene and Harris is unafraid to provide his characters the space to engage in provocative and highly charged debates.

In *Black Exhibition*, which premiered at Brooklyn's Bushwick Starr performance space in 2019, Harris wrote under the pseudonym @GaryXXXFisher. It is a 60-minute play loosely based on the obscure black gay writer Gary Fisher, who died of AIDS in 1994. Harris also performed in the play, which included additional actors performing iconic queer roles, such as Yukio Mishima, Kathy Acker, and Samuel Delany. Harris described this experimental play as a "choreopoem," a tribute to the late playwright Ntozake Shange. His latest play, *A Boy's Company Presents: Tell Me If I'm Hurting You*, was scheduled to premiere in the spring of 2020 at Playwrights Horizons, but, like every other theatrical production, became a casualty of the COVID-19 pandemic. Playwrights Horizons announced its season for the return to live theatre in 2021, but Harris's play was not included, leaving its future uncertain. Harris wrote on Twitter that he was no longer in discussions to stage the play at Playwrights Horizons and that his treatment at the theatre had been "disrespectful."

Harris has used his fame to consistently advocate for the performing arts and, despite his celebrity, he is deeply interested in championing the works of others. He has donated a collection of Black plays to a public library in each of the 50 states in order to raise awareness of African American theatre. He also created two $50,000 commissions for new plays by Black women administered through NYTW and produced online streaming productions of two recent Pulitzer Prize finalists in Drama: Will Arbery's *Hero of the Fourth Turning* (2020) and Michael Breslin and Patrick Foley's *Circle Jerk* (2021). Harris's celebrity extends beyond the theatre and includes influence and visibility in the fashion, film, and social media worlds: he received a fashion spread in the August 2021 issue of *Harper's BAZAAR* and has appeared in *Vogue* and *GQ*; and he also released a fashion collection in collaboration with SSENSE. A parody of *Slave Play* even appeared in the fourth season of the television series *The Good Fight*. Without a doubt, Harris occupies a unique position in the US cultural landscape that many playwrights rarely, if at all, achieve.

In every arena he inhabits, Harris pushes the culture forward with audacious creativity and dramatic flair. In fall 2021, for example, Harris threatened to pull the Broadway production of *Slave Play*, which was scheduled to have its regional theatre premiere at the prestigious Mark Taper Forum in Los Angeles as part of their 2021–2022 season. Harris was protesting the theatre's shortage of women playwrights in their programming and, outraged by the exclusion of women playwrights, used his various social media platforms and rising cultural power to call out the theatre, which immediately responded with an apology and a promise to rectify the problem. His move brought even more heat to the controversy when various women playwrights, appreciative of Harris's advocacy, couldn't help but observe that it took a man's complaint to hold the theatre accountable. This incident demonstrates Harris's tremendous cultural influence and media savvy. He is not afraid of controversy and is willing to put himself out on a limb for a cause beyond his own fame or fortune. In doing so, he models a new form of queer celebrity in the theatre, one thoroughly engaged and endlessly inventive, one politically responsible and artistically unpredictable.

NOTE

1 Jeremy O. Harris. Twitter post. October 15, 2020, 2:04 PM. https://twitter.com/jeremyoharris/status/1316802162203209729

FURTHER READING

Cunningham, Vinson. "The Bel Air Battleground of Daddy." *New Yorker*, March 11, 2019.
Holdren, Sara and Barfield, Tanya. "*Slave Play* Nearly Demands a Conversation. So We Had One." *Vulture*, October 6, 2019.
Wilson, Imogen. "Music and Queered Temporality in *Slave Play*." *Current Musicology*, Vol. 106 (2020), 9–27.

RACHEL HAUCK
(Worcester, Massachusetts, 1968–)
Stacy Wolf

Rachel Hauck is among the most influential, creative, and bold set designers working in the US today. She has worked in almost every off-Broadway venue in New York City (including the Public Theater, Signature, New York Theatre Workshop, and Playwrights Horizons), in many regional theatres across the country, and internationally.

Unlike many of her set designer peers, Hauck is self-taught. She attended UCLA as an undergraduate, but did not go to graduate school, nor was she an assistant to an established designer. When Hauck began working in the theatre after a few years designing for television shows, "I was on a steep learning curve," she said. "I wasn't taught how to draft. I didn't know anything about budgets."[1] Her lack of formal design education meant that, as she said, "I found my own path, and I invented my own way of working." Hauck started working as a set designer in Los Angeles in 1992, practicing both the rough, experimental aesthetic of the Actors' Gang, and the established, mainstream style of plays produced at the Mark Taper Forum. She was awarded both an NEA/TCG Design Fellowship (1998–2000) and a Princess Grace Award for Theater (1998).

Starting in 1998, Hauck began dividing her time between Los Angeles and New York, then moved fully to New York in 2007, and her career expanded in the city and across the US. Hauck served as resident set designer at the O'Neill Playwrights Conference from 2005 to 2014, where she fostered a design-focused dramaturgy on the work of more than 70 playwrights. In 2016, Hauck received an Obie Award for Sustained Achievement in Design.

Hauck has designed sets for extant and classic plays and is best known for her work on world premieres. Her artistic process is multifold, grounded in close dramaturgical analysis, extensive research and image-gathering, countless conversations and image-culling with directors, model-building and rebuilding, and gut instinct. As she told Victoria Myers at *The Interval*, "But that part of like, 'How do you make the actual design,' I don't know, that stuff's magic, right? It comes from that squishy other place that you can't really define."[2]

Hauck's style is eclectic, as she envisions and builds a vast range of theatrical worlds. She describes her primary aesthetic as minimalist. "In a minimalist design, everything that you put on that stage has intensity and meaning," she said. "The absence invites the audience to invest in a different way." "Minimalism," she said, "is not for the faint of heart."

In June of 2015, Hauck joined director Rachel Chavkin as the set designer for *Hadestown*. The musical, based on the 2010 concept album by Anaïs Mitchell, contemporizes and intertwines the classic Greek myths of Orpheus and Eurydice and Hades and Persephone, touching on environmentalism, labor practices, and class inequities as well as the myths' themes of true love, music, and storytelling. After runs at the off-Broadway New York Theatre Workshop, in Edmonton, Canada, and in London, *Hadestown* opened on Broadway in April 2019. *New York Times* reviewer Jesse Green described Hauck's "high concept," "single set [that] depicts a recognizable idea of place: a basement jazz joint that miraculously turns into the furnace room of Hades' factory."[3] The musical won eight Tony Awards, including one for Hauck for Best Scenic Design of a Musical.

That same season, Hauck designed Heidi Schreck's *What the Constitution Means to Me*. Her set, which functioned as a character in the play, represented an American Legion Hall with a few chairs, a worn carpet, and a wall covered with 163 framed photos of American Legion members. Green described *Constitution* as "nothing less than a chronicle of the legal subjugation of women by men, as experienced in the day-to-day injustices of living while female and in the foundational American document that offers paltry recourse."[4]

These two acclaimed Broadway shows in the 2018–2019 season propelled Hauck to a new stage of her career. "The difference between Broadway and off-Broadway is vast," she said. "When the Broadway shows opened, some people asked where I came from, as if I'd appeared out of nowhere, and the answer was, I've been working off-Broadway for 20 years!"

Hauck, who is equally comfortable with the identifiers "lesbian," "gay," or "queer," came of age in Los Angeles. "I've lived my life delightfully openly," she said, so "I've never felt a need to really speak to [my sexuality] too specifically one way or the other." Still, she said that when she saw *Fun Home*, the 2015, Tony Award-winning, Jeanine Tesori and Lisa Kron musical based on the graphic novel by Alison Bechdel, "I was stunned by the experience. I had never seen myself on stage."

Hauck has designed several plays and musicals that feature queer characters, including three directed by Leigh Silverman: *The Beebo Brinker Chronicles* (2007) by Kate Moira Ryan and Linda S. Chapman, adapted from the famous series of 1950s lesbian pulp novels; Colman Domingo's *A Boy and His Soul* (2009); Christopher Shinn's *Where Do We Live* (2001) and *Picked* (2011); Tanya Barfield's *Bright Half Life* (2015); and Madeleine George's *Hurricane Diane* (2019), among others. As exemplified through collaborations like these, Hauck sees herself as part of an ecosystem of queer theatre makers.

Throughout her career, Hauck has chosen projects based on several factors. First and foremost, she must like and connect with the script when she reads it. "I wanted to do work that I wanted to be known for doing. I wanted to shape in a direction. And so I pursued the work that I was excited about," she said.[5] This passion, commitment, and integrity defines Hauck's "brand," equaled by her formidable creativity and her warm and generous collaborative spirit.

She sees herself as a political person whose first agenda is to create work that she believes in. Her sexuality is fundamental to who she is as an artist—"I've never been straight for one second," so "everything is filtered through that lens"—but it doesn't define her. The effect of her experience is openness, which is revealed through the varied, imaginative theatrical worlds she creates. "I think there's a lot less judgment," she said.

Second, and as important, Hauck will sign onto any project with her longtime collaborators, including director Leigh Silverman and Hauck's life partner, director Lisa Peterson, with whom she worked on many of her first plays. Many of Hauck's closest collaborators are lesbians, and most of the directors who hired her in the early years of her career were women. Hauck credits numerous artists with inspiring and supporting her, including the Five Lesbian Brothers, David Zinn, Clint Ramos, and Bill Rauch. She is always excited to design plays by emerging writers.

Although Hauck doesn't want to be identified as a "woman set designer," she is well aware that only 20 percent of the set designers at regional theatres are women and that personal, gendered networks launch and sustain careers.[6] She worked with an all-female design team handpicked by director Ruben Santiago-Hudson for *Othello* at the Public Theater in 2018. Hauck said, "Directors have long relationships with collaborators … They're deep and they're rich, and it's not for nothing that they go back to their team."[7]

Hauck is also a teacher, mentor, and activist. She's lectured and taught masterclasses around the US and teaches regularly at Princeton University. She understands that her status and visibility in the field can help to launch young designers; perhaps she's especially sensitive because she didn't have a queer mentor in college. She said, "Theater design is one of the few professional apprenticeships still out there ... so who you bring with you as your associate, as your assistant, as your intern—those are all people that you're getting into the room."[8] She went on, "If those opportunities aren't going to women and people of color, then they aren't ready to take the next step."[9] She also joined a group of off-Broadway designers to write the first collective bargaining agreement for off-Broadway theatre artists.

In 2021, Hauck described her career so far: "If you look at the work, you can see that it's long and steady, strong and slow. I'm not outspoken and am rather open and unwavering." She told a story of a friend who walked into the theatre to see *Bright Half Life*, saw the set, and said, "'Oh, somebody's ripping off Rachel Hauck,' and then he was like, 'Oh, it's Rachel Hauck!'"[10]

NOTES

1 Personal interview, May 20, 2021. All of Hauck's quotes are from this interview, unless specified otherwise.
2 Victoria Myers, "An Interview with Set Designer Rachel Hauck," *The Interval*, May 21, 2019. www.theintervalny.com/interviews/2019/05/an-interview-with-set-designer-rachel-hauck/
3 Jesse Green, "Review: The Metamorphosis of 'Hadestown,' From Cool to Gorgeous," *New York Times*, April 17, 2019. www.nytimes.com/2019/04/17/theater/hadestown-review-broadway-anais-mitchell.html
4 Ibid.
5 Quoted in Cory Pattak, *In 1: the Podcast. The Lives of Theatrical Designers*, #71 Rachel Hauck, April 28, 2017. www.in1podcast.com/71-rachel-hauck. This quote was edited for clarity.
6 Quoted in Arabella Hau, "Set Designer Speaks on Women in the Art World," *Iowa State Daily*, October 16, 2019. https://tinyurl.com/bdcdax6v
7 Quoted in Sonia Weiser, "The Women Empowering 'Othello'," *New York Times*, June 7, 2018: C1. www.nytimes.com/2018/06/06/theater/othello-theater-tech-jobs-women.html
8 Ibid.
9 Ibid.
10 My thanks to Marissa Michaels for her research assistance.

FURTHER READING

"Rachel Hauck, Tony Award Nominee, Best Set Design, *Hadestown* on Broadway," *All Arts TV*, June 3, 2019, www.youtube.com/watch?v=O8GwSOuXnwk

"Take a Tour Way Down *Hadestown* with Rachel Hauck and Rachel Chavkin," *Theatermania*, June 4, 2019, www.youtube.com/watch?v=mCWZsq6TIUY

Talenti, Pier Carlo. "Rachel Hauck," *Art Restart*, Thomas S. Kenan Institute for the Arts, University of North Carolina School of the Arts, February 22, 2021, www.uncsa.edu/kenan/art-restart/rachel-hauck.aspx#pandemic

CHISA HUTCHINSON
(Queens, New York, 1980–)
La Donna L. Forsgren

"If change doesn't happen, it won't be for my lack of trying," Chisa Hutchinson remarked in a 2017 interview with actor and director Rodney Gilbert. "Even if all I have to offer is words. I'm going to try every which way to wield those words to see what they can produce, what ripples they can make."[1] As an award-winning Black queer feminist playwright, Hutchinson arms herself with the weapon of words, striking out to reveal and dismantle oppressive forces that would render Black girls—cis, trans, queer, or otherwise—invisible within the Black freedom struggle and US society more broadly. In this endeavor, she belongs to a lineage that spans from Angelina Weld Grimké to Lorraine Hansberry to Tanya Barfield and Tracey Scott Wilson.

Hutchinson's works have been produced at theatres off-Broadway, off-off-Broadway, and regionally, including *Somebody's Daughter* (2017) at Second Stage Theater, *Proof of Love* (2019) at New York Theatre Workshop, and *Surely Goodness and Mercy* (2019) at Keen Company. She has received many awards and honors for her Black queer feminist efforts, including the Lilly Award (2010), GLAAD Media Award for *She Like Girls* (2010), New York Innovative Theatre Award for *This is Not the Play* (2012), Helen Merrill Award (2013), Paul Green Award (2013), and Lanford Wilson Award (2015), as well as being elected a member of New Dramatists (2013–2020). Similar to the work of dramatists Robert O'Hara and Jeremy O. Harris, Hutchinson privileges Black queer identity and uses dark comedy to explore issues of race, gender, sexuality, and power in US society. However, Hutchinson's dramas remain unique in that they privilege the experiences of Black queer girls and women who are often marginalized within Black, queer, and women's histories.

Hutchinson's early experiences navigating the world as a poor Black queer girl inspired her mission to use art to promote Black queer visibility, agency, and empowerment. Born in Queens, New

York, to "young, irresponsible parents," Hutchinson was raised in poverty with her (unofficial) adopted family in Newark, New Jersey.[2] At the age of 14, she received a scholarship to attend the private girl's college-preparatory day school, Kent Place School. Her experience moving from a poor inner-city neighborhood to an elite boarding school taught her the importance of representation and agency.

> Early on I got the message, "Okay, you can't succeed here. You have to go somewhere else. You have to rely on the kindness of strangers. You have no agency." I want to flip that script. I want to show people—little kids and cranky ol' lunch ladies with no health insurance—that we can help each other. We don't have to rely on the government.[3]

Rather than internalize the erroneous belief that Black America should wait for liberal whites to "save" them, Hutchinson encourages Black agency and empowerment through self-definition. Her dramatic works mirror this queer Black feminist thought by privileging Black queer girl subjectivity and the pursuit of self-definition. In so doing, Hutchinson breaks ground by simply *normalizing* Black queer girl existence.

Hutchinson has produced nearly a dozen original works, all of which demonstrate a deep commitment to empowering heretofore marginalized voices in US society. She received formal training from Vassar College (BA Dramatic Arts) and New York University's Tisch School of the Arts (MFA Dramatic Writing). Still, she credits the Pulitzer Prize-winning dramatist Lynn Nottage for helping her continue to hone her craft.[4] While making each play stylistically unique—Hutchinson draws from dark comedy, musical theatre, science fiction, and revenge-horror genres—each story centers the experiences of Black, Indigenous, and people of color (BIPOC). As a politically engaged artist, Hutchinson crafts works that allow BIPOC characters to explore issues most pertinent to their lives, including queer sexuality, transgender identity, intracultural conflict, assisted suicide, infanticide, child abuse, slavery, white supremacy, gentrification, exploitation, mortality, morality, and stereotypes. As BIPOC characters grapple with these complex issues, they gain a new understanding of themselves, empowering them to speak their truth to a seemingly more powerful force within their community.

Hutchinson's representative works—*She Like Girls* and *Dead and Breathing*—exemplify her Black queer feminist praxis, which refers to the political theory and practice of centering the concerns of marginalized members of the Black community within the Black liberation struggle.[5] Hutchinson's first major play, *She Like Girls*, premiered off-off-Broadway in 2010 and was inspired by the true-life story of Sakia Gunn, a 15-year-old Black girl who was murdered while waiting at a Newark bus stop on May 11, 2003. When Gunn refused the advances of a Black man, telling him that she was a lesbian, he retaliated by stabbing her to death.[6] In *She Like Girls*, 16-year-old Kia Clark struggles to accept her sexual attraction to her classmate, Marisol Feliciano. Kia and Marisol eventually fall in love despite familial and societal forces that try to separate them. However, just as Kia learns to accept her identity as a Black queer girl, she too falls victim to a hate crime when she declines sexual advances from a boy at a bus stop. The play concludes with Kia declaring that she is a lesbian and refusing to remain silent. "I *know* what the fuck I am!" Kia tells her assailant. "NO! I WILL NOT SHUT THE FUCK UP! I! WILL NOT! SHUT! THE FUCK UP," she yells.[7] Hutchinson follows this moment with a blackout and the sound of a gunshot.

Dead and Breathing—produced at the Contemporary American Theater Festival in West Virginia (2014), the National Black Theatre in New York (2015), and Arch 468 in London (2018)— also concludes with the death of a Black woman, this time a wealthy hospice patient named Carolyn Whitlock. As Carolyn tries to convince her irreverent Christian nurse, Veronika, to assist her in her suicide, audiences learn about Veronika's transgender identity and her past struggles to mother a child dying of AIDS. Both plays—written before the formation of the Black Lives Matter movement in 2015—attest to the resiliency of Black girls, reveal the forces that harm them, and issue a call for the Black community to include them within the Black liberation struggle.

In addition to her work as a playwright, Hutchinson has written and performed with the New York Neo-Futurists experimental theatre troupe, including a monologue called "Legacy of Love," reflecting on the experience of having her religious mother attend the production of *She Like Girls*.[8] Her plays have also reached broader audiences in other media: *Proof of Love* has been recorded for Audible listeners and presented as a live online streaming event by Black Lives, Black Words, and Hutchinson adapted her play *The Subject* into a film that won awards at multiple festivals in 2020. While continuing to write new plays for the theatre, with productions scheduled for *Whitelisted* and *Amerikin*, Hutchinson is also developing new works for film and television with Disney, Paramount, and Showtime.

Ultimately, Hutchinson's dramatic oeuvre inspires Black girl empowerment and community action. She asserts,

> I also want to show people that no matter what situation you find yourself in, what your circumstances are, you can always find your agency. You can always find some way to empower yourself and empower others around you. So you don't always have to wait.[9]

By recognizing that *none* of us are free until *all* of us are free, Hutchinson reimagines the Black radical tradition in terms of collective liberation.

NOTES

1. Chisa Hutchinson and Rodney Gilbert, "Shoestrings: A Conversation with Chisa Hutchinson and Rodney Gilbert." *Theatre Topics* vol. 27 no.2 (2017): 163–168.
2. Chisa Hutchinson, "Bio," accessed June 1, 2021. www.chisahutchinson.com/bio.html
3. Hutchinson and Gilbert, 166.
4. Andrea Lepcio, "Dramatists Guild Fellows Off-Broadway." *The Dramatist* vol. 19 no. 5 (2017): 50–55.
5. Charlene A. Carruthers, *Unapologetic: A Black, Queer, and Feminist Mandate for Radical Movements*. Boston: Beacon Press, 2018, 10.
6. Timothy Stewart-Winter and Whitney Strub, "The Murder of Sakia Gunn and LGBT Anti-Violence Mobilization," *OutHistory*, accessed May 3, 2021. https://outhistory.org/exhibits/show/queer-newark/murder-of-sakia-gunn
7. Chisa Hutchinson, *She Like Girls*. New York: Playscripts, 2010, 53.
8. Chisa Hutchinson, "For Pride …," accessed May 3, 2021. www.chisahutchinson.com/for-pride.html
9. Hutchinson and Gilbert, 166.

FURTHER READING

Myers, Victoria. "An Interview with Chisa Hutchinson," *The Interval*, February 25, 2015. www.theintervalny.com/interviews/2015/02/an-interview-with-chisa-hutchinson/

Svich, Caridad. "Sex Takes a Stage: A Virtual Roundtable." *The Dramatist* vol. 15 no. 6 (2013): 30–39.

MICHAEL R. JACKSON
(Detroit, Michigan, 1981–)
Aviva Helena Neff

The surreal world of Michael R. Jackson, or "the Living Michael Jackson" as he puts it, has taken US theatre by storm. Jackson's contributions to contemporary theatre range from new musicals such as *Only Children* (2007) to adaptations of cult horror B-movies (*Teeth*, 2019). Jackson's off-Broadway musical debut, *A Strange Loop* (2019), thrust the playwright, composer, and lyricist into the New York City and national spotlights and won him a number of awards. Yet it is his early years in the Midwest that helped shaped his artistic vision. Jackson was born in Detroit in 1981—in the midst of Coleman Young's historic tenure as the city's first Black mayor—to Henry E. Jackson Jr., a former police officer and Mary L. Jackson, a former employee of General Motors. As a child, Jackson performed with the highly respected Brazeal Dennard Youth Chorale, which was founded in Detroit in 1972 to "remember, discover, and preserve the spiritual music of the African American experience and culture."[1] Like many notable Black artists from the Motor City, Jackson attended Cass Technical High School, where his writing was nurtured by InsideOut Literary Arts, a Detroit based nonprofit.

When Jackson moved to New York City in 1999, he was already a published writer with a strong, authorial voice, thanks to encouragement from his mentors in high school. After completing his BFA in playwriting in 2003 at New York University, Jackson wrote a monologue called "Why I Can't Get Work," which he credits as the origin of his lauded musical. "*A Strange Loop* started off as a monologue that I wrote in between undergrad and grad school," he explains.

> I was feeling very lost and alienated, and I wrote this long, rambling monologue about a young black man walking through New York and observing things, and the feelings he had about family and about the world—this is a little bit post-September 11th—and about his queerness and race, and just a bunch of things.[2]

In 2003, Jackson returned to New York University to earn an MFA in musical theatre, where he focused on book and lyric writing. While sharpening his skills with composer Mike Reid, Jackson wrote a song called "Memory Song," which would later become a part of *A Strange Loop*. During his evolution from playwright to lyricist and composer, Jackson was invited to do a concert at Ars Nova in 2007, where his song "Periodically" was performed. It was during this time that Jackson met Adam Wiggins, a music director and arranger, who would quickly become Jackson's "right hand" and copyist on *A Strange Loop*.

A Strange Loop reflects the circuitous nature of US national and local New York politics by framing events through the main character of Usher, a man named for his job as an usher at Broadway's *The Lion King*. The musical is a metatheatrical experience in which Usher, identified as "too black, too fat, too feminine," weathers the storms of the so-called "white gaytriarchy" while writing a musical about "real life" called *A Strange Loop* about a Broadway usher named Usher writing a musical about his life, which he titles *A Strange Loop*.[3] Jackson identifies Usher as "at war with who he is which is shaped by his experiences as a black, queer man/artist."[4] As such, the play turns toward the anxiety of identity and the weight of carrying the label of being a "Black writer." Jackson asks us to critically consider the impact of tokenism on Usher: representing his family, representing Black writers, and trying to discover a truthful way of representing himself. *A Strange Loop* marks an important turn toward the absurd and surreal, while foregrounding a decidedly Black, queer identity.

Throughout the show, Usher battles the thin, white-dominated queer communities of New York City and the heteronormativity of his own family. The role of Usher was originated by queer actor Larry Owens, who went on to earn the Lucille Lortel Award for Outstanding Lead Actor in a Musical, the Drama Desk Award for Outstanding Actor in a Musical, and was an honoree for Outstanding Actor in a Musical by the Outer Critics Circle. Reflecting on his experience as a fat actor in theatre, Owens said,

> For some reason, our society thinks that fat people have brought this on themselves, and if they wanted to change they could, and there's no reason that anyone would want to be fat, so why would we listen to their stories?[5]

In its staging, the image of a fat, queer, Black man as the lead challenges the theatre's preconceived notions of who can star in an "American musical."

Throughout the play, Usher struggles with six intrusive, internal Thoughts—personified beings portrayed by actors—who form a chorus who endlessly torment him with self-loathing, reckless spending, and punishment for his sexuality. Usher battles his Thoughts by channeling his "inner white girl," particularly through the music of Liz Phair.[6] Usher's relationship with his family is strained at best, embodying the pressures faced by some queer, Black children as they navigate their identity with socially conservative parents. Usher's folks are particularly religious and embrace his career aspirations only when he is asked to ghost-write a Tyler Perry gospel play, which they celebrate, saying "Tyler Perry writes real life." Perry—who is considered by some to be a controversial figure for his stereotypical depictions of Black American culture—is a theatre, film, and television mogul whose work seeks to speak to Black American humor and experiences.

Jackson deftly navigates the dizzying collision of Perry's and Usher's Blackness through the soaring gospel songs, "Writing a Gospel Play" and "Precious Little Dream/AIDS is God's Punishment." Within these dynamic numbers, Usher brainstorms his stock characters for Perry, which places the audience in Jackson's merry-go-round of Black/queer/Christian friction. Usher's ghost-written imaginings of Tyler Perry characters reach toward minstrelsy, which earns him the label of "race traitor" and "ass licker." Jackson positions Usher as "other" from his family and the rest of the mainstream heterosexual Black community by deftly indicating Usher's marginalization as a queer person. Through the heady chaos of repetition, Jackson offers a timely lesson for audiences—*A Strange Loop* suggests that the solution to breaking the cycle of anxiety is self-love. Jackson reflects:

> [*A Strange Loop* is] about what it means to be a self in general and what it means to be a black queer self in particular so [*A Strange Loop's*] message of self-love and self-acceptance, and also self-disavowal, both speaks to these times specifically and not at all.[7]

Ten months after the conclusion of its off-Broadway run, *A Strange Loop* earned Jackson a Pulitzer Prize in Drama (2020), making him the first Black musical theatre writer to receive the honor and the first time a musical was awarded this prestigious award without a Broadway performance.[8] Jackson was further recognized for the show with a Drama Desk Award, Outer Critics Circle Award, Obie Award, New York Drama Critics' Circle Award, and Lambda Literary Award for Drama. This is especially significant, given the 2016 report by the Asian American Performers Action Coalition (AAPAC), which noted that during 2016–2017 only 13.2 percent of all plays produced on and off-Broadway were written by playwrights of color, and 18.6 percent of actors cast were Black Americans.[9] It is also worth noting that *A Strange Loop* was developed amidst the burgeoning Black Lives Matter movement, whose effect was felt from the streets to the stages, urging production companies to consider how to support meaningful representation, rather than white-authored ideations of Black lives. In a 2015 article, Jackson urged the theatre community to look beyond statistics and look for work that "aims to decenter whiteness as the primary reference point in the stories nonwhite bodies populate."[10]

Jackson's surreal dramedies are meant to be wrestled with in order to fully appreciate both their humor and complexity. His work reiterates the oft-invisible boundaries that queer Black people must navigate in contemporary society—especially in the realm of white theatre. Without a doubt, his full impact on US theatre is yet to be fully seen, although his effort places Black culture in a crucible of belonging in ways that white-authored texts that feature Black characters are often found wanting. Jackson—like his contemporaries in theatre, Branden Jacobs-Jenkins, Jeremy O. Harris, James Ijames, and Donja R. Love—creates art that deconstructs mainstream imaginings of Black identity by queering hetero-Christian Blackness and confronting the specter of AIDS in the Black community: "I'm very much about creating as much expansiveness for black identity as possible while at the same time respecting it."[11]

NOTES

1. Brazael Dennard Choir, "About." www.brazealdennard.com/about.html
2. Shoshana Greenberg, "Michael R. Jackson: What If," *American Theatre,* March 28, 2019. www.americantheatre.org/2019/03/28/michael-r-jackson-what-if
3. Michael R. Jackson, *A Strange Loop* (New York: Theatre Communications Group, 2020).
4. Jonathan Mandell, "Playwright Michael R. Jackson (A Strange Loop) on Self-Love and Self-Acceptance in These Turbulent Times," *DC Theatre Scene,* June 8, 2020. https://dctheatrescene.com/2020/06/08/playwright-michael-r-jackson-a-strange-loop-on-self-love-and-self-acceptance-in-these-turbulent-times
5. David Goldberg, "Larry Owens on Broadway's Beauty Standards as a Queer Black Man of Size," *Dazed Digital,* August 2, 2019.

www.dazeddigital.com/beauty/body/article/45478/1/larry-owens-on-broadway-s-beauty-standards-as-a-queer-black-man-of-size
6 Jennifer Krasinski, "Round and Round," *Artforum*, July 25, 2019, www.artforum.com/performance/jennifer-krasinski-on-michael-r-jackson-s-a-strange-loop-80393
7 Mandell, "Playwright Michael R. Jackson."
8 Pulitzer Prize, "*A Strange Loop*, by Michael R. Jackson," May 4, 2020. www.pulitzer.org/winners/michael-r-jackson
9 "AAPAC Report Reveals Larger Pattern of Inequities in NY Theatre," *American Theatre Magazine*, October 1, 2020. www.americantheatre.org/2020/10/01/aapac-report-reveals-larger-pattern-of-inequities-in-ny-theatre
10 Michael R. Jackson, "Unpacking 'Diversity' in Musical Theatre," *HowlRound*, September 30, 2015. https://howlround.com/unpacking-diversity-musical-theatre
11 "Artist Interview: Michael R. Jackson," Playwrights Horizons, June 17, 2019. www.playwrightshorizons.org/shows/trailers/artist-interview-michael-r-jackson

FURTHER READING

Jackson, Michael R. www.thelivingmichaeljackson.com/
Krasinski, Jennifer. "Round and Round," *Artforum*, July 25, 2019. www.artforum.com/performance/jennifer-krasinski-on-michael-r-jackson-s-a-strange-loop-80393

BILL T. JONES
(Bunnell, Florida, 1952–)
Ariel Nereson

Bill T. Jones (William Tass Jones) has profoundly influenced the development of contemporary US performance through his work in concert dance, musical theatre, dramatic theatre, opera, and performance art. Termed "the political lion of modern dance," Jones's commitments to both formalism and social intervention have forged a body of work that emphasizes themes of identity, freedom, collision, and belonging.[1] Importantly, his oeuvre celebrates experiences and representations of intersectional queer identity, where queerness and Blackness wedge open spaces of excess, opacity, and relationality that function as vital alternatives to hegemonic culture and its logics of compulsory heterosexuality and white supremacy.

Jones's early life was shaped by family lore, including stories about his parents' vibrant courtship, often told with great showmanship by his father Gus Jones, and stories about slavery's enduring violences and the burdens carried by Black women, offered to him and his ten siblings by his mother, Estella Jones (who became a frequent co-performer in her son's later works), and his grandmother, Anna Edwards. During his childhood, Jones's family labored as migrant farmworkers with a home base in Florida; the family later settled in upstate New York. Labor and accomplishment were emphasized both within the family's daily experiences and by Estella Jones's commitment to ensuring her children's academic success, including educating them in the quotidian racisms they would encounter as schoolchildren. These experiences created a background hum of desire, violence, work, and care that eventually found its way into the foreground of Jones's choreography.

In 1970, Jones attended SUNY Binghamton, initially recruited to run track, and met Arnie Zane. Together they flourished romantically and creatively. Appalled by the United States' Vietnam-era violences and homophobia, Jones and Zane sought refuge in Amsterdam, where they became involved in an interdisciplinary avant-garde art scene.

Upon their return to the US, and after a brief sojourn in San Francisco, the pair returned to Binghamton and established, with Lois Welk, the American Dance Asylum in 1974.

Before forming the Bill T. Jones/Arnie Zane Company in 1982, Jones and Zane created a rich repertoire of duets that staged their obvious physical differences (in height, in build, in race) in order to subvert the stereotypes attached to their bodies. These dances—among them *Monkey Run Road* (1979), *Valley Cottage* (1980), *Blauvelt Mountain* (1980), and *Rotary Action* (1982)—developed movement vocabularies of speed, challenge, fast footwork, innovative partnering emphasizing momentum shifts, the visuality of shape and line, and the incorporation of live spoken text that would come to define the company's aesthetic for its first two decades. This series of works has also functioned as an enduring choreographic blueprint, reimagined in several other works and restaged in its entirety in 2011 as the concert-length *Body Against Body*. In this way, Jones and Zane's partnership, as expressed through relational movement, has functioned as an ongoing method of community and artistic formation as the company persists, without Zane.

Arnie Zane died in 1988 at the age of 39, in Jones's arms at their home in Valley Cottage, New York. Zane had been ill since 1984 with what would eventually be identified as AIDS-related lymphoma. The company, defined publicly by Jones and Zane's romance, had become a hub for queer performance makers, and sadly Zane was not the only loss from their ranks. Shortly after Zane passed, company member Damien Acquavella fell ill during the making of a new work, what would become the canonical *D-Man in the Waters* (1989), and died from AIDS complications shortly after its premiere, where he was carried and held on stage by Jones as he completed the choreography with his upper body. The work remains a staple of the company repertory, though Acquavella's role is seldom recast and his absent figure marks the work's signature asymmetry.

What is often described as Jones's signature choreographic meditation on race, *Last Supper at Uncle Tom's Cabin/The Promised Land* (1990), was profoundly impacted by Zane's death and gestures of queer care extended to Jones while he nursed Zane. The work became notorious as the culture wars of the early 1990s heated up because of its final section, "The Promised Land," which was inspired by a deck of pornographic playing cards playfully gifted to Jones and Zane in 1988 by company member Seán Curran. In every city that hosted *Last Supper*, presenters were tasked with finding 60 community participants for the final section: a communal procession, back and forth across the stage, as participants disrobed, eventually ending nude (or almost). Jones commented that this choice was meant to affirm belonging and commonality in the face of dehumanizing isolation that met his and many other queer people's revelations that they were HIV-positive.

Jones's HIV-positive status and his experiences caregiving for members of his community influenced the development of the company's most well-known work, *Still/Here* (1994). *Still/Here* is renowned for not only its performed content but also its method of generating choreography and its controversial reception. The work was created through a series of "survivor workshops" held in several cities across the US wherein Jones worked with chronically ill and dying people to generate movement maps of their lives and a gestural vocabulary of their feelings about sickness and death. These workshops not only functioned therapeutically for a vulnerable population, they also served to frame HIV/AIDS as one of several ways a person might fall seriously ill; in effect, they worked to depathologize AIDS during a cultural moment when queer life remained hegemonically construed as deviant. Additionally, *Still/Here* ignited a critical firestorm, as seen in Arlene Croce's infamous "nonreview," wherein she denigrated the work as victim art and refused to see it.[2] Her screed brought broad attention to cultural hierarchies of high and low dance, and to the ways that the whiteness of the critical establishment sought to constrain how choreographers addressed gender, race, class, and sexuality in their works.

From the mid-1990s through the mid-2000s, the company continued to produce innovative work, much at the intersection of dance and new technologies, and some that referenced queer aesthetics in style rather than content, for example in the high-camp aesthetics of *A Quarreling Pair* (2007). Following a lauded series of works about Abraham Lincoln (2006–2009), in 2010 Jones and his associate artistic director Janet Wong merged the company with Dance Theater Workshop to create New York Live Arts, a producing and presenting entity for which BTJ/AZ became the house company. Through his administrative labor at Live Arts, Jones has continued to support the work of queer artists of color, from artist residencies to Pride month programming to the annual Live Ideas festival, which celebrates the expression of ideas through aesthetic practice.

During this period, Jones choreographed his first Broadway production, the critically acclaimed avant-garde rock musical *Spring Awakening* (2006). Through offering a choreographic score composed predominantly of abstract gestures, pedestrian movement, and simple manipulations of facings and timings, Jones "ushered in a postmodern/contemporary dance aesthetic" to the commercial stage.[3] Jones won Tony Awards for Best Choreography for *Spring Awakening* and the 2009 production *Fela!*, which he also directed and which featured a movement vocabulary that drew upon postmodern aesthetics in its assemblage of African diasporic forms and modern dance idioms. Jones's work in the commercial theatre locates his artistic practice in a network that includes other queer theatre choreographers, including Alvin Ailey, Jack Cole, and Jerome Robbins, who made works for both concert and commercial venues throughout their careers. In this way, Jones's career exemplifies minoritarian art-making strategies that refuse dichotomous understandings of genre, seeing both concert and commercial forms as viable outlets for artistic expression.

The significance of Jones's work to queer aesthetic and cultural production was reaffirmed in 2020, when the COVID-19 pandemic necessitated virtual programming during June, the month of Pride. A former NYC Pride Parade grand marshal, Jones's presence was summoned again to joyfully represent queer life in all of its complexities, as the Brooklyn Academy of Music (BAM) celebrated Pride by making freely available its archive of BTJ/AZ performances. The primary focus of this archival footage was the 1984 premiere of *Secret Pastures*, a work whose creation and performance enacted queer coalitional worldmaking. In an interview with frequent interlocutor Bill Moyers in July 2020, Jones reflected on what freedom means for Black, queer citizens of the US: "What is free? I can kiss my male lover on the mouth in public. That's free."[4] Indeed, while BAM's footage offers several compelling moments, the *Secret Pastures* curtain call lingers on an embrace between Jones and Zane, pointing to the continued need, as Jones articulated in 2020, to affirm queer desire and care in the public sphere.

NOTES

1 Kaufman, Sarah, "Bill T. Jones, Who Brought the Avant-garde to Broadway," *Washington Post*, December 3, 2010, www.washingtonpost.com/wpdyn/content/article/2010/12/03/AR2010120302765.html. The four themes of identity, freedom, collision, and belonging were used as summations of Jones's career achievements when he received the Kennedy Center Honors from President Barack Obama in 2010.
2 Croce, Arlene, "Discussing the Undiscussable," in *Writing in the Dark, Dancing in the New Yorker* (New York: Farrar, Straus, and Giroux, [1994] 2000), pp. 708–719. See Nereson, A., "Embodying the Undiscussable:

Documentary Methodology in Bill T. Jones's *Still/Here* and the Culture Wars," *Studies in Musical Theatre* Vol. 5, No. 3 (2011), pp. 297–304, for analysis of Croce's review.
3 Gennaro, Liza and Stacy Wolf, "Dance in Musical Theater," p. 163. In *The Oxford Handbook of Dance and Theater*, ed. Nadine George-Graves (New York: Oxford University Press, 2015), pp. 148–168.
4 Jones, Bill T., Interview with Bill Moyers, *Moyers on Democracy*, July 11, 2020, https://billmoyers.com/story/bill-t-jones-talks-with-bill-moyers-about-race-and-revolution-george-floyd-and-a-cabin-boy-named-pip/

FURTHER READING

Jones, Bill T. *Last Night on Earth*. With Peggy Gillespie. New York: Pantheon Books, 1995.

Nereson, Ariel. *Democracy Moving: Bill T. Jones, Contemporary American Performance, and the Racial Past*. Ann Arbor: University of Michigan Press, 2022.

MOISÉS KAUFMAN
(Caracas, Venezuela, 1963–)
Bess Rowen

At first glance, director, playwright, screenwriter, teacher, and activist Moisés Kaufman seems to have little in common with Matthew Shepard, the young university student who was murdered in Laramie, Wyoming, in 1998, aside from their queerness. But Kaufman's theatrical legacy will forever be tied to Shepard through *The Laramie Project* (2000), a piece of documentary theatre that Kaufman created with his company Tectonic Theater Project to explore the town's social environment in the aftermath of Shepard's murder. Eight actors—including other queer theatre makers like Leigh Fondakowski, Greg Pierotti, and Kelli Simpkins—transformed verbatim interviews into over 60 characters from Laramie. The play premiered at the Denver Center Theatre Company and then moved to New York with moderate success before being made into an HBO movie that catalyzed its popularity. *Laramie*'s power partially stems from its ubiquity: there have been over 2,200 professional, amateur, and school production licenses issued in the past decade.[1] The play participated in a larger social and cultural movement surrounding hate crimes legislation that led to President Barack Obama signing The Matthew Shepard and James Byrd Jr. Hate Crimes Prevention Act into law in 2009.

And yet *The Laramie Project* is just one of the many examples of how Kaufman tells queer stories from a unique theatrical perspective. As Stephen Bottoms writes,

> We need more of Kaufman's queerness—by which I mean not so much the subject matter he has gravitated toward as a gay man, but the "outsider" awareness that his multiply-othered subject position as a gay, Jewish, Venezuelan living in New York has given him on the language and identity assumptions that some other "documentarians" simply take for granted.[2]

Kaufman's aesthetic is undoubtedly influenced by these aspects of his identity, but his challenges to the form and content of the queer stories he brings to life gain new resonance when viewed specifically through a queer lens.

Growing up, Kaufman says that his queerness marginalized him within his Jewish community:

> But dealing with that within the context of a conservative, Catholic, *machista* Latin American society made it doubly so. However, the Jewish community had taught me well. There was a part of me that understood that being different was just that: being different![3]

Kaufman left Venezuela in 1987 to attend New York University as part of their Experimental Theatre Wing. Here his aesthetic was greatly influenced by avant-garde theatre makers such as Jerzy Grotowski, Robert Wilson, and Joseph Chaikin. He also followed in the steps of other queer documentary theatre pieces such as Jonathan Ned Katz's survey of queer history and liberation, *Coming Out* (1972), and Emily Mann's exploration of Harvey Milk's murder, *Execution of Justice* (1985).

In the first years of Tectonic Theater Project—which was officially founded in 1991 with his husband, Jeff LaHoste—Kaufman directed *One Arm*, an adaptation of Tennessee Williams's 1948 short story and screenplay of the same name. The story follows Ollie Olsen, a former sailor and boxing champion who loses his right arm in a car accident. He turns to sex work with older men until he murders a client after an escalating altercation. *One Arm* is characterized by Williams's penchant for male hustlers, physical "mutilations," and society's punishment of male sensitivity. And yet Kaufman's direction works against the potential melodrama of the story and instead focuses on the humanity of the characters.

Kaufman credits *One Arm* as a key step toward Tectonic's methodology as he "developed techniques for rehearsing, researching and staging plays, and [began] to call these 'tectonic' techniques (the word refers to the art and science of structure)."[4] The most well-known aspect of Tectonic's process is Moment Work, a trademarked technique that

> [explores] the theatrical potential of all the elements of the stage (props, sound, architecture, lights, costume, etc.) in order to create strong theatrical and dramatic narratives. The technique is

our attempt to create theatrical narratives from the ground up—in other words, "write performance" as opposed to "writing text."[5]

The embodied, experiential impulse of this work resonates with a queer history that is all too often erased or elided in the historical record. In this sense, Kaufman's Moment Work builds a queer repertoire to supplement the incomplete queer archive.

Kaufman's interest in the archive is evident from his first major success, *Gross Indecency: The Three Trials of Oscar Wilde* (1997), a documentary play comprising court transcripts and Wilde's letters. The play follows Wilde's trials and conviction for gross indecency in 1895 through primary documents that help narrativize the impact these events had on his life and legacy. Through a negotiation with the many different perspectives and perceived truths that comprise any history, *Gross Indecency* begins the process of a queer historiography that continues with *The Laramie Project*, where it shifts to work with living subjects and history. Both plays focus on important moments in history that not only explore the queer figures at the center, but also a cross-section of individual reactions to the events that befall them.

Kaufman says of both plays,

> I focused on what I call "watershed historical moments." These are times when all the ideas, beliefs and ideologies that are the pillars of a certain culture at a certain time surface around a specific event. When this happens, the event itself operates as a lightning rod that allows us to see clearly for a brief moment, what ideas that society is made of.[6]

It is significant that Kaufman chose the hardships faced by two queer men to be the "watershed moments" that serve as barometers of their respective societies. Although he has other marginalized identity markers, Kaufman continually uses queer stories as his way into studying and confronting the societal norms associated with the dominant culture.

Kaufman is consistently attracted to multilayered dramatic narratives that resist simple conclusions. Another important work from his impressive directorial resume is Doug Wright's Pulitzer Prize-winning *I Am My Own Wife* (2003), a one-person show that explores the ethically complex story of Charlotte von Mahlsdorf, a transgender woman from Germany who lived through the Nazi and Soviet regimes. He even returned to the Shepard story to create *The*

Laramie Project: 10 Years Later (2009), which follows Tectonic Theater Project company members as they return to Laramie, revisiting former interview subjects and speaking to new residents both young and old. The Brooklyn Academy of Music presented the resulting two-play work, "The Laramie Cycle," in 2013 to critical acclaim. In 2018, Kaufman directed a pared-down revival of Harvey Fierstein's *Torch Song Trilogy* (1982), which the *New York Times* characterized as having "an irresistibly compelling gravity beneath the glibness ... Mr. Kaufman turns out to be just the man for eliciting the sting within the soap bubbles of *Torch Song*."[7] More recently, Kaufman continued to plumb the intersections of his identity with his 2020 adaptation of fellow Venezuelan Jonathan Jakubowicz's novel *Las Aventuras de Juan Planchard* (*The Adventures of Juan Planchard*).

Moisés Kaufman's impact as an artist has resulted in coveted accolades such as the National Medal of Arts, which was presented to him in 2016 by President Obama, and the prestigious Guggenheim Fellowship. But he has also won several important queer-specific awards such as the Human Rights Campaign's Artistic Integrity Award, a GLAAD Media Award, and the Lambda Book Award. Kaufman has made substantial contributions to queer theatre, both in terms of subject matter and artistic methods, by examining dark moments of queer history through devising and documentary theatre techniques informed by queer critical perspectives. It is clear that (following Stephen Bottoms) the theatre world still needs more of Kaufman's (Jewish, Venezuelan) queerness.

NOTES

1 John Moore, "The Enduring Legacy of *Laramie*, Two Decades Later," *American Theatre*, February 26, 2020.
2 Stephen Bottoms, "Putting the Document into Documentary: An Unwelcome Corrective?" *TDR: The Drama Review*, 50, no. 3 (Fall 2006): 67.
3 Caridad Svich, "Moisés Kaufman: 'Reconstructing History Through Theatre'—An Interview," *Contemporary Theatre Review*, 13, no. 3 (2003): 71.
4 Svich, "Moisés Kaufman," 69.
5 "The Moment Work Institute," Tectonic Theater Project, accessed April 21, 2021, www.tectonictheaterproject.org/#MWI
6 Svich, "Moisés Kaufman," 70.
7 Ben Brantley, "A *Torch Song* Burning with Emotion Behind the Laughs," *New York Times*, October 19, 2017.

FURTHER READING

Brown, Rich. "Moisés Kaufman: The Copulation of Form and Content," *Theatre Topics*, 15, no. 1 (March 2005): 51–67.

Reyes, Raul. A. "Legendary Playwright Moisés Kaufman Talks About Art, LGBTQ Activism," *NBC News*, October 26, 2016, www.nbcnews.com/news/latino/legendary-playwright-mois-s-kaufman-talks-about-art-lgbtq-activism-n672736

TONY KUSHNER
(New York City, 1956–)
Virginia Anderson

"God: A cure would be nice." Tony Kushner stood at a podium in the Cathedral Church of St. John the Divine on October 9, 1994, delivering a sermon for the Episcopalian National Day of Prayer for AIDS.[1] Wearing a vestment, he addressed the congregation that filled the cathedral, one of the five largest church buildings in the world, "and delivered this blasphemous thing!"[2] He called for the protection of all those infected with HIV and for kids discovering sex. He demanded the enlightenment of Pope John Paul II and other religious leaders. In a style that represented much of his dramatic success, Kushner's words mingled political accusation with desperate humanity, engendering tears and laughter and culminating in a series of challenges for both his divine and congregated audience. He demanded of God,

> So a cure for AIDS. For racism too. For homophobia and sexism, and an end to war, to nationalism and capitalism, to work as such and to hatred of the flesh ... If you cannot do these things for us, we will do them for ourselves, but slowly, because we can't see far ahead. At least give us time to accomplish the future.

Kushner's landmark play, *Angels in America*, was running on Broadway when Archbishop Paul Moore had invited him to speak at the cathedral. He recalled:

> I felt like it was something that I should do ... People were being allowed to pretend this thing wasn't happening ... We were being told we didn't count, that we were not humans. We were not people that other people could be expected to feel compassion or concern for. I think that was part of the impulse of the prayer: to say, "be angry!"[3]

Tony Kushner was born in Manhattan to musician parents in 1956. When he was 2 years old, he moved with his family to Lake Charles, Louisiana. "There wasn't any visible gay culture when I was growing up," Kushner recalls.[4] An agnostic, he credits Judaism with helping him to forge his identity:

> Being Jewish is how I learned how to be gay, because it was a way of understanding what it meant to have an identity that a lot of people hated but that you yourself knew to be an important source of being, and to learn not to apologize for being something even if the majority of people surrounding you felt that this thing that you were was wrong or evil.[5]

Embarking on higher education, Kushner was interested in theatre and sought "a place where I could be with other people like me."[6] New York City offered him both. He earned a BA in Medieval Studies at Columbia University and an MFA in Directing from New York University's Tisch School of the Arts. There he studied with Carl Weber, a collaborator of Bertolt Brecht's; both practitioners would provide exceptional and enduring influence on his work.

Still, it is Tennessee Williams whom Kushner describes as "all-in-all my favorite playwright and probably all-in-all our greatest playwright."[7] Along with crafting stage dialogue that is at once poetic and realistic, James Fisher has argued that both playwrights share an "appreciation of the fragility of beauty" and create stories in which "the sensitive outsider renders a profound heartbreak for his most memorable characters," often asking, "What is the relationship between sexuality and love? Is sexuality an expression of love or power?"[8] Kushner has also acknowledged the influence of Larry Kramer, explaining, "I was indebted to him as a gay man and as a citizen. As a person who tries to stay politically engaged, I was in awe of him." Kushner describes Kramer's *The Normal Heart* (1985), one of the earliest plays to confront the AIDS epidemic, as

> a theatrical polemic that described the present moment with harrowing exactitude; an incredibly crafted, gorgeous, funny, devastating masterpiece of theatrical realism; and also—and this is very rare—a work of art that provably moved its audiences to political action.[9]

The influence of Williams and Kramer can be felt within *Angels in America: A Gay Fantasia on National Themes*, Kushner's most popular and influential play.

Angels has received extraordinary critical acclaim, including the 1993 Pulitzer Prize for Drama and the 1993 and 1994 Tony Awards for Best Play. Adapted into an Emmy Award-winning television miniseries for HBO (2003) and an opera (2004), the play has been successfully revived on the West End (2017) and Broadway (2018). The two-part play places the AIDS epidemic within a sweeping political, medical, religious, and social context. Intertwining the stories of a gay man who abandons his HIV-positive partner, a closeted Mormon and his distraught wife, and the nefarious Roy Cohn, *Angels* revealed the fusions and the fissures of the personal with the political and influenced the national conversation concerning AIDS. David Ehrenstein explains,

> AIDS made it impossible not to talk about gayness ... *Angels in America* tied it into the huge arc of the American story; the gay community was no longer an isolated group. We needed a big play about this, and he gave us an epic ... What Kushner did was introduce the epidemic to a whole lot of people who weren't paying attention. And for those of us who were, he gave us a whole new context.[10]

Angels offered high-profile achievements in the careers of other queer theatre artists, including director George C. Wolfe, who directed its Broadway premiere and later directed Kushner's semi-autobiographical musical *Caroline, or Change* (2003), and regular Kushner collaborator Stephen Spinella, who earned two Tony Awards for his portrayal of Prior Walter. Spinella reflected on *Angels*: "at the core of its power was the daily tenacious determination of LGBTQ people to take their place as equal players on the stage. It remains the artistic achievement of my life I am proudest of."[11] Another frequent collaborator has been director Michael Grief, who helmed Kushner's *A Bright Room Called Day* (1991), *The Intelligent Homosexual's Guide to Capitalism and Socialism with a Key to the Scriptures* (2009), and the 2010 off-Broadway revival of *Angels*.

Kushner's career has spanned plays, musicals, adaptations, and screenplays, creating works often rooted in complex histories, such as the films *Munich* (2005), *Lincoln* (2012), and the remake of *West Side Story* (2021), all directed by Steven Spielberg. Yet his oeuvre is bound most forcefully with themes that represent the convergence of politics, fury, and love. These themes, which fueled his prayer in

1994, found manifestation following the mass shooting at Pulse, a gay nightclub in Orlando, in June of 2016. He explains,

> I was watching the news last night and this MSNBC anchor showed people having a vigil in Boston. [A woman] asked, "Why are the weapons of war in the hands of the mentally ill in this country? Why does any citizen have access to this?" And they immediately go back to the news anchor who said, "but mostly it was messages of love"—like *that* was a political opinion, but the *real* thing is about loving. And it's like, no! Love is a part of history, too. Love is part of the fabric of time ... There may be divine love that lives beyond what we know, but love is what happens in our lifetimes as we coexist with one another. And that's also politics: what happens in our lifetimes as we coexist. Nothing is exempt from it. Our ability to love has *everything* to do with assault weapons. I just gave some money to a woman in New York, who's trying to bring her son's body home from Orlando. Tell *that* woman that love isn't about a ban on assault weapons. Otherwise it's just sentimentality.[12]

Across his work as a writer and an activist, Kushner presents this multivalent approach to love—one mixed with politics and fury and always resulting in fierce hope for the future.

NOTES

1 Tony Kushner, "A Prayer." *Thinking About the Longstanding Problems of Virtue and Happiness: Essays, a Play, Two Poems and a Prayer.* New York: Theatre Communications Group, 1995, 215.
2 Tony Kushner, interview with the author. June 13, 2016.
3 Ibid.
4 Tony Kushner, interview with Gus Weill, *Louisiana Legends*, May 10, 1998. YouTube video, 21:12, posted by Louisiana Public Broadcasting. December 26, 2019. www.youtube.com/watch?v=R2dcATyiFwk
5 Tony Kushner, interview with Terry Gross. *Fresh Air.* Audio. December 9, 2003. 25:45. https://freshairarchive.org/segments/playwright-tony-kushner
6 Kushner, interview with Weill, 6:06.
7 Robert Vorlicky, ed. *Tony Kushner in Conversation.* Ann Arbor: University of Michigan Press, 2011, 235.
8 James Fisher, *The Theater of Tony Kushner: Living Past Hope.* 2nd edition. London: Routledge, 2021, 11.

9 Tony Kushner, "Tony Kushner: Larry Kramer Spoke the Truths We Needed to Hear." *New York Times*, May 29, 2020. www.nytimes.com/2020/05/29/opinion/larry-kramer.html
10 Quoted in Mary McNamara, "How *Angels in America* Changed the National Conversation." *Los Angeles Times*. November 10, 2012. www.latimes.com/entertainment/arts/la-xpm-2012-nov-10-la-et-cm-critics-notebook-angels-20121111-story.html
11 Stephen Spinella, "Stephen Spinella on Tony Kushner's 'Homo Song of American Sissies and Queers, Closet-Cases and Nasty Queens'." *Playbill*, June 18, 2015. www.playbill.com/article/stephen-spinella-on-tony-kushners-homo-song-of-american-sissies-and-queers-closet-cases-and-nasty-queens-com-351460
12 Kushner, interview with the author, edited for clarity.

FURTHER READING

Scott, A.O., "Tony Kushner: Oracle of the Upper West Side," *New York Times*, November 30, 2021, www.nytimes.com/2021/11/30/t-magazine/tony-kushner-caroline-west-side.html

Steindler, Catherine. "Tony Kushner, The Art of Theater No. 16." Interview. *Paris Review* 54.201 (Summer 2012). www.theparisreview.org/interviews/6153/the-art-of-theater-no-16-tony-kushner

TINA LANDAU
(New York City, 1962–)
David Román

Tina Landau is an interdisciplinary theatre artist whose prolific career defies categorization. She creates large-scale theatrical spectacles and intimate unplugged performances in traditional and non-traditional settings. As a director, Landau is as comfortable working with the classics as she is with contemporary playwrights. As a writer, she is equally wide-ranging in terms of content and form. She's written the book for several award-winning off-Broadway musicals, including collaborations with innovative composers of her generation such as Adam Guettel (*Floyd Collins*, 1996) and Ricky Ian Gordon (*Dream True*, 1998). Landau's own plays include *Space*, which *Time* magazine listed as one of the top ten works of 1996. Landau is interested in exploring new forms of artistic expression through music, text, and design.

Landau was born in New York City; her parents, both film producers, moved to Los Angeles when she was 14. Landau graduated from Beverly Hills High School and attended Yale University, where she directed several undergraduate productions, including plays by Shakespeare. She received further training at Harvard's Institute for Advanced Theater Training, a program affiliated with American Repertory Theater.

Landau was among the first wave of successful women directors in late twentieth-century US theatre and she was among the first queer women to direct on Broadway. She made her Broadway debut in 1998 with the revival of Comden and Green's *Bells Are Ringing* starring Faith Prince. Landau was most recently on Broadway in 2017 with *The SpongeBob Musical*, which was nominated for 12 Tony Awards including Best Director and Best Musical. Her work on the production won the Drama Desk Award and Outer Circle Critics Award for Best Director of a Musical.

Her work has been seen in a wide range of venues including most of the regional theatres throughout the United States and several off-Broadway theatres. In 1997, Landau joined the ensemble of the world-famous Steppenwolf Theatre in Chicago where she has directed nearly 20 productions, including her own plays. Some of these productions have been remounted in other regional theatres with Landau at the helm and the creative team and cast retained. Among her most accomplished productions with Steppenwolf are her 2002 revival of William Saroyan's classic play *The Time of Your Life* (1939) and the world premiere of Tarell Alvin McCraney's *Head of Passes* (2013)—both of which were presented at other regional theatres—and Tracy Letts's *Superior Donuts* (2008), which moved to Broadway in 2009.

Each new Landau production is a unique theatrical experience; the only guarantee is a surplus of artistic creativity from Landau and the diverse set of collaborators she brings into her projects. While it's routine to claim theatre is a collaborative enterprise, Landau's aesthetics are deeply tied to collaboration and the individual contributions of playwrights, designers, and actors. Throughout her distinguished career she has worked with major theatre figures, including Charles L. Mee, whose plays she directed at En Garde Arts; Bill Irwin, the MacArthur and Tony Award-winning performer, whom she directed in *Old Hats* (2013) with David Shiner; and Paula Vogel, the Pulitzer Prize-winning playwright, on *A Civil War Christmas* (2008).

In 1994, in association with En Garde Arts, Landau presented her epic site-specific multimedia play *Stonewall: Night Variations*, which revisits the 1969 Stonewall rebellion that sparked the modern lesbian and gay movement. The play, marking the 25th anniversary of Stonewall, was performed outdoors on Pier 25 on West Street, overlooking the Hudson River, and featured a cast of nearly 60 performers, including a choir, representing a diverse array of queer characters. Landau's work itself was queer in its refusal to adhere to the conventions of traditional theatre. *Stonewall* paid tribute to queer pioneers both real and imagined through radically innovative theatrics and deep-rooted community-based politics. As Ben Brantley, in his *New York Times* review described, the pier was transformed into "a hallucinogenic swirl of side-show attractions" and "the Greenwich Village of 1969 seemed to come to life, in all its motley variety, in some surreal, trans-historical heaven."[1] At the end of the play, the cast read names of famous LGBTQ people honoring the legacy of Stonewall. For this production, she also collaborated with composer Ricky Ian Gordon and filmmaker Jennie Livingston.

Landau's practice of collaboration is paramount to her artistry. She has collaborated with several queer artists throughout her career, including her former partner, the director Ann Bogart, with whom she published *The Viewpoints Book: A Practical Guide to Viewpoints and Composition* (1994), which theorizes collaboration and the creative process. Her most sustained collaboration, however, has been with playwright Tarell Alvin McCraney, which began in 2004. She has directed several of his world premieres, including his celebrated queer plays *Wig Out!* (2008), *The Brother/Sister Plays* (2009), and most recently *Ms. Blakk for President*, which opened at Steppenwolf in 2019. Over the years, Landau and McCraney have become one of the most compelling creative teams on the scene, and one of the few lesbian and gay partnerships in American theatre. Of course, it needs to be noted that Landau is white and McCraney is Black, offering yet another element to their unique bond.

This queer alliance was at the heart of *Ms. Blakk for President* in nearly every aspect of the production. The play recuperates the forgotten life of Joan Jet Blakk and the queer communities from which this once legendary Chicago drag queen emerged and thrived before her dramatic 1993 presidential run. The play focuses on Terence Alan Smith, a real-life working-class Black gay man who created Joan Jett Blakk as his drag persona, but it also reaches further into the political culture of Chicago's dynamic queer community. It tells the story of Chicago's Queer Nation and the city's early 1990s queer club scene, AIDS activism and drag culture, intergenerational Black queer kinship, and multicultural political alliances. Landau's work is deeply invested in historical research, and, while *Ms. Blakk for President* was not a documentary play, it would be difficult to leave the production without having learned about queer life in the 1990s, and even earlier pioneering figures from the Stonewall era such as Marsha P. Johnson. For the Steppenwolf production, McCraney performed the role of Joan Jett Blakk supported by a queer and non-binary cast. The celebrated scenic designer (and frequent Landau collaborator) David Zinn created the set for the play, which began in the theatre's lobby. Zinn, himself an out gay man with a long history in the theatre (he won the 2018 Tony for Best Scenic Design of a Musical for his work on *The SpongeBob Musical*), offered a visually explosive scene that transported audiences back into the early 1990s. The lobby was transformed into a repository of Queer Nation memorabilia—posters, stickers, photographs—that allowed audience members of all backgrounds and generations to immerse themselves in the period's radical aesthetics and queer politics before even entering into the actual theatre.

In the program notes to the Steppenwolf production of *Ms. Blakk for President*, Landau writes about her resistance to traditional theatre conventions, explaining that she creates what she promotes as queer theatre:

> Queer to me is more than about sexuality or gender—it's also a mode of existence, a philosophy, an aesthetic, a way of life, a political statement. That which is queer resists categorization—it can be fluid, slippery, contradictory. Its form is not a binary This-or-That, but a non-binary This-AND-That (-and Maybe-Everything-Else-Too). So just as a person might identify as Queer, so might a show.[2]

Landau's distinctive take on theatre's innately queer potentiality has led to a career of highly imaginative and politically enlightening work. For over 30 years, Landau has been at the forefront of queer theatre, creating spaces where the audience is invited into the performance and not sequestered outside of it. In short, she extends the community outward, always building the community from the inside out.

NOTES

1 Brantley, Ben. 1994. Review of *Stonewall: Night Variations*. June 25, 1994, Section 1, p. 13.
2 Honold, Greta. 2019. "An Interview with Ensemble Members: Tina Landau and Tarell Alvin McCraney." Steppenwolf Theatre Program for *Ms. Blakk for President*. Chicago, 2019.

FURTHER READING

Bogart, Anne and Landau, Tina. 2004. *The Viewpoints Book: A Practical Guide to Viewpoints and Composition*. New York: Theatre Communications Group.
Román, David. 2005. "Afterword: The Time of Your Life." In *Performance in America: Contemporary US Culture and the Performing Arts*. Durham, NC: Duke University Press.

NATHAN LANE
(Jersey City, New Jersey, 1956–)
James F. Wilson

By the time Nathan Lane was an established star on stage and screen, he had played a number of queer characters, most famously the flamboyant drag performer Albert in the 1996 film *The Birdcage*. Still, he coyly avoided the subject of his sexuality in press interviews and talk-show appearances and, as his stardom increased, he faced some pressure to publicly come out as a gay man. In a 1999 cover story for *The Advocate*, he told Bruce Vilanch, "I've never hidden anything, but that apparently is not enough." Describing himself as "really not political," Lane was privately motivated to speak out after the murder of 21-year-old Matthew Shepard. The incident aroused his political consciousness, and Lane felt a personal and professional responsibility to take a stand. He explained, "If I do this story and say I'm a gay person, it might make it easier for somebody else. So it seems stupid not to."[1]

His announcement had no apparent effect on his box office appeal, and he continued to move effortlessly from popular comedies and big-budget musicals to canonical works by playwrights including Eugene O'Neill, Samuel Beckett, and Simon Gray. Lane's formidable and highly lauded success reflects the possibility for LGBTQ performers to overtly acknowledge their personal identities and principles without being artistically pigeonholed and relegated to the fringes of show business.

Lane made his Broadway debut in the 1982 revival of Noël Coward's *Present Laughter* (1942) directed by and starring George C. Scott. Over the next decade he appeared in numerous Broadway and off-Broadway plays and musicals, but his performance as Nathan Detroit in the 1992 revival of *Guys and Dolls* (1950) made him a major box office draw. He received his first of six Tony Award nominations for the role, and he headlined a string of hit shows, such as *Laughter on the 23rd Floor* (1993), the 2000 revival of *The Man Who Came to Dinner* (1939), the 2005 revival of *The Odd Couple* (1965),

The Addams Family (2010), and the 2016 revival of *The Front Page* (1928). He won a Tony Award for Best Leading Actor in a Musical for the 1995 revival of *A Funny Thing Happened on the Way to the Forum* (1962) and again in 2001 for his indelible performance as Max Bialystock in *The Producers*. With his impeccable comic timing and his larger-than-life stage persona, Lane is a direct descendant of musical theatre clowns like Bert Lahr, Phil Silvers, and Zero Mostel. Moreover, in a spate of exaggerated, gay character parts, he evoked the effeminate stock figures of burlesque and vaudeville, as well as the subversive camp performances created by Charles Ludlam's Ridiculous Theatrical Company in the 1960s and 1970s. Lane, however, distinctively imbues his over-the-top representations with layers of sadness, bitterness, and outrage—sometimes simultaneously.

Lane's multifaceted queer characterizations have been created in collaboration with other queer theatre artists, including the directors Joe Mantello, Jack O'Brien, and George C. Wolfe. Most notably, he had a 30-year artistic association with playwright Terrence McNally, who referred to Lane as his "muse." Lane remembers,

> Early on in our relationship [McNally] explained to me that he had recently lost his two closest friends and collaborators: actor, director and former partner, Bobby Drivas, and the inimitable character actor, Jimmy Coco. He said he felt I was sent to replace them, by God or William Morris, I suppose, and that he wanted to write plays for me.[2]

Between 1989 and 2016, Lane appeared in six McNally plays, as well as the film adaptation of *Frankie and Johnny* (1991) and the television film *The Last Mile* (1992). Lane has said of McNally, "He gave me some of the best and most important roles of my career … His work inspired and brought out the best in me."[3]

In fact, McNally's *The Lisbon Traviata* (1989), their first collaboration, provided a major boost to Lane's career. He played Mendy, an obsessed opera queen, and he was both hilarious and heartbreaking. Mel Gussow wrote, "Mr. Lane deserves the highest praise for a brilliant performance as a man doomed to live an ordinary life while aspiring to the ecstasy of opera."[4] Five years later, Lane once again balanced camp and emotional depth in his performance of Buzz Hauser, an angry, lonely, and musical-theatre-obsessed costume designer with HIV, in McNally's Tony-winning play, *Love! Valour! Compassion!* (1994).

Lane's star power helped to propel the work of other queer playwrights. For instance, he appeared in two works by Jon Robin Baitz, *The Film Society* (1988) and *Mizlansky/Zilinsky or "Schmucks"* (1998), and in 2013 he was the driving force behind Douglas Carter Beane's *The Nance*. Beane's play examines burlesque performances of the 1930s and focuses on Chauncey Miles, a gay actor and diehard Republican, who plays stereotypically "nance" comedy parts on stage. In addition to foregrounding the queer elements of burlesque and vaudeville theatre, *The Nance* also reveals the legal jeopardy LGBTQ people faced in the 1930s. The play received mixed reviews, but most critics hailed Lane's performance. Jesse Green wrote,

> Rarely have his innate qualities of pathos and quacking cheer been put to better use; it's hard to decide whether Beane has given him a part he was born to play or he has given Beane a role he was born to write.[5]

Not long afterward, Lane received critical raves as another conflicted gay Republican. In 2018, he won his third Tony Award, this time as Best Featured Actor in a Play, for his portrayal of Roy Cohn in a revival of Tony Kushner's *Angels in America* (1993). The show transferred to Broadway from London's National Theatre, and Ben Brantley described his interpretation as a "career-high performance."[6] Since Lane was known for playing loveable scoundrels and sympathetic oddballs, the choice was a considerable departure. When he accepted the Tony, Lane explained that, leading up to the production, he was determined "to shake things up" and that he "needed to scare [himself] again and challenge [himself] more."[7] In his approach to the villainous Cohn—who was in real life Joseph McCarthy's chief counsel, Ronald Reagan's informal adviser, and Donald Trump's mentor—Lane combined his expert comic timing with grotesque ferocity and glimmers of poignancy. The result, as Sara Holdren described, was "an all-too-human monster with a master comedian's timing."[8]

He continued to shake things up the following season when he assumed the title role in Taylor Mac's *Gary: A Sequel to Titus Andronicus* (2019). Lane played a servant-in-training (and minor character in *Titus Andronicus*) tasked with clearing the residual dead bodies, entrails, and human waste. *Gary* required Lane to make the exceedingly dark humor, scatological jokes, and numerous gags involving cadavers' erect penises palatable for Broadway audiences.

Although the theatre is Lane's primary artistic home, he regularly appears in film and television. For example, he supplied his voice to

The Lion King (1994) and *Stuart Little* (1999), and he had recurring roles on *Modern Family* (2009–2020) and *The Good Wife* (2016). Aside from occasional darker roles in *The People v. OJ Simpson: American Crime Story* (2016) and *Penny Dreadful: City of Angels* (2020), he typically has not been offered the range of parts he receives from theatre producers. He claims, "In film and television, I have no power, but in the theater, I have a little bit of power where I could call someone and say, 'Let's do *The Iceman Cometh*'."[9]

It seems impossible to imagine an out gay actor of a previous generation with the body of work, professional respect, and mainstream popularity that Lane has achieved. Rumors and gossip were enough to limit, if not destroy, promising careers through the late twentieth century. In his more than four decades in the commercial theatre, Lane also has become more political and outspoken. At first hesitant to forthrightly divulge his sexual orientation, he later took a public stand on politics and social oppressions in the United States, and in 2015 he announced his marriage to longtime partner Devlin Elliott. Arguably, Lane's success helped pave the way for a succession of crossover theatre stars, like Neil Patrick Harris, Cynthia Nixon, Jim Parsons, Sarah Paulson, Zachary Quinto, and many others, who have publicly embraced their LGBTQ identities and have had thriving careers on the stage.

NOTES

1 Quoted in Bruce Vilanch. "Citizen Lane," *The Advocate*, February 2, 1999, 37.
2 Nathan Lane. "Nathan Lane: Terrence McNally Changed My Life as an Actor," *Time*, March 31, 2020. https://time.com/5813230/terrence-mcnally-coronavirus-nathan-lane/
3 Ibid.
4 Mel Gussow, "Agony and Ecstasy of an Opera Addiction," *New York Times*, June 7, 1989.
5 Jesse Green, "Theater Review: *The Nance* Makes Ideal Use of Nathan Lane," *Vulture*, April 15, 2013. www.vulture.com/2013/04/theater-review-the-nance.html
6 Ben Brantley, "On the Wings of Despair, Uplift," *New York Times*, March 25, 2018.
7 *72nd Tony Awards*, directed by Glenn Weiss, hosted by Sara Bareilles and Josh Groban, aired June 10, 2018, CBS.
8 Sara Holdren, "Theater Review: *Angels in America* Punches Through the Roof Again," *Vulture*, March 25, 2018. www.vulture.com/2018/03/theater-angels-in-america-punches-through-the-roof-again.html

9 Quoted in Clarence Moye, "Nathan Lane Explores His Darker Side in *City of Angels*," *Awards Daily,* July 3, 2020. www.awardsdaily.com/2020/07/03/nathan-lane-explores-his-darker-side-in-city-of-angels/

FURTHER READING

Kenny, Ursula. "This Much I Know: Nathan Lane," *Guardian*, March 11, 2017. www.theguardian.com/lifeandstyle/2017/mar/11/nathan-lane-i-have-played-a-lot-of-morally-questionable-people-not-sure-why

Lane, Nathan, Devlin Elliott, and Dan Krall. *Naughty Mabel*. New York: Simon & Schuster Books for Young Readers, 2015.

Riedel, Michael. *Singular Sensation: The Triumph of Broadway*. New York: Avid Reader Press, 2020.

HARUNA LEE
(Hong Kong, 1985–)
Jessica Del Vecchio

A Taiwanese, Japanese, and American nonbinary performer and playwright, Haruna Lee has thwarted expectations their entire career, and it is the boldness with which they flout norms—not only of theatre making, but more importantly of gender and sexuality—that renders their work an innovative example of queer experimental performance. Their very first theatre experience was queer: Lee played Lewis in a middle-school musical about Lewis and Clark's nineteenth-century expedition through the western United States. Playing that role, Lee realized that theatre could provide a means to resist their predominantly white community's expectations of how Asian American women should behave.[1] Decades later, Lee's theatre making continues this exploration of the possibilities outside of racial stereotypes and normative gender and sexuality.

After growing up between Japan and Seattle, Lee graduated from the Experimental Theatre Wing at Tisch School of the Arts at New York University and soon found success as an actor in experimental work in downtown New York City. In 2010, at age 25, they won the prestigious Van Lier Fellowship in Playwriting from New Dramatists but repeatedly encountered criticisms of their plays' "messiness" and lack of structure, as well as dubiousness about their ability to pursue writing and performing simultaneously. Interdisciplinary artists Taylor Mac and Young Jean Lee were encouraging, however, and Lee found support for their experimental style in the MFA Playwriting Program at Brooklyn College.[2] Lee also found fellow travelers in Greg Laffey, Stivo Arnoczy, Karen Boyer, Sarah Lurie, Andrew R. Butler, Lauren Swan-Potras, and Sasha Arutyunova, an "ensemble of theater makers and designers who collaborated across artistic disciplines" and formed the harunalee theater company in 2010. The company "created epic visual landscapes" for six of Lee's plays before "lovingly disbanding" in 2020.[3]

These "epic visual landscapes," which bring the audience into the fantasy worlds Lee creates through their texts, are a crucial part of the work's queerness, as is its intentional "messiness." The costumes are extravagant and campy, their over-the-top, hodgepodge aesthetic pointing to the construction of gender. Lee's works are often musical, featuring live bands on stage and requiring actors to belt out original pop tunes. The plays are funny, containing overtly sexual, frequently raunchy, humor. They reference fucking and masturbation, and words like "hole" and "box" serve as double entendres—jokes, yes, but also metaphors that offer insight into the plays' themes. Though critics have dismissed Lee's humor as "sophomoric," this explicit queer sexuality flouts the conventions of "serious" experimental drama and situates Lee's work in a history of irreverent queer experimental performance. Queer sexuality is also part of its world-making potential. Lee sees themself as a "fierce human who loves sex in all different kinds of ways" but who "wasn't allowed to express that in any liberated way."[4] Lee's plays demonstrate how, as historian Amy Sueyoshi writes, "embracing queerness can be liberating and transformational within an API [Asian and Pacific Islander] community besieged and belittled by white American standards of gender and sexual ideals."[5]

The critical dismissals also tend to undervalue the intellectual force of Lee's work, which is rooted in literary and theoretical source material. Lee cites Adrienne Kennedy's *Funnyhouse of a Negro* as inspiration for *Suicide Forest* (2019). *to the left of the pantry and under the sugar shack* (2016) and *Memory Retrograde* (2015–2018) were influenced by Frances Yates's *The Art of Memory* and Gaston Bachelard's *The Poetics of Space*. *War Lesbian* (2014) is a loose adaptation of a queer Inuit myth that also makes reference to Filippo Tommaso Marinetti's *Futurist Manifesto*. Lee and writer-performer Jen Goma cite a range of "auto-theorists" such as Audre Lorde, Assata Shakur, Claudia Rankine, Maggie Nelson, and Roland Barthes, whose work inspired their duet *plural (love)* (2017), a performance installation that explores the limits of society's sexual norms and includes pop songs with lyrics by Jean-Paul Sartre.

Lee's plays interrogate the construction of femininity, parody masculinity, and question binary gender. As Lee points out, Asian American femininity is "codified by this white gaze." They explain, "My relationship to my own body and my own sex and sexuality has—from the moment I stepped foot in this country—been defined by somebody else."[6] Their work is an attempt to define their sex and sexuality in and on their own terms. In *drunkfish oceanrant* (2013), for example, a collaboration with the company Built for Collapse based on Japanese Rakugo performance, Lee plays with media stereotypes of Asian women and those that render Asian men the butt of the joke. In it, Lee portrays a Japanese storyteller who sports a thin glittery goatee and who transforms from a drunken fisherman into a romantic ballad singer in a flowy blue chiffon dress, and finally into a J-Pop star in a bedazzled bra top—goatee still in place throughout.

War Lesbian, Lee's pop opera produced by Dixon Place in 2014, offers a vision of "lesbian" as a "limitless body"—a person beyond the confines of traditional gender and sexuality. Sedna, the titular war lesbian played by queer performance artist Erin Markey, is born of her mother, Womb, a vapid housewife in a towering white wig; punished by her father Mitch, a dogsled champion who sings about eating raw steak and the thrill of feeling the wind on the underside of his balls; and trained by a demonic Ellen DeGeneres in how to capitalize on her identity and burgeoning celebrity. Ellen, as played by Lee in a white suit and blond wig, critiques the commodification of queerness as she acknowledges that she represents an "Acceptable Butch Form" and explains, "I used to not fit into a box, so I created this box of my own. Now, I sell this box. I make money off my box," gesturing toward her vagina. In the foreword of the unpublished script, Lee notes that they envision Sedna as

> an enormous woman because her very existence doesn't fit inside any given, prescribed box ... the norms that society has to offer can never fill her up. So she goes searching for more, always searching for larger spaces she can inhabit and become her own.

Lee, too, seems to be searching for larger spaces to inhabit. Their most acclaimed piece, *Suicide Forest*, is an exploration and explosion of Japanese and Japanese American gender and sexual roles. Premiered at the Bushwick Starr in 2019 and remounted off-Broadway as a co-production with the Ma-Yi Theater Company in 2020, the piece was touted as "highbrow/brilliant" by *New York Magazine*, garnered Lee an Obie Award for Playwriting and Conception, and was published by 53rd State Press. Directed by Aya Ogawa and performed by a Japanese and Japanese heritage cast, the piece features Lee acting alongside their mother, Aoi Lee, a Butoh dancer who plays a spirit that is haunting Lee's character, Azusa, a 16-year-old Japanese schoolgirl. In Act 2 of the production, Lee once again thwarts expectations in content and form. After a scene set in the "suicide forest" at Mount Fuji, lights come up on stage and the performers "*drop their characters, becoming themselves.*"[7] Lee addresses the audience, taking responsibility for the play and asking the performers to share "their percentages"—to quantify how Japanese and how American they feel at that particular moment in time. As the show falls into another register of theatricality, Lee reveals their "real kink"—their desire "to deserve it all, all the pain that is mine," before engaging in a gentle and intimate conversation with their mother that demonstrates the challenges of communication across language and culture.[8] The audience's expectations are thwarted, but the play's themes crystalize as we watch Lee navigate the many parts of themself in real time during these final moments of the play.

In "Why Queer Asian American Studies?" Amy Sueyoshi argues for the liberational potential of Asian America embodying what she calls a "queer frame of mind."[9] "By resetting to a queer frame of mind," she writes,

> Asian America could move out of the shadows of inadequacy that often defines our existences and create new standards of "excellence" ... This is the transformative power of queer to fuel not just self-acceptance and liberation but also community cohesion and political power.[10]

Lee is defining new standards of excellence in experimental theatre in both content and form. Like Sedna, they do not fit in any prescribed box; they defy expectations, critique the limitations of gender and sexual norms, and present transformational worlds in which queerness knows no bounds.

NOTES

1 Rachel Lin, interview with Haruna Lee, *Upstage Left*, podcast audio, March 19, 2020, https://therachellin.com/upstage-left (19:37–22:18).
2 Lin, interview (35.30–39.26).
3 "About – Company," Haruna Lee, 2020, www.harunalee.com/company
4 Lin, interview (47:00–49:29).
5 Amy Sueyoshi, "Why Queer Asian American Studies? Implications for Japanese America," *Pan-Japan* 12, no. 1/2 (2016): 113.
6 Lin, interview (47:00–49:29).
7 Haruna Lee, *Suicide Forest* (Brooklyn, NY: 53rd State Press, 2019), 75.
8 Ibid., 78.
9 Sueyoshi, 113.
10 Ibid., 114.

FURTHER READING

Gawlak, Emily. "Interview: Kristine Haruna Lee on Feminism, Gertrude Stein, and *War Lesbian*'s Demonic Ellen DeGeneres." *Stage Buddy*. December 19, 2014, https://stagebuddy.com/theater/theater-feature/interview-kristine-haruna-lee-feminism-gertrude-stein-war-lesbians-demonic-ellen-degeneres

Tella, Caitlyn. "The Impossible Realm of Embodiment: On the Work of Haruna Lee." *Quarterless Review*. February 12, 2021, https://thequarterlessreview.com/Haruna-Lee

JOAN LIPKIN
(Chicago, Illinois)
Gad Guterman

Joan Lipkin is an interdisciplinary artist and activist. As a playwright, director, producer, and political advocate, her goals are to foster public conversations and urge civic action. For over three decades, she has mined the entertaining power of the arts to empower marginalized populations and spotlight injustices. The desire to turn private discussions into public dialogues and bring people together to explore shared issues underlies Lipkin's artistic practice. When she received the Ethical Humanist of the Year Award from the Ethical Society of St. Louis (2007), Lipkin stressed how the arts forge connection, to ourselves and to others. The feeling of togetherness, Lipkin suggested, propels positive transformations.[1]

In 1989, Lipkin founded That Uppity Theatre Company in St. Louis, Missouri, an organization she still helms as artistic director. She "take[s] great pleasure in being part of a tradition of people who have historically been called uppity—blacks, gays, women, anybody who steps out of line."[2] One of the company's early successes was *Some of My Best Friends Are ...* (1989, music/lyrics by Tom Clear), the first theatre piece about gay and lesbian lives staged in Missouri. *SoMBFA* exemplifies key strategies Lipkin utilizes in much of her work; she relies on humor to comment on and transcend oppression. Lipkin views comedy as "a force for social and political transformation" and laughter, especially laughter born from pain, as a unifying, energizing force.[3] Carnivalesque strategies, such as having a straight couple navigate a heterophobic environment, epitomize the humor in *SoMBFA*. Biting comedy also arises from self-conscious stereotypes, popular culture references, and direct address. The musical opens with "No Billing," in which "Joan" must convince reluctant actors to participate in a gay-themed revue. Although pushed to an extreme, "No Billing" simultaneously reflects the struggles Lipkin faced casting the show in that era and celebrates the collective effort behind what became a sold-out success.

The revue's collage-like approach offered a kaleidoscopic view of LGBTQ+ lives, including but also expanding beyond a trend of focusing narratives on the AIDS crisis. Driven by what Lipkin calls a "politics of inclusion," *SoMBFA* expressly composed its company and audience of "people of all preferences," part of the show's subtitle.[4] Decades later, when Lipkin produced Briefs: A Festival of Short LGBTQ+ Plays (2012–2017), collage again served to feature a plurality of voices. Although she acknowledges the need for separatist performance spaces, Lipkin gravitates toward projects that forge bridges across communities. Both Briefs and *SoMBFA* animated communion. The projects invited direct intervention in a common cause: at performances of *SoMBFA*, the company asked audiences to sign a petition to repeal Missouri's homophobic Sexual Misconduct Law and, at Briefs, audiences fundraised for local charities, from Metro Trans Umbrella Group to the Islamic Foundation. When possible, Lipkin further encourages community by providing convivial cabaret seating; for her, employing a local bartender for the event can be as important as casting the play. And casting, in her view, optimally centers individuals who have traditionally faced silence and diminished visibility. Lipkin thus illuminates intersections among queerness, gender, race, age, and disability.

Lipkin propagates Uppity's mission through myriad partnerships and collaborations. Her intergenerational, interdisciplinary work ranges from a commission with the NYC Gay Men's Chorus that premiered at Lincoln Center to a devised performance in a church basement with a St. Louis chapter of PFLAG. She also established several performance groups to build communal spirit and engage diverse audiences. In the early 2000s, for instance, Lipkin directed As American as Apple Pie, an ensemble focused on elevating LGBTQ+ youth through collective creation, and The Louies, which offered support and community to gay men through performance-based projects. Since 2015, her direction of Playback Now! St. Louis builds on the improvisational work of Jonathan Fox and Jo Salas to foster autobiographical storytelling.

Notably, Lipkin cofounded the DisAbility Project (DP) in 1995 with occupational therapist Fran Cohen. Fusing artistry and activism, the mixed-ability ensemble promotes authentic representation and advances anti-ableist policies. The DP highlights intersectional identities. "It is interesting and troubling that sexuality is often erased when disability is in the room," Lipkin shares in a conversation with mentee Ryan Haddad.[5] As does Haddad's autobiographical *Hi, Are*

You Single? (2017), Lipkin's work with the DP often highlights queer lives within disabled communities.

As a producer, Lipkin embraces collaborative efforts that engage fellow artists and private and public agencies. Uppity's *Big Fat LGBT Show*, for example, has toured corporations and schools to spread awareness about LGBTQ+ issues. With the Alternate Currents/Direct Currents (AC/DC) Series (1992–2000), Uppity fostered the work of queer performance artists including Quentin Crisp, Michael Kearns, and Holly Hughes, as well as After Rodney, a poetry performance group organized by Lipkin that cultivated discussion among white women and women of color. AC/DC provoked controversy when it presented Tim Miller's *My Queer Body* in 1992. Along with Hughes, Miller was part of the "NEA Four" artists whose depictions of gender and sexuality drew national attention when the National Endowment for the Arts, spurred by Congress, rescinded funding. The Supreme Court eventually upheld the NEA's decision, and the battle amplified how queer artists struggled in the 1990s to resist homophobia and misogyny disguised as morality. In conservative Missouri, Lipkin confronted the threats around producing Miller's show by partnering with the Regional Arts Commission, prompting their approval of a freedom of expression policy. Lipkin models and argues that artists need to rescue themselves and each other, learning to navigate within and against bureaucracies to make art happen.[6]

Lipkin's plays emerge from a need to tell stories she finds absent on the stage. *Small Domestic Acts* (1992), for example, focuses on a straight and a lesbian couple to explore how spousal and social roles can conflict with sexual identity and attraction. The parallel journeys of Lesbian Sheila and Straight Sheila, each in a problematic partnership, trouble essentialist conceptions of gender and relationships. *He's Having Her Baby* (1990, music/lyrics by Tom Clear) imagines how a teenage boy becomes pregnant after one date and ultimately recognizes the necessity for reproductive choice. The original production faced antagonistic reviews and even incited a bomb threat. Lipkin successfully confronted the hostility by encouraging both cast and audiences to invest in the high-stakes issue and "[see] themselves as active, collective partners in social change."[7] Lipkin embraces the label of "feminist writer" and believes that feminism must include other forms of marginalization in its quest for change. Her advocacy for queer communities likewise stems from a belief that "queer" is a politically motivated category and that queer liberation must combat inequity in all forms.

Yet, Lipkin avoids simplistic affiliations; her plays embrace contradictions and unapologetically juxtaposing points of views. For instance, *The State of Marriage* (2010) advocates for everyone's right to marry while recognizing marriage as a chauvinistic, historically contingent institution. *Ferguson* (2015) and *Our Friends* (2016, part of After Orlando: an international theatre action present intimate struggles faced by couples who see advocacy and resilience in the face of tragedy differently. Such invitations to explore conflict illustrate Lipkin's inclusionary project. "Our survival," Lipkin says, "depends upon people learning how to listen to each other and to appreciate, or at least tolerate, each other's differences."[8] Moreover, survival requires constant reprioritization. In the advent of Trump's presidency, Lipkin put Briefs and other projects on hold to amplify Dance the Vote, an award-winning project she founded that utilizes the arts to promote voter registration and democracy.[9]

A devoted participant in the politics and artistic life of St. Louis, Lipkin has successfully exported her intergenerational, community-based approach to a variety of locations and organizations across the United States and abroad. Since 2016, she has served LGBTQ+ communities in Belgrade and Sarajevo, where she has directed *The Queer Café*, a project woven from dialogues facilitated in collaboration with Belgrade Pride and the Civil Rights Defenders. *Queer Café* attests to Lipkin's core belief that the ability to "craft and own [one's] narratives and get them out in the world" galvanizes individuals and communities.[10] Such efforts—rooted in defending gender equality, LGBTQ+ lives, disability, immigration reform, racial justice, voting rights, climate action, reproductive choice, or gun sense—embody Lipkin's core belief that artists are essential for civic health.

NOTES

1 Matthew Hile, "2007 Humanist of the Year: Towards a Democracy of Art," Ethical Society of St. Louis, 15 April 2007, www.ethicalstl. org/2007-humanist-year-towards-democracy-art-joan-lipkin-founder-artistic-director-uppity-theatre-company2007-humanist-year-towards-democracy-art-joan-lipkin-foun/
2 Lipkin, "Rabble-Rousing in St Louis with That Uppity Theatre," interview by Lizbeth Goodman, *New Theatre Quarterly* 9, no. 36 (1993): 367.
3 Domnica Radulescu, *Women's Comedic Art as Social Revolution* (Jefferson, NC: McFarland & Company, 2012), 222.
4 Lizbeth Goodman, *Contemporary Feminist Theatres* (London: Routledge, 1993), 146. The full subtitle is "A Gay and Lesbian Revue for People of All Preferences."

5 Joan Lipkin and Ryan Haddad, "'Be Fierce, Believe in Yourself, and Find Your People': A Roundtable Discussion about Disability and Performance," *Journal of Literary & Cultural Disability Studies* 12, no. 2 (2018): 232. Haddad studied with Lipkin at the Trinity/La MaMa program.
6 Lipkin, "Visionary Dialogues: Creativity in Crisis," De Nichols blog, August 30, 2020, www.denichols.co/blog/visionary-dialogues-creativity-in-crisis
7 Lipkin, "Aftermath: Surviving the Reviews," in *Upstaging Big Daddy: Directing Theater as if Gender and Race Matter*, ed. Ellen Donkin and Susan Clements (Ann Arbor, MI: University of Michigan Press, 1993), 321.
8 Lipkin, "Rabble-Rousing," 374.
9 Lipkin coproduces Dance the Vote with Ashley L. Tate. In 2021, Dance the Vote received an IDEA Award from St Louis's Arts and Culture Accessibility Cooperative for its commitment to inclusion, diversity, equity, and accessibility as well as FOCUS St Louis's What's Right with the Region Award for Fostering Creativity for Social Change. CBS featured the project in *Every Vote Counts: A Celebration of Democracy*.
10 Lipkin and Haddad, "'Be Fierce'": 226.

FURTHER READING

"Outspoken: Oral Interviews with LGBTQ Pioneers," interview by Steven F. Dansky, Vimeo, 10 July 2019, https://vimeo.com/347356550

"Who Speaks and Who Is Spoken For?" interview by Iris Smith, *The Drama Review* 38, no. 3 (1994): 96–127.

CHARLES LUDLAM
(Floral Park, New York, 1943–1987)
Joe E. Jeffreys

To be ridiculous is to be worthy of ridicule. And ridicule is ultra-vicious criticism.
To be called ridiculous is something most people avoid. Charles Ludlam, however, embraced the label, and, in so doing, this playwright, actor, director, philosopher, and all-around theatrical dynamo became a foundational figure in queer theatre. As the creator of the Ridiculous Theatrical Company, from the 1960s through the 1980s Ludlam wrote 29 plays that he often starred in and directed, reveling in a devious aesthetic, lush references high and low, and an arch sense of humor. Like Shakespeare and Molière before him, Ludlam established a longstanding company housed in a theatre devoted to the repertory production of his many plays, and the fact that these works are unabashedly queer makes this singular achievement even more remarkable. The Ridiculous Theatrical Company won numerous awards and garnered critical praise from mainstream publications like the *New York Times* and *Time* magazine, as well as grants from institutions including the National Endowment for the Arts and the Ford Foundation.

Born and raised in several Long Island townships, even as a young person Ludlam was always already a theatrical impresario. He gave puppet shows in his home basement, was a fixture of his high school drama program, and acted as well as directed children's shows with his local community theatre. Perhaps most remarkable, when he was still a teenager, he rented space one summer above a liquor store and staged a dramaturgically dense selection including Strindberg's surrealist *A Dream Play* and a Noh drama. Ludlam attended Hofstra University, where he majored in dramatic literature. While he acted in numerous productions staged by the college's theatre department, the young odd duck was rarely cast in lead roles.

After Hofstra, Ludlam moved to New York City, and it is here that the great Ridiculous work begins. Experimental theatre was everywhere in New York during this period, from The Living Theatre, which Ludlam saw and admired, to The Open Theater, and vibrant off-off-Broadway spaces like La MaMa and Judson Poets' Theater. His New York City stage debut came in a Ronald Tavel play directed by John Vaccaro for the Play-House of the Ridiculous. Competing origin myths surround the naming of Vaccaro's troupe and their zeroing in on the word "ridiculous" as an uber-apt descriptor of themselves, but it is in and from this group that an unmistakably queer approach to theatre germinates. With seeds planted as far back as Aristophanes to more recent sprouts cultivated by Jack Smith, notions of farce, tragedy, triumph, trash fabulousness, carnivalesque inversions, and outsider stances flower into the Ridiculous. Other Ridiculous grafts in this era's garden include the Cockettes' glittering genderfuck on the West Coast and John Waters' early low-budget film work in Baltimore.

In 1966, Ludlam wrote and acted in the anarchic *Big Hotel*, staged by Vaccaro. The following year, during rehearsals for Ludlam's second play for the group, Vaccaro fired Ludlam from his own play. Ludlam left, taking eight of the cast with him, including Lola Pashalinski, underground film star and drag performer Mario Montez, and his former Hofstra classmate Susan Carlson, whom Ludlam rechristened Black-Eyed Susan and made a key member of his Ridiculous universe. They formed their own group, the Ridiculous Theatrical Company, and staged their own version of Ludlam's sci-fi tragedy mash-up *Conquest of the Universe* (1967) or, as it is freshly renamed, *When Queens Collide*. From this point until his death Ludlam worked tirelessly to sustain and create for his Ridiculous Theatrical Company. They tramped from space to space, gay bar to porn theatre, and toured Europe several times performing his works until 1978, when they leased a fabled basement entertainment space at One Sheridan Square, a stone's throw away from where the Stonewall uprising unleashed less than a decade earlier.[1]

Ludlam's 29 published plays, and there is also a bulging archive of abandoned works, range widely in style. An outsider viewpoint, however, remains hard-core. His early plays, like *Big Hotel* (1966) and *The Grand Tarot* (1969), offer experimental nonlinear structures and stand as collage epics built upon unbridled direct quote mash-ups of far-flung sources, from Christopher Marlowe's *Tamburlaine the Great* (1588) to newspaper help wanted ads. Later works, like his Flaubert-inspired *Salammbô* (1985) and *The Artificial Jungle* (1986), his riff on Zola's *Thérèse Raquin*, continue a dizzying reference base from the kitsch to the sublime but are increasingly more traditional in their well-made play construction.

What never becomes dramaturgically staid is his plays' comedic perspective. Most Western theatre offers a dominant position, ridiculing and encouraging laughter at nonconformity. Ludlam flips this script and focuses on the world as seen by the outsider, asking his audience to laugh and experience liberation with and through it. To be Ridiculous is to empower the ridicule, claiming and reversing the criticism. During the 1960s' increasing sexual liberation, the Ridiculous movement spun an outcast sensibility into serious yet salaciously outspoken artistic expression. They weaponized queer aesthetics, like drag and extravagance, as coruscating compasses pointing to messages of equality and compassion. "Basically the catch phrase for my movement would be 'virtuoso maximalism,' enemy of minimalism," Ludlam philosophized.[2]

Foundational to queer theatre, Ludlam distinguished his work from lesbian or gay theatre. None of Ludlam's plays truck in coming out narratives and only a few offer lesbian or gay characters. Queer or outsider characters and ideas, however, abound. "Gay theatre," Ludlam stated,

> is really a political movement to show you that gay people can be admirable, responsible members of the community. It shows their problems. I don't do that. "Queer theatre" embraces more variation, and the possibility of something being odd or peculiar rather than just simply homosexuality.[3]

As Ludlam repeatedly proved through his works like the pan sexuality of his *Bluebeard* (1970), his country-western musical *Corn* (1972), or his "tear-jerker" *Camille* (1973), a queer play does not require LGBT subject matter or even sexually queer characters.

Queer theatre can be a function of aesthetics and acting style, and, in the Ridiculous, extravagance in any form is mandatory. Ridiculous performers are metatheatrically aware of their performances and capable of simultaneously transmitting an opinion about that performance. This acting approach is grounded in an all-too-frequent queer reality—being different but perhaps unable to present your true identity, and thus presenting as something other but with slips and a clear attitude about it. Some might talk about this as a result of alienation. Others might call it out as camp. Nowhere was this *seltsame Verfremdungseffekt* (queer alienation effect) more evident than in Ludlam's portrayal of Dumas fils's tragic courtesan Camille. With his hairy chest flowing out of low décolletage gowns, by the play's end Ludlam's enactment of Camille's consumptive deathbed scene invariably brought tears in the audience who had fully invested in the seemingly incongruous image as a full person.

Ludlam died of AIDS-related complications in 1987 at age 44, and his passing was reported on page one of the *New York Times*. After his death, Ludlam's life and work partner Everett Quinton advanced the Ridiculous genre at One Sheridan Square and far beyond its subterranean walls as well. Less than a decade after Ludlam's death, his work saw numerous productions, with his two-actor, eight-character, quick-change, penny dreadful play *The Mystery of Irma Vep* (1984) becoming one of the most produced plays in America. Parts of Ludlam's spirit and impact manifested during his lifetime in the works of fellow thespians Charles Busch and Ethyl Eichelberger. Today, the Five Lesbian Brothers and Taylor Mac carry parts of Ludlam's vibrant legacy, and Tony Kushner acknowledges Ludlam as "our great antecedent."[4]

Who's ridiculous now?

NOTES

1 The space had served as home to everything from a speakeasy, to a magic theatre, and, in the late 1930s, a space called Café Society, where Billie Holiday, Sarah Vaughn and Lena Horne performed. Closer to Ludlam's 1978 lease, it had served as a jazz club where Jimi Hendrix played, and as a gay bar, The Haven, that witnessed its own violent raid and destruction by the New York City Police Department. Since 1998, One Sheridan Square has served as home to the Axis Theatre Company.
2 Ludlam, Charles and Steven Samuels. *Ridiculous Theatre: Scourge of Human Folly: The Essays and Opinions of Charles Ludlam* (New York: Theatre Communications Group, 1992), 222.
3 Ibid., 230.
4 Kushner, Tony. "Foreword: Notes Toward a Theatre of the Fabulous," in *Staging Gay Lives: An Anthology of Contemporary Gay Lives*, ed. John Clum (Boulder, CO: Westview Press, 1996), vii.

FURTHER READING

Brecht, Stefan. *Queer Theatre*. Frankfurt am Main: Suhrkamp, 1978.
Edgecomb, Sean. *Charles Ludlam Lives! Charles Busch, Bradford Louryk, Taylor Mac, and the Queer Legacy of the Ridiculous Theatrical Company*. Ann Arbor, MI: University of Michigan Press, 2017.
Kaufman, David. *Ridiculous! The Theatrical Life and Times of Charles Ludlam*. New York: Applause, 2002.

TAYLOR MAC
(Laguna Beach, California, 1973–)
Sean F. Edgecomb

In 2000, Taylor Mac (né Taylor Mac Bowyer) summered in Provincetown, Massachusetts. Located on the tip of Cape Cod, "Ptown," a historic and storied gay resort, was a place where Mac could escape from the hustle of New York City. Following their graduation from the American Academy of Dramatic Arts in 1996, Mac had begun a career as an actor in touring productions while also writing original one-act plays (including the *Dilating Cycle*: *Okay*, *Maurizio Pollini*, *The Levee*, and *A Crevice*), but frustration with the casting system inspired their escape to this queer enclave. It was in Ptown that Mac began experimenting with cabaret-style, solo performances, featuring original songs (self-accompanied on the ukulele) and monologues. Aesthetically, Mac used what they could access to create a character—a "stage-worthy version of [Taylor Mac]"— relying on a creative assemblage of trash and thrifted materials for original "metaphoric" costumes and clownish white face paint, highlighted with drugstore makeup and glitter.[1]

These early drag performances would establish Mac's signature messy aesthetic, but also began garnering comparisons to queer downtown performers of an older generation, including Jack Smith, Charles Ludlam, and Ethyl Eichelberger. Upon returning to New York City that autumn, Mac began immersing themself in the plays and archived performances of these three key figures in the development of American LGBTQ+ theatre as a genre with distinct individual styles. In addition to drag, camp, improvisation, and curated amateurism, all three performers contributed to the Theatre of the Ridiculous which parodied heteronormative culture through performances "used as vehicles for social commentary and/or humor."[2]

Mac's early research on these queer Ridiculous forebears inspired new solo performances that spoke to queer life in the contemporary United States—including criticism of the George W. Bush administration and its response to the 9/11 terrorist attacks—while also continuing the queer legacy of Smith, Ludlam, and Eichelberger, three artists who had all tragically succumbed to AIDS-related complications. Mac's foundational performances took place in various sites in lower Manhattan, including The Slide Bar and HERE Arts Center, helping to establish them as an up-and-coming queer voice in post-millennial New York City. It was also during this period that Mac became acquainted with boylesque performer James Tigger! Ferguson, who would become a longtime collaborator.

In 2002, Mac presented their first official performance art cabaret, *The Face of Liberalism*, which led to an invitation to collaborate on *Live Patriot Acts: Patriots Gone Wiiiiildd!*, in response to the Republican National Convention, which took place at Madison Square Garden the following year. Simultaneously, several of Mac's one-act plays found productions in small theatres across Manhattan. Additionally, Mac premiered their solo show, *Cardiac Arrest or Venus on a Half Clam* (2004), at the Fez before transferring it to headline the Queer at HERE Festival. Mac's ceaseless work ethic and growing fame resulted in their selection as the winner of P.S. 122's inaugural Ethyl Eichelberger Award. The associated funding was used to write and produce *Red Tide Blooming* (2006), which was written in the style of Ludlam's Ridiculous and tackled themes such as transphobia, capitalism, and the threat of climate change.

Following a much-lauded run of a new, pastiched, one-person show, *The Be(a)st of Taylor Mac* (2006), at the Edinburgh Festival Fringe, Mac began to tour regularly while completing their autobiographical play, *The Young Ladies of ...* (2007), which also premiered at HERE. Mac's ongoing relationship with HERE led to a commission for *The Lily's Revenge* (2009), a five-hour, five-act durational play inspired by the structure of Japanese Noh drama. The show, which took up marriage equality by linking intolerance to nostalgia, called for an extensive creative team and introduced composer-arranger-pianist Matt Ray, costume designer Machine Dazzle, and guitarist Viva DeConcini as ongoing collaborators. Mac's interest in rejecting nostalgia as a trait of nationalist prejudice was further explored in the cabaret show *Comparison is Violence: The Ziggy Stardust Meets Tiny Tim Songbook* (2010), which opened at Joe's Pub before touring as far as Australia. After winning an Obie Award for *The Lily's Revenge*, Mac, Ray, and Dazzle began to imagine and conceive a much longer durational production that would examine the violence of American history through its popular music, covering a period of 240 years (1776–2016) in a 24-hour performance.

While workshopping what would become *A 24-Decade History of Popular Music* through ongoing concerts and fellowships, including Sundance Theatre Lab, Mac engaged in a series of collaborative performances with other companies. In 2011, Mac teamed with Paul Zimet and Ellen Maddow of Talking Band to present *Walk Across America for Mother Earth* at La MaMa Experimental Theatre Club. A *commedia dell'arte*-influenced show in style, *Walk* was based on an antinuclear protest walk that Mac had participated in as a young man. It was during this period that Mac was also cast in a variety of productions, including the roles of Puck/Egeus in the Classic Stage Company's production of *A Midsummer Night's Dream* (2012), as the Emcee in PlayMakers Repertory Company's production of *Cabaret* (2013), as Shin Te/Shui Ta in the Foundry Theatre's production of *The Good Person of Szechwan* (2014), and in collaboration with Mandy Patinkin in *The Last Two People on Earth: An Apocalyptic Vaudeville* (2015) at the American Repertory Theatre in Cambridge, Massachusetts. It was also during this period that Mac introduced "judy" as their preferred gender pronoun in performance—inspired, in part, by gay icon Judy Garland.

As Mac garnered critical acclaim, including *TimeOut New York* proclaiming Mac as a "future theatre legend,"[3] as well as earning the Peter Zeisler Memorial Award for "ingenuity, artistic integrity … and exemplifying pioneering practices in theatre," they also continued writing scripts in which they would not appear.[4] Inspired by the Dionysia Festival in ancient Athens, Mac began a cycle of four plays. Part 1: *The Fre*, originally commissioned for the Children's Theatre Company of Minneapolis, premiered at The Flea Theater in 2020. Part II: *Hir* premiered at San Francisco's Magic Theatre in 2014 before inspiring a new production off-Broadway at Playwright's Horizons the following year, directed by Niegel Smith and starring Kristine Nielsen. Thereafter, Smith would become Mac's director of choice. Part III: *The Bourgeois Oligarch* has yet to be produced. Part IV: *Gary: A Sequel to Titus Andronicus*, in a 2019 Broadway production starring Nathan Lane and directed by George C. Wolfe, opened to mixed reviews but received seven Tony Award nominations, including Best Play.

Perhaps Mac's most celebrated project to date is *A 24-Decade History of Popular Music*, which, after years of marathon-style training (with ever-lengthening performances), culminated in a 24-hour performance at St. Ann's Warehouse in Brooklyn, New York, October 8–9, 2016. The immersive performance, which included Ray, Dazzle, Ferguson, Smith, and DeConcini, was inspired by an early AIDS walk that Mac had participated in as a teenager in San Francisco. Mac reminisces that the event embodied "a community coming together [as] it was being torn apart."[5] The concert reframed this memory within the format of a "radical faerie realness ritual sacrifice" intending to symbolically purge the violence and intolerance of America's difficult past through performance in order to communally envision a more inclusive future for its marginalized people.[6] In addition to critical and scholarly praise, Mac was selected for the Edward M. Kennedy Prize, a Guggenheim Award, the Doris Duke Award (2016), a MacArthur Genius Grant, a Special Citation Obie, and a selection as finalist for the Pulitzer Prize (2017).

In addition to touring a truncated version of *A 24-Decade History* around the globe, Mac and Ray conceived an annual seasonal show, *Holiday Sauce* (2017), which premiered at Town Hall in Manhattan. Beyond carrying on the legacy of the marathon concert, Mac also dedicated the show to their late drag mother, Flawless Sabrina, who gained cult fame in the documentary film *The Queen* (1968). Through the COVID-19 pandemic, Mac continued to produce new virtual work including a pre-recorded *Holiday Sauce* (2020) and, through a residency at ALL ARTS, a series of short films that explore the queerness of Walt Whitman (2021). In 2020, Mac was also presented the prestigious Ibsen Award, marking the first time that a US artist was selected from a global list for bringing new artistic dimension to the world of drama or theatre.

NOTES

1 Sean F. Edgecomb. "The Ridiculous Performance of Taylor Mac," *Theatre Journal* 64:4 (2012), 553.
2 Stephen J. Bottoms. *Playing Underground: A Critical History of the 1960s Off-Broadway* (Ann Arbor, MI: University of Michigan Press, 2006), 215.
3 Courtnie Mele, "2014 TCG National Conference Awards and Final Programming," *BroadwayWorld*, June 1, 2014. www.broadwayworld.com/article/2014-TCG-National-Conference-Awards-and-Final-Programming-619-21-20140616
4 "The Latinx Theatre Commons' Peter Zeisler Memorial Award Acceptance Speech," *HowlRound*, June 14, 2017. https://howlround.com/latinx-theatre-commons-peter-zeisler-memorial-award-acceptance-speech
5 WFMT Blog, "How 1 Artist is Condensing 24 Decades of American Popular Song into a Single, 24-Hour Performance," April 12, 2016. http://blogs.wfmt.com/offmic/2016/04/12/how-1-artist-is-condensing-24-decades-of-american-popular-song-into-a-single-24-hour-performance/
6 Maddie Hopfield, "Taylor Mac: Distilling the Past to Imagine a Future," *Theatre Philadelphia*, June 25, 2018. www.theatrephiladelphia.org/theatre-news/taylor-mac-distilling-the-past-to-imagine-a-future

FURTHER READING

Román, David, Kalle Westerling, and Dan Venning, with Jennifer Buckley, Miriam Felton-Dansky, Kim Marra, César Alvarez, and Erik Patterson. "Subjective Histories of Taylor Mac's 'Radical Faerie Realness Ritual' History," *Theatre Journal* 69:3 (September 2017), 403–415.

Svich, Caridad. "Glamming it Up with Taylor Mac," *American Theatre* (November 2008), 36–38.

Weiss, Sasha. "Taylor Mac Wants Theater to Make You Uncomfortable," *New York Times Magazine,* April 2, 2019. www.nytimes.com/2019/04/02/magazine/taylor-mac-gary-broadway.html

JOE MANTELLO
(Rockford, Illinois, 1962–)
James F. Wilson

In the annals of popular theatre, Joe Mantello may be best known for directing the mega-hit musical *Wicked* (2003). The show, which chronicles the backstory of the witches of Oz, has played more than 7,000 performances while making more than $1 billion on Broadway and has been produced around the world. Among cultural studies scholars, however, Mantello's impressive body of work surely will be measured by his contributions to queer theatre and performance. Mantello, as an actor and director, has been associated with many of the iconic works by LGBTQ playwrights of the late twentieth and early twenty-first centuries. He simultaneously embraces queer legacies while charting new courses for the popular American theatre.

Mantello was not initially drawn to a life in the arts, claiming he "was deeply ashamed" of theatre as an adolescent. He correlated his own gay identity with acting in school plays and community productions: both were freighted with immense stigma. He says, "Where I grew up, boys played sports. When Mrs. Windsor wrote in my yearbook, 'Have you ever considered a career in the theater?' it was literally like she wrote the word 'faggot'."[1] Nevertheless, after high school, he attended the University of North Carolina School of the Arts (UNCSA) and majored in drama. The BFA program changed his life, and he says attending UNCSA was "like being raised by apes and then coming to a city and seeing other humans."[2] More important, he was able to comfortably merge his gay identity with his theatre pursuits.

After graduation, he relocated to New York City in 1984. Along with fellow UNCSA alums Mary-Louise Parker, Peter Hedges, and K. Todd Freeman, he founded Edge Theater. The enterprise was short-lived, but the experience provided a supportive environment to develop as an actor. Beginning in 1989, he found a similarly encouraging milieu as a member of the esteemed off-Broadway theatre group, the Circle Repertory Company. Mantello's affiliation evinces a direct link to the wellspring of queer theatre in New York City and helped launch his career as an actor and director.

Circle Rep was founded in 1969 by veterans of the legendary Caffe Cino: Marshall W. Mason, Lanford Wilson, Rob Thirkield, and Tanya Berezin. In the 1990s, when it was an artistic home for Mantello, Circle Rep nurtured a cadre of LGBTQ writers, such as Jon Robin Baitz, Keith Curran, William M. Hoffman, Craig Lucas, Paula Vogel, and Wilson. Characteristically, the company's notable plays and productions tended to eschew dramatic realism and blended loopy theatricality with dark undertones. For instance, Mantello's first acting role with Circle Rep was a small part in Curran's *Walking the Dead* (1991), which Berezin, the company's artistic director, described as being "about a lesbian who has a sex-change operation and becomes a heterosexual man who puts on a dress for his estranged mother's second wedding, only to be discovered by two would-be rapists—which leads to a surprise ending."[3]

Mantello's next role was in Vogel's AIDS play *The Baltimore Waltz* (1992), which presents an alternately whimsical and nightmarish odyssey of a terminally ill schoolteacher and her brother. Demonstrating his quick-change acting abilities, Mantello played a number of characters in the duo's whirlwind travels. He received excellent reviews, including from Frank Rich, who wrote that Mantello "winningly performs a potpourri of burlesque turns in cameo roles of several nationalities and sexual dispositions."[4] He was nominated for Best Debut Performance by the Outer Critics Circle Awards committee.

Circle Rep also provided Mantello opportunities to pursue his greater passion, directing. His most prominent success at Circle Rep was Baitz's *Three Hotels* (1993), which comprises three monologues and concerns an American businessman and his estranged wife. Mantello and Baitz were partners at the time, and they separately noted the impact their personal lives had on their professional success.[5] The couple ended their romantic relationship in 2002, but they continued to work together, and Mantello directed Baitz's highly lauded *Other Desert Cities* (2011).

Mantello made his Broadway acting debut in Tony Kushner's *Angels in America* (1993) as Louis Ironson, an overwrought legal word processor, who deserts his AIDS-afflicted partner. Mantello was nominated for a Tony Award, and Rich praised his "combustible amalgam of puppyish Jewish guilt and self-serving intellectual piety."[6] Acting in *Angels* gave him a chance to work with director George C. Wolfe, who became a professional role model. According to Mantello, Wolfe "sees very clearly what he wants, and you end up there—but feeling that you've done it all on your own."[7] Artistic clarity as well as cohesiveness of all of the production elements are integral to Mantello's own approach to directing.

These qualities were evident in his elegant and spare staging of Terrence McNally's *Love! Valour! Compassion!* (1994), which concerns a group of gay men who gather at a country home over three separate summer weekends. Mantello was nominated for a Tony Award, and McNally won for Best Play. Critic Charles Isherwood wrote that Mantello "has a painter's eye for visual space ... and a musical sense of rhythm."[8] After helming the film adaptation in 1997, he went on to direct several more works by McNally, including the controversial *Corpus Christi* (1998), the opera *Dead Man Walking* (2000), and the musical *A Man of No Importance* (2002). McNally confirmed that Mantello's meticulous attention to detail distinguishes him from other directors. He remarked, "What makes him thunderously good is that he cares desperately about what his plays look, sound, smell and taste like. They have a wonderful sensuality but are never overripe."[9]

Mantello has brought this sensuous lyricism to numerous plays that tackle weighty issues related to LGBTQ experience. For instance, he directed Marc Wolf's one-person play *Another American Asking and Telling* (1999), which focuses on gay men in the military, and Alexi Kaye Campbell's *The Pride* (2010), a play that shows the devastating effects of sexual repression in shifting scenes taking place in 1958 and 2008. In 2003, he won his first Tony Award for his direction of Richard Greenberg's *Take Me Out*, a drama exploring homophobia and racism in professional sports, which also won the Tony for Best Play. Mantello won his second Tony for directing the 2004 revival of Stephen Sondheim and John Weidman's musical *Assassins* (1990).

While directing *Casa Valentina* (2014), Harvey Fierstein's play about a group of cross-dressing men in the Catskills in the early 1960s, Mantello addressed the complexities of gender expression and sexual orientation. Ben Brantley admired the "liquid staging" and stated that the production was "directed with unexpected ripples of beauty."[10] Even when not addressing LGBTQ topics directly, Mantello has applied his distinctive directorial precision to plays by a new generation of queer playwrights including Adam Bock, Stephen Karam, and John Logan.

After an absence of nearly two decades, Mantello returned to acting, starring in the 2011 revival of Larry Kramer's groundbreaking AIDS play, *The Normal Heart* (1985). Co-directed by Joel Grey and Wolfe, the production confirmed the play's fierce urgency, and Mantello plumbed rich and emotional layers in his performance of Ned Weeks. He was nominated for a Tony Award, and taking on the role demonstrates his commitment to projects that explore LGBTQ histories and revitalize classic plays by queer writers. For example, he played Tom in the 2017 revival of Tennessee Williams's *The Glass Menagerie* (1944) and directed the 2018 revivals of Edward Albee's *Three Tall Women* (1990) and Mart Crowley's *The Boys in the Band* (1968).

Although he had once bristled at the connection between gay identity and theatre, within Mantello's credits they are intricately intertwined. This, however, may be purely serendipitous. Surveying his prolific record, he says:

> I become involved with things that speak to me and move me and make me laugh and frighten me. It just randomly happens that I have been involved with some of the most seminal gay plays of the last 50 years.[11]

NOTES

1 Jacob Bernstein, "Broadway Joe," *New York Times* (June 2, 2013), 26.
2 Bruce Weber, "Couple of the Moment in New York Theater," *New York Times* (October 30, 1994), H1.
3 Alex Witchel, "On Stage and Off," *New York Times* (May 3, 1991), C2.
4 Frank Rich, "Play About AIDS Uses Fantasy to Try to Remake the World," *New York Times* (February 12, 1992), C15.
5 Weber, "Couple of the Moment."
6 Frank Rich, "Embracing All Possibilities in Art and Life," *New York Times* (May 5, 1993), C15.
7 Donald G. McNeil Jr., "George Wolfe and His Theater of Inclusion," *New York Times* (April 23, 1995), H1.
8 Charles Isherwood, "Legit Reviews: *Love! Valour! Compassion!*," *Variety* (December 12, 1996), https://variety.com/1996/legit/reviews/love-valour-compassion-3-1117436950/
9 Maureen Dowd, "Director Joe Mantello, Broadway's Invisible Wizard," *New York Times* (May 31, 2018), D1.
10 Ben Brantley, "A Place to Slip into Something Comfortable," *New York Times* (April 24, 2014), C1.
11 Dowd, "Broadway's Invisible Wizard."

FURTHER READING

Tepper, Jennifer Ashley. *The Untold Stories of Broadway*, vol. 4. New York: Dress Circle Publishing, 2021.

Weinert-Kendt, Rob. "Joe Mantello: The Way We Do Things the Way We Do," *American Theatre* (April 19, 2018), www.americantheatre.org/2018/04/19/joe-mantello-the-way-we-do-the-things-we-do/

TARELL ALVIN McCRANEY
(Miami, Florida, 1980–)
Isaiah Matthew Wooden

Tarell Alvin McCraney's plays are rich with examples of Black queer kinship and belonging. In the years since he made his professional debut as a playwright in 2007, McCraney has produced an impressive body of work that is as striking for the complex representations of Black queer life and experience it renders as it is for the immense praise it has generated from critics and audiences in the United States and internationally. Born October 17, 1980, and raised in Miami's Liberty City neighborhood, McCraney developed a deep affection for theatre and performance at an early age. He spent his formative years training as an actor and dancer at institutions such as Miami's New World School of the Arts and The Theatre School at DePaul University, where he earned his BFA in Acting in 2003. Part of what drew McCraney to the performing arts were the opportunities they afforded him to create and embody new worlds, casting a spotlight on lives and stories that might otherwise go unremarked upon or under-recognized. When McCraney entered the MFA in Playwriting program at the Yale School of Drama in 2004, he shifted focus away from being a player in other people's theatrical narratives to creating dramatic texts that resonated with his own experiences as a Black queer artist.

The question of what it means to come of age as a Black queer person in the twenty-first century is one that McCraney explores in several of his plays, including the acclaimed trilogy *The Brother/Sister Plays* (2009), *Wig Out!* (2008), and *Choir Boy* (2013). He has also explored similar themes in the projects he has created for the big and small screens. The much-celebrated film *Moonlight* (2016), which garnered McCraney an Oscar for Best Adapted Screenplay in 2017, and the equally acclaimed television series *David Makes Man* (2019), both feature Black queer youth characters who struggle to navigate some of the pleasures and perils of their everyday lives. Perhaps most notable about McCraney's Black queer protagonists are the ways that, even when confronted with conditions and circumstances that feel bleak or unwieldy, they manage to claim joy and forge strong affective ties.

Take, for example, the queer father-son duo Elegba and Marcus Eshu, who feature prominently in *The Brother/Sister Plays*, the triptych that helped introduce audiences to some of the concerns that have become hallmarks of McCraney's work, including his investments in exploring the dramaturgical possibilities of Black queerness. The first two plays, *In the Red and Brown Water* and *The Brothers Size*, chart Elegba's transition from adolescence to adulthood. Much like the Yoruba deity with whom he shares a name, a trickster figure known for his elusiveness, unpredictability, and sexual exploits, Elegba stands out in the plays for the ways he flouts the logics and impositions of hegemonic norms, particularly those aimed at disciplining Black desire. His refusal to conform or capitulate to the rules of social propriety is what, in part, renders him an object of scorn in the eyes of the law. But it is also what distinguishes him as a beloved member of the fictional San Pere community where McCraney sets the trilogy.

While Elegba's sexual fluidity is mostly only hinted at, Marcus's sexuality becomes a major point of conflict in *Marcus; Or the Secret of Sweet*. Turning attention to the next generation of San Pere residents, the trilogy's third play primarily centers on its titular character's efforts to come to terms with and make sense of the meanings and implications of his queer sexual identity. Of particular concern for the youth are the relationships he shares with his mother, Oba, and his two best friends, Osha and Shaunta Iyun. Outwardly expressing and embracing his queerness, he fears, might alter their closeness. His apprehensions are not wholly unfounded. Oba, for example, refuses to tell her son much about his father, opting to keep details about the man a mystery. He is likewise afraid of disappointing Osha, who is quite vocal about her romantic interests in him. While Shaunta Iyun attempts to explain early in the play that she already knows that he is "sweet," a euphemism she uses to describe his queerness, it does not allay the youth's fears. Ultimately, it is through a series of transformative encounters at the swampy edges of San Pere (including a sexual tryst with a charming visitor from the Bronx named Shua) and in his drag-filled dreams that Marcus comes to know and appreciate the expansiveness of his friends and family's love and support for him.

Like Marcus, the spirited youth who animate *Wig Out!*, which first premiered at London's Royal Court Theatre in 2008 and was subsequently produced off-Broadway at the Vineyard Theatre in 2009, also negotiate doubts about where and how they fit into the world. Indeed, motivating their respective desires to participate in the drag/ballroom houses at the center of the colorful fantasia McCraney crafts are the harms and abuses many of them suffered at the hands of relatives who refused to accept or acknowledge their sexuality, gender expression, and/or gender identity. Ballroom culture traces its origins to Harlem's LGBTQ community in the late nineteenth and early twentieth centuries and includes the competitive drag balls where participants "walk" in categories such as "runway," "face," "butch queen realness," and "femme queen realness." The rituals and practices of house/ballroom culture afford each character safe haven to express their queerness freely and, importantly, to cultivate relationships that are at once meaningful and affirming. As with Jennie Livingston's consequential documentary *Paris is Burning* (1990) and the groundbreaking television series *Pose* (2018–2021), *Wig Out!* renders and reveals the ballroom community as "an enduring social sanctuary for those who have been rejected by and marginalized within their families of origin, religious institutions, and society at large," to echo scholar Marlon Bailey.[1] The play also reflects McCraney's longstanding dedication to creating characters and stories that frustrate the disciplining logics of both hetero- and homonormativity.

McCraney further reveals this commitment to affirming queer ways of being and loving in *Choir Boy*, which also premiered at the Royal Court Theatre in London (2012) and was subsequently produced off-Broadway (2013) and on Broadway (2018) by Manhattan Theatre Club. Set in the fictional Charles R. Drew Prep School for Boys, *Choir Boy* dramatizes the coming-of-age experience of Pharus Jonathan Young, a student leader of Drew's renowned choir who is often made to feel out of place by his peers and school administrators because of his effeminacy and presumed queer sexuality. Aiding in Pharus's efforts to make Drew into a locus of belonging are the relationships—one romantic, the other platonic—that he shares with two of his classmates, David Heard and Anthony Justin "AJ" James. At first blush, David and AJ seem to have very little in common with each other or with Pharus, with David maintaining a singular focus on deepening his religious faith and AJ relishing the social advantages afforded to him as a star athlete. Yet, both, in their own way, confirm for Pharus that he is worthy of love. These relationships are not without friction. Indeed, David's feelings for Pharus ultimately turn violent when he fears that another peer has discovered the truth of the pair's years-long sexual relationship. By having Pharus and his schoolmates complicate conventional gender and sexual norms in the play, McCraney invites reflection on the endurance of certain definitional binarisms and illuminates their fundamental incapacity to account for the complexities of human difference.

As more recent works such as *Ms. Blakk for President* (2019), which he co-wrote with longtime collaborator Tina Landau, attest to, McCraney continues to make bringing Black queer narratives to the stage and screen a priority. The play, which had its premiere at Steppenwolf Theatre Company, gives fresh theatrical life to the pioneering work of Black queer activist Terence Alan Smith. A co-founder of the Chicago chapter of Queer Nation, Smith ran for mayor of Chicago and President of the United States as his drag persona Joan Jett Blakk in the 1990s to agitate for the end of the AIDS crisis and to combat rising homophobia, serophobia, and queer antagonism. In reflecting on what inspired him to dramatize Smith's activism, McCraney explained, "It's a Chicago story, it's a queer story, and a Black story … What these folks at Queer Nation and ACT UP did during that time, I'm just reaping the benefits of it."[2] What surely marks McCraney as one of the most important theatre makers of the twenty-first century is his unwavering belief in the power of art to honor Black queer pasts and presents. The compelling ways he heralds Black queer futures throughout his ever-growing body of work offers further evidence of his significance to modern theatre history.

NOTES

1 Marlon M. Bailey, *Butch Queens Up in Pumps: Gender, Performance, and Ballroom Culture in Detroit* (Ann Arbor: University of Michigan Press, 2013), 6.
2 See Kris Vire, "After Moonlight," *Chicago Magazine*, May 13, 2019. www.chicagomag.com/Chicago-Magazine/May-2019/Tarell-Alvin-McCraney-Ms-Blakk-for-President/

FURTHER READING

Luckett, Sharrell D., Román, David, and Wooden, Isaiah Matthew, eds. *Tarell Alvin McCraney: Theater, Performance, and Collaboration* (Evanston: Northwestern University Press, 2020).
Román, David. "The Distant Present of Tarell Alvin McCraney," *American Quarterly*, 66, no. 1 (2014): 181–195.
Wooden, Isaiah Matthew. "*Ms. Blakk's* Radical Queer History," *PAJ: A Journal of Performance and Art*, 124 (2020): 64–70.

TERRENCE McNALLY
(St. Petersburg, Florida, 1938–2020)
Virginia Anderson

Over a career spanning five decades, Terrence McNally was responsible for over 80 plays, musicals, and opera librettos. His legacy, however, is not only tied to his prolific writing for the stage across genres, but his advocacy for LGBTQ individuals through their representation in his work. McNally was an openly gay playwright when he launched his seismic career in the early 1960s, a time when others feared the consequences of such public identification. His plays were similarly groundbreaking; producer Paul Libin described McNally's *And Things That Go Bump in the Night* (1965) as "the first Broadway play with a positive, confident, openly gay character." Attorney and LGBTQ activist Roberta Kaplan observed, "he started so early to show Americans who gay people are, that we have the same hopes, dreams and struggles as everyone else. Terrence did it before anyone else. He did it better than anyone else."[1]

McNally was born in St. Petersburg, Florida, but grew up in the conservative Christian town of Corpus Christi, Texas, a working-class area sustained by the oil industry, farming, and its Naval Air Station. His father was a beer distributor and his parents were heavy drinkers, but they introduced their son to theatre, taking him to see *Annie Get Your Gun* (1946) and *The King and I* (1951) on Broadway when he was a child. By the time he was a teenager, he was producing operas in his family's garage. His creative writing was encouraged by Maurine McElroy, his high school English teacher and a trusted mentor and friend for decades to come. She nurtured his love of classical music and urged him to leave Texas to further his education.

While a student at Columbia University, McNally accompanied writer John Steinbeck and his family on a trip around the world as a tutor to Steinbeck's children. It was on this trip that McNally began to write *And Things that Go Bump in the Night*. In 1961, Steinbeck asked McNally to collaborate on several projects and the writer provided early encouragement.

The exchange of influential ideas would find another conduit through McNally's romantic relationship with playwright Edward Albee. Together several years, including while Albee was writing *Who's Afraid of Virginia Woolf?* (1962), they had different views on how to publicly present their sexuality. "Edward didn't want to be reviewed as a gay playwright and was never comfortable coming out," McNally told the *San Francisco Chronicle* in 2018.

> That's one of about a million reasons why that relationship was never going to go anywhere. I became invisible when press was around or at an opening night. I knew it was wrong. It's so much work to live that way.[2]

Although *And Things that Go Bump in the Night* was a critical failure and ran for only 16 performances, McNally continued to write at a furious pace. Success came with *Next* (1968), starring James Coco and directed by Elaine May, and his next several plays presented provocative absurdist satires on American society. By the 1970s, McNally shifted his style to comedy and farce, perhaps most memorably with *Bad Habits* (1974) and *The Ritz* (1975), a door-slamming farce set in a gay bathhouse.

Writing for the mainstream theatre of Broadway and off-Broadway, McNally introduced many audiences to complex characters and nuanced situations they had not previously encountered in the commercial theatre. Many of his plays mirrored the social changes that many gay men were experiencing contemporaneously. As the AIDS epidemic took hold during the 1980s and 1990s, McNally captured pain, intimacy, and homophobia while celebrating life through minutiae of generosity and humor. McNally wrote from personal experience and observation of the world around him. Speaking at the AIDS Walk New York, he shared,

> I'm always startled when I'm asked why I chose to write about AIDS. There was no choice. An artist responds to their world and tries to make sense of it, even the bad things. What else was I going to write about, the weather? ... I am bewildered and more than a little angry by the artists who did nothing but fiddle while their own, this great city, burned.[3]

McNally directly addressed the impact of the AIDS epidemic in *Andre's Mother* (1988), *Lips Together, Teeth Apart* (1991), *Love! Valour! Compassion!* (1994), and *Mothers and Sons* (2014).

The homophobia that fueled so much of the cruelty and disconnection during the early years of the AIDS epidemic flared in 1998 with the premiere of McNally's controversial play *Corpus Christi* at Manhattan Theatre Club (MTC). Protests outside the theatre, bomb threats, and death threats took place because McNally's telling of the Passion Play, set in Corpus Christi, Texas, reimagined Jesus and his disciples as gay men. Pendulum swings of cancelations and reinstatement resulted in nightly protests organized by religious leaders that forced MTC to ask audience members to pass through metal detectors before each performance. The controversy surrounding *Corpus Christi* may have garnered more attention than the play itself, but McNally has indicated that it was an artistic experience and moment in his life that he treasured.

Celebrated as a librettist as much as a playwright, McNally has written several award-winning musicals, including collaborations with John Kander and Fred Ebb (*The Rink*, 1984; *Kiss of the Spider Woman*, 1993; *The Visit*, 2015), Lynn Aherns and Stephen Flaherty (*Ragtime*, 1998; *A Man of No Importance*, 2003; *Anastasia*, 2017), and David Yazbek (*The Full Monty*, 2000). His opera *Dead Man Walking* (2000), with composer Jack Heggie, is one of the most frequently produced contemporary American operas around the world. McNally received four Tony Awards prior to a 2019 Tony Award for Lifetime Achievement in the Theatre, with two awards for Best Play (*Love! Valour! Compassion!*, 1995; *Master Class*, 1996) and two awards for Best Book of a Musical (*Kiss of the Spiderwoman*, 1993; *Ragtime*, 1998). In 2018, he was elected to the American Academy of Arts and Letters, one of the highest honors bestowed for artistic merit in the United States.

McNally's popular success is matched by his influence on multiple generations of theatre artists. McNally often wrote for actor Nathan Lane, who credits McNally for a career with opportunities beyond comedy alone. Their collaborations began with *The Lisbon Traviata* (1989) and continued for the remainder of McNally's lifetime. The playwright also helped to launch the directing career of Joe Mantello in the years following his success as an actor in Tony Kushner's *Angels in America,* naming Mantello a "McNally director"[4] and frequently emphasizing his contributions to *Love! Valor! Compassion!* and the 2002 Broadway revival of *Frankie and Johnny in the Clair de Lune* (1987).

McNally's impact as a playwriting mentor continues to be felt. Matthew López began a professional relationship with McNally as his assistant on a workshop of his musical *A Man of No Importance*. In exchange, McNally read one of López's plays. López cites McNally's encouragement and constructive criticism as "the permission I felt I needed to pursue a career as a writer"; and McNally and his husband Tom Kirdahy provided key support for the Broadway opening of López's Tony Award-winning play, *The Inheritance* (2019). "Without Terrence's example and his role in my life, I would never have been able to write *The Inheritance*," López insists. He clarifies the lineage of his own landmark play, which brought stories of gay men facing the past, present, and future of the AIDS epidemic into the twenty-first century:

> People always think I was chasing after Kushner with *The Inheritance*, but nothing could be further from the truth. It was Terrence I was watching and learning from as a student and later as a friend and mentee. *Love! Valour! Compassion!* was the spiritual ancestor to *The Inheritance*, not *Angels in America*.[5]

Looking to the future, less than a year before he died from complications related to COVID-19 within the first months of the pandemic, Terrence McNally reflected on his place in the continuum of theatre as he accepted his Tony Award for lifetime achievement:

> I love it when I remember theatre changes hearts. That secret place where we all truly live. I love my playwright peers, past, present, and especially future. You're chomping at the bit for your turn. Your diversity is long overdue and welcome.[6]

NOTES

1 *Terrence McNally: Every Act of Life*. Directed by Jeff Kaufman, *American Masters*. Season 33, episode 8. PBS, 2018.
2 Jesse Green and Neil Genzlinger. "Terrence McNally, Tony-Winning Playwright of Gay Life, Dies at 81." *New York Times*, March 24, 2020. www.nytimes.com/2020/03/24/theater/terrence-mcnally-dead-coronavirus.html
3 *Terrence McNally: Every Act of Life*. 01:24:56.
4 Toby Silverman Zinman. "Interview with Terrence McNally." *Terrence McNally: A Casebook*. New York: Routledge, 1997, 5.
5 Stephen Karam, Andrea Lepcio, and Matthew Lopez. "The Influence of Terrence McNally." *The Dramatist*, January 1, 2021. www.dramatistsguild.com/thedramatist/influence-terrence-mcnally

6 "Terrence McNally: Theatre Changes Hearts." *American Theatre*, March 24, 2020. www.americantheatre.org/2020/03/24/terrence-mcnally-theatre-changes-hearts

FURTHER READING

Frontain, Raymond-Jean. *The Theater of Terrence McNally: Something About Grace*. Vancouver, BC: Fairleigh Dickinson University Press, 2019.

McNally, Terrence. *Muse of Fire: Reflections on Theater*, ed. Raymond-Jean Frontain. Vancouver, BC: Fairleigh Dickinson University Press, 2019.

MURIEL MIGUEL
(Brooklyn, New York, 1937–)
Christy Stanlake

Muriel Miguel, whose Indigenous names are Bright Sun and Waga Nadili, descends from two Native nations: Kuna from Kuna Yala (located off the coast of Panama) on her father's side and Rappahannock from Virginia on her mother's. Born and raised in Brooklyn, New York, Miguel is the youngest of her Star family's (or clan's) three children: her older sisters are Elizabeth "Lisa" Mayo and Gloria Miguel.[1] Miguel is an actor, director, dancer, choreographer, playwright, educator, and activist, who is best known for being the founder and artistic director of Spiderwoman Theater, which began in 1975 (making Spiderwoman the oldest continually performing feminist theatre company in North America). Although the three sisters have been Spiderwoman's core, performers have varied over the years to meet the needs of each show the group creates. Other members have included Lois Weaver and Peggy Shaw, who later formed the queer feminist performance group Split Britches in 1980; Elvira and Hortensia Colorado, Chichimec/Otomi sisters and creators of Coatlicue Theatre Company; and the second generation of Spiderwoman Theater, Gloria's daughter Monique Mojica (Kuna/Rappahannock) and Muriel's daughter Murielle Borst (Kuna/Rappahannock), both of whom are also professional, independent theatre artists.

Spiderwoman Theater is named for the Hopi deity, Spiderwoman, who wove the world into existence, then taught people how to weave. The group's technique for creating plays is called "storyweaving." Through it, each member of a production shares stories that are personal, traditional, or from popular culture. By workshopping the stories' key themes, phrases, images, and gestures, the ensemble discovers points of connection that create a weblike structure of narratives that branches out, circles, and overlaps in ways that allow each individual's story to become part of a larger, collective one. The plays developed through storyweaving are multidimensional, nonlinear,

DOI: 10.4324/9781003203896-34   165

poetic, and athletic works of art that juxtapose humor with mourning, the political with the personal, and the idiosyncratic with the global.

While Miguel's dear friend and early Spiderwoman Theater collaborator Josephine Mofsie (Hopi/Winnebago) inspired storyweaving, Native nations generally share the concept that stories have the ability to transform the material world; consequently, they honor the generative power of spoken, embodied language.[2] Part of what made Spiderwoman Theater revolutionary, and what keeps the company relevant and exciting today, is its commitment to transforming the world through voicing stories that people often keep silent. Miguel recounts, "There are so many stories that as soon as you start it, people say, 'She can't tell that story.' And ... once you tell the story, it's a freedom! It's freedom!"[3] In Native philosophies, both storytellers and listeners share equal responsibility in creating meaning; accordingly, audiences of Spiderwoman Theater leave the performances knowing that they, too, now carry and continue the story. This reciprocity between Spiderwoman Theater and its audiences has been present since the group's inception, when women attending *Women in Violence* (1976) lingered in the theatre to share their own stories of having survived abuse. More recently, Indigenous male viewers of *Material Witness* (2016) joined the post-performance gatherings to discuss the responsibility they feel for bringing an end to the epidemic of murdered and missing Indigenous women.

Miguel's commitment to voicing silenced stories extends to her longstanding openness about being a two-spirit person. Across Native communities, the term "two-spirit" refers to LGBTQ people—individuals who possess elements of both male and female identities. Until settler-colonizers imposed Christianity upon Native peoples with the intent of eradicating Native cultures, two-spirit people were frequently celebrated within Native societies for being spiritually gifted with unique abilities to understand men and women alike. Two-spirit people are reclaiming both their identities and honored place within Indigenous nations across North America. Indigenous Canadian playwright Tomson Highway (Cree), celebrated author of *The Rez Sisters* (1986) and *Dry Lips Oughta Move to Kapuskasing* (1989), has written essays about the violence Christianity has enacted against Indigenous understandings of sexuality, gender, and spirituality.[4] In 2013, the book *Two-Spirit Acts* featured works by two-spirit performers: Miguel, Kent Monkman (Cree), and Waawaate Fobister (Anishnaabe). Fobister's *Agokwe* (2008) specifically recounts and reclaims the Anishnaabe tradition of celebrating two-spirit people as revered spiritual leaders. All of these artists can look to Miguel for having boldly theatricalized her stories of being two-spirit from as early as 1981 in Spiderwoman's *Sun, Moon, and Feather*.

Sun, Moon, and Feather presents the memories and coming-of-age stories of the three sisters through scenes that explore their childhood poverty, family dynamics, and determined dreams. One scene focuses on Miguel's first flirtations with another woman and the way her sisters responded:

> LISA: When Gloria first found out, she cried all night.
> GLORIA: What happened? What went wrong? I don't want her to be that way.
> LISA AND GLORIA: Gay.
> ...
> GLORIA: It doesn't matter. I love her anyway.
> LISA: I love her.[5]

Staging both Miguel's experience and her sisters' reactions voiced two types of stories often kept secret in the early 1980s—a coming-out story and the story of family members choosing love over their initial bewilderment. Miguel continued to make her two-spirit identity a part of Spiderwoman's plays. *Reverb-ber-ber-rations* (1990), an intimate look at the sisters' spirituality and the connections they feel extending from their mother to their own children, ends with personal statements that claim each sister's place in the world. Miguel closes the play stating:

> I am a woman with two daughters, a granddaughter
> I am a woman with a woman lover
> I am here now
> I am saying this now because to deny these events about me and my life
> Would be to deny my children.[6]

Significantly, Miguel's statement intertwines her lineage, spirituality, sexuality, Native identity, and motherhood to show that each is an indispensable, interrelated element of the other.

In addition to Spiderwoman's ensemble plays, Miguel has created several one-woman shows, two of which focus specifically on two-spirit stories. Both *Trail of the Otter* (1996) and *Hot'n'Soft* (1991) connect Miguel's personal stories and identity to characters from Native American creation stories. *Trail of the Otter* relates the silencing and repression of two-spirit people to the destruction of the earth and water and to the proliferation of diseases that threaten humanity. Since Otter is both a creation figure and a two-spirit character in the play, to reject Otter's two-spirit existence is to forget the Earth's creation myths. *Hot'n'Soft* is an audacious play weaving Miguel's personal encounters with coyote trickster tales. In Native mythologies, tricksters are both creative and destructive—they have voracious appetites for food and sex, and they have the ability to transform their shape, species, and gender. Through the use of humor, tricksters demonstrate the extremes of human potential. Likewise, Miguel's *Hot'n'Soft* is wildly funny, encompassing both erotica and vulnerability, as it situates two-spirit people within the long tradition of Native epistemologies.

Miguel's work exists at the heart of US experimental theatre (she was an early member of Joseph Chaikin's Open Theater), modern dance (she trained with Alwin Nickolais, Erick Hawkins, and Jean Erdman), Indigenous theatre (she was a founding member of the Native American Theatre Ensemble), contemporary Native dance performance (she co-founded Thunderbird American Indian Dancers), feminist theatre, and queer performance. She uses these experiences to advance Native performance and activism for Indigenous, feminist, and queer issues. She originated the roles of Philomena Moosetail in *Rez Sisters* and Aunt Shadie in Marie Clements's (Métis) *Unnatural and Accidental Women* (2000), as well as served in artistic leadership positions for Native Earth Performing Arts, Banff Centre for the Arts, Turtle Gals Performance Ensemble, and Raven Spirit Dance Company. Additionally, Miguel mentors upcoming generations by serving as a faculty member of the Centre for Indigenous Theatre's professional theatre conservatory and as program director for CIT's summer courses. Her dedication to developing the stories of young people is reflected in her work with the Minnesota Native American AIDS Task Force, where she and Native youth develop shows about HIV/AIDS. She also served as program director for Banff's Aboriginal Dance Program.

Miguel's contributions have earned her a Guggenheim Fellowship (2016) and Rauschenberg Residency (2015). With Spiderwoman Theater, she also received the Otto René Castillo Award for Political Theatre (2013), Lifetime Achievement Award from the Women's Caucus for Art (2010), and Honoring the Spirit Award from the American Indian Community House (2009). In 1997, Miguel and her sisters received honorary doctorates from Miami University in Oxford, Ohio, where the Native American Women Playwrights Archive houses Spiderwoman Theater's official papers.[7]

NOTES

1 Muriel Miguel, "Muriel Miguel: Artistic Director and Founding Member of Spiderwoman Theater," interview by Jo Reed, *2017 NEA Podcast*, National Endowment for the Arts, October 12, 2017. Transcript, www.arts.gov/stories/podcast/muriel-miguel#transcript
2 Jill Carter, "The Physics of the Mola: W/righting Indigenous Resurgence on the Contemporary Stage," *Modern Drama* 59, no. 1 (2016): 10.
3 Miguel, "Muriel Miguel."
4 Tomson Highway, *Comparing Mythologies*, Charles R. Bronfman Lecture in Canadian Studies (Ottawa: University of Ottawa Press, 2003).
5 Spiderwoman Theater, "Sun, Moon, and Feather," in *Contemporary Plays by Women of Color*, ed. Kathy Perkins and Roberta Uno (New York: Routledge, 1996), 305.
6 Spiderwoman Theater, "Reverb-ber-ber-rations," in *Staging Coyote's Dream*, ed. Monique Mojica and Ric Knowles (Toronto: Playwrights Canada Press, 2003), 132.
7 Spiderwoman Theater, NAWPA Spiderwoman Theater Archive, Walter Havighurst Special Collections and University Archives, Miami University, Oxford, Ohio. https://spec.lib.miamioh.edu/home/nawpa-spiderwoman-theater/

FURTHER READING

Miguel, Muriel. "Hot'n'Soft." In *Two-Spirit Acts*, edited by Jean O'Hara, 1–31. Toronto: Playwrights Canada Press, 2013.
Miguel, Muriel. "Trail of the Otter." In *Staging Coyote's Dream*, vol. 2, edited by Monique Mojica and Ric Knowles, 171–184. Toronto: Playwrights Canada Press, 2008.

CHERRÍE MORAGA
(Whittier, California, 1952–)
Alicia Arrizón

Born in Los Angeles, and raised in the San Gabriel Valley, Cherríe Moraga is an internationally recognized playwright, poet, essayist, activist, and memoirist. Moraga's commitment to voicing feminist, queer, indigenous, and identity politics that counteract social injustice and neocolonialism is persistent across her work. After 20 years as an artist-in-residence at Stanford University, in 2017 Moraga became a tenured professor in the Department of English at the University of California, Santa Barbara. There, "La Maestra," as Moraga is known, along with her artistic partner, Celia Herrera Rodríguez, instituted Las Maestras, a Center for Xicana Indigenous Thought and Art Practice. She is also a founding member of La Red Xicana Indígena (2002), an advocacy network of Xicanas working in education, the arts, spiritual practice, and Indigenous women's rights. Characterized as a network of Xicanas indígenas, group members are based in Arizona, New Mexico, and California. Their agenda may involve political, educational, and cultural work that serves to raise Indigenous consciousness and supports the social justice struggles of people of indigenous American origins North and South.

Throughout her published works, Moraga's critical thinking evolves as she examines her subjectivity as a biracial Chicana, lesbian lover, mother, daughter, dramatist, and US third world feminist.[1] While Moraga is best known for co-editing, with Gloria Anzaldúa, the anthology of feminist thought *This Bridge Called My Back: Writings by Radical Women of Color* (1981, 1983, 2015), her theatre legacy has developed as a result of her overall concerns represented in her writings since the publication of *Loving in the War Years* (1983) and after the first production of *Giving Up the Ghost* (first published in 1985, and staged in 1987). She has published three volumes of plays: *Heroes and Saints & Other Plays* (1994), *The Hungry Woman: A Mexican Medea & Heart of the Earth: A Popol Vuh Story* (2001), and *Watsonville/Circle in the Dirt* (2002). In her dramatic works, as in her overall writings, Moraga draws attention to the transitory sense that is part of the complexity of identity which plays an important role in the formation of community. Overall, Moraga's theatre has opened the doors for discussion of lesbian sexuality within the Latinx community. This is the case with *Giving Up the Ghost*, in which she expands earlier articulations expressed in *Loving in the War Years* about gendered and sexualized subjectivities and the effects of cultural taboos against both lesbian and heterosexual women. In this play, the representation of lesbian desire is contrasted against restrictive construction of gender and the effects of heteronormativity. Moraga's two-act play represents the sexual relationship of two women, Marisa (her younger self Corky) and their lover Amalia. While the marginalization of their identities as Chicana lesbians is central to the dramatic plot, the play challenges a targeted audience (Chicana/Latinas and women) to question their sexuality while confronting expressions of the gender binary and heterosexism perpetuated by societal and cultural norms.

Moraga, who studied with María Irene Fornés in 1983 and 1984 in her New York workshops for Hispanic playwrights, had benefited tremendously from her generosity and wisdom. She began writing *Shadow of a Man* in Fornés's workshops. Fornés not only liked the play, but also offered to direct it herself at San Francisco's Eureka Theatre in 1990. In *Shadow*, Moraga depicts a family struggling under the "shadow" of machismo in 1960s Los Angeles. The bilingual play offered Fornés an opportunity to explore the complexities of Latino culture, which include the bicultural and bilingual technique and sensibilities of her own cultural experience.

Moraga's premiere collection of theatre publication, *Heroes and Saints & Other Plays*, brought together *Shadow of Man*, *Heroes and Saints*, and her first produced play, *Giving Up the Ghost*. The collection showcases the result of ten years of producing theatre and writing plays and Moraga's priorities as a writer, director, and producer of Latinx theatre—lesbian desire, AIDS, religion, pesticide poisoning, family, and community are themes developed in this collection. Since the production of her first play, Moraga's gendered subjectivities in theatre and in the discursive configurations of her writing as a whole demonstrate that the construction of nation, authority, history, and tradition are deeply sexualized and therefore depend upon a particular appropriation of space. Her recognition of this structure, of everyday reality, and her understanding of its implications are perhaps most illustrated in *The Hungry Woman: A Mexican Medea*. In this collection, Moraga also includes *Heart of the Earth: A Popol Vuh Story*, in which Moraga presents a feminist reimagining of the Quiché Maya Popul Vuh. Written in collaboration with master puppet maker Ralph Lee, the script was originally produced at the Public Theater in New York in 1994. From mythological knowledge to activism, the concerns in Moraga's theatre are well connected to her ideological perspectives developed in her earlier writings. The activism advocated in her prose writing is evident in *Heroes and Saints* (1994), *Watsonville: Some Place Not Here* (2000, 2002), and *Circle in the Dirt: El Pueblo de East Palo Alto* (2002). All these plays confront social problems such as labor and land rights.

One of Moraga's unpublished manuscripts, *Digging up the Dirt: Prison Correspondence from Poet to Pervert* (produced in 2010), looks at the themes of love, art, and death (it was directed by Moraga and Adelina Anthony). Here, as in most of her plays, the playwright uses the imagined landscape of the Southwest to explore the taboo questions that continue to impact Chicano culture. And, as a unifying theme in Moraga's work, such depictions ultimately become an exploration of lesbian/queer desire.

The sacred geography of the Indigenous Americas has inspired Moraga and her primary collaborator Celia Herrera Rodríguez in the creation of *New Fire: To Put Things Right Again* (2012). As collaborators in this project, Moraga and Celia traveled the West, participating in and recording indigenous spiritual practices. *New Fire* is a "ceremonial performance"—a combination of documentary video and live performance, of reality and fiction, of ceremonial practices and the performance of myth. The central character in the play, a native Chicana named Vero, celebrates her 52nd birthday as a coming-of-age year for women in the Mesoamerican tradition. During a one-night healing ceremony, she attempts to cure herself of the poisonous residue of violence done against her. By juxtaposing the healing ceremony with realistic flashbacks that provide insight into Vero's personal past, as well as with representative traditional spiritual practices, Moraga and Rodríguez have structurally connected the history and suffering of an individual to the history and suffering of her collective people.

In *The Mathematics of Love* (produced 2008, 2010, 2015, and 2017), written in collaboration with Ricardo Bracho, Moraga revisits the Malinche paradigm (the Aztec woman who served as the translator, adviser, and slave-mistress to Hernán Cortez during the Spanish conquest of Mexico) as a cultural legacy embedded in her personal narrative. While the dramatic trajectory of the play takes us on a journey through pre-conquest Mexico City, Mission-era California, and contemporary Los Angeles, the play reflects the classic narrative of the brown woman and the white man, like Malinche and Cortez (and like Moraga's parents). In the context of Malinche's narrative, Moraga situates her own narrative in relation to the narrative of her mother. The reiteration of motherhood is unequivocally intertwined in the symbolism of the play. As a prevalent theme in most of Moraga's writings, through the motherhood signifier, the understanding of love is fundamentally an act of self-acceptance.

Moraga is a prominent contributor to a US Latina theatre renaissance emerging after the Civil Rights and women's liberation movements. In particular, her overall contributions have been crucial to the theorization of queer feminist of color critique. Moraga has expressed an urgency to write and produce her own dramatic works. She has expressed eloquently:

> a writer will write with or without a movement; but at the same time, for Chicano, lesbian, gay and feminist writers—anybody writing against the grain of Anglo misogynist culture—political movements are what have allowed our writing to surface from the secret places in our notebooks into the public sphere.[2]

For Moraga, writing and producing is a personal and political journey reconfigured through the collective memory and contradictions of her people, including her kin relations, Chicano history and nationalism, sexuality, and indigeneity. In a nostalgic tone, she insists that the act of writing memorializes the past and "allude[s] to a future for which we must prepare … May we continue to make art that incites censorship and threatens to bring the army beating down our desert door."[3]

NOTES

1 These include her earlier solo publications—*Loving in the War Years: lo que nunca pasó por sus labios* (1983), *The Last Generation* (1993), and *Waiting in the Wings: Portrait of a Queer Motherhood* (1997)—to *A Xicana Codex of Changing Consciousness: Writings, 2000–2010* (2011) and *Native Country of the Heart* (2019).
2 Cherríe Moraga, *The Last Generation: Prose and Poetry* (Boston, MA: South End Press, 1993), 58–59.
3 Cherríe Moraga, *A Xicana Codex of Changing Consciousness: Writings 2000–2010* (Durham, NC: Duke University Press, 2011), 17.

FURTHER READING

Jacobs, Elizabeth. "Shadow of a Man: A Chicana/Latina Drama as Embodied Feminist Practice." *New Theatre Quarterly*, 31:1 (February 2015), 49–58.

Moraga, Cherríe. "And Frida Looks Back: The Art of Latina/o Queer Heroics." In *Cast Out: Queer Lives in Theater*, ed. Robin Bernstein (Ann Arbor, MI: University of Michigan Press, 2006), 79–90.

Yarbro-Bejarano, Yvonne. *The Wounded Heart: Writings on Cherríe Moraga* (Austin, TX: University of Texas Press, 2001).

Ybarra, Patricia. "The Revolution Fails Here: Cherríe Moraga's *The Hungry Woman* as a Mexican Medea." *Aztlán: A Journal of Chicano Studies*, 33:1 (Spring 2008), 63–88.

DAAIMAH MUBASHSHIR
(Birmingham, Alabama)
Adam Ashraf Elsayigh

Daaimah Mubashshir—a Black, queer, and Muslim playwright—was born in Birmingham, Alabama, and raised in Houston, Texas. She describes the community she grew up in as one that embodied Black pride but that, like any other community, "was not without its dysfunctions"—primarily its (then) staunch homophobia.[1] These experiences undoubtedly influenced her writing and, while her plays are thematically queer, her inclusion in this anthology is pertinent for reasons well beyond the themes of her plays or the sexual orientations of her protagonists. When asked how she defines queer theatre, Mubashshir says,

> If we think about queer, we automatically think about gender and we think about sexual orientation. At the base of it, I think, is this work fun? If it's got a little bit of tongue-in-cheek and shake our ass to the establishment, then yes, it's queer.

Every work by Mubashshir is a queering and subversion of dominant narratives about Black, queer, and Muslim identities and their intersectionalities. As such, she is positioned as a rather unique artist within US theatre.

Not one to go about things in a "traditional" way, Mubashshir also experiments with content and form in her process. For example, *The Immeasurable Want of Light* is a collection of short plays that emerged from her approach to writing that she called "Everyday Afroplay." According to art historian Rachel Valinsky, "Beginning in 2016, Mubashshir developed a daily writing practice in response to Chris Ofili's Afro Muses painting series, offering a sustained meditation on Blackness and the Black body."[2] The collection, developed at the MacDowell Colony and published by 3 Hole Press, is a testament to the eclectic ways Mubashshir's writing embraces history and complicates its retelling by rejecting the unities of time and space. Set on the faraway galaxy of Capaurisces, the central dramatic tension in *Immeasurable* arises from a shifting perspective on what it means to live in Black skin. The forces informing Capaurisces are a heightened version of those informing our own—namely, the visceral and tangible effects of history on the characters, which include Ella Fitzgerald, Nell Painter, Hilton Als, and Fred Moten. As Valinsky explains,

> In her exploration of the politics of representing the Black body, Mubashshir also incorporates mythic questions of origin and artistic creation. She turns to the stars as a framework, charting their transformation from dark matter to exploding supernovas through the central character, Maker.[3]

Maker guides us through this phantasmagorical world by still invoking debt and capital; she describes the mass of the world of Capaurisces as "continuing to grow" and "accrued at an interest rate." These references and allusions to an oppressive and exploitative late-stage capitalist reality that disproportionately affects Black and queer bodies are interspersed within an otherwise poetic rhetoric in Mubashshir's work. Even more so, she highlights the ways in which marginalized and policed bodies are affected by the worlds they inhabit and how these realities then affect how the Black body can function in space. In the play, Mubashshir also critiques the sociopolitical realities of representation: for instance, she refers to some of her characters as "the Black body" or names them Black Person 1, 2, and 3.

Mubashshir's writing is especially pertinent, as it bridges queer theatre with identities seldom represented on the stage. In *Room Enough (For Us All)*—which was presented at the Playwrights' Center in Minneapolis, Magic Time at Judson Memorial Church in New York City, and featured on the 2019 Kilroys' List—she dramatizes the tensions between queerness and Black Muslim identity through dark comedy, employing the genre of the family drama to explore how a family reconciles after having abandoned a queer child in their formative years. In *Room Enough*, Mubashshir not only situates herself within a canon of queer Muslim work, which includes playwrights like Mashuq Mushtaq Deen, Adam Ashraf Elsayigh, and Sharifa Yasmin (to name a few), but further complicates that canon by depicting a Black, Muslim family that practices its faith in a manner significantly distinct from those depicted by queer Muslims from the Middle East, North Africa, and South Asia. While a play like Ayad Akhtar's *The Who and the What* (2014) seeks to capture a diasporic Muslim subjectivity, Mubashshir's, *Room Enough* offers a distinct perspective through its autobiographic nature. It presents a milieu where Jamillah, the protagonist, experiences marginalization both within and outside the domestic space, creating a situation where catharsis comes from a celebration of the maternal figure, Fatimah, as she attempts to right the wrong of abandoning her queer daughter.

Mubashshir's artistic practice is queer not only in its themes but in *how* and *why* she writes and the way she speaks of herself within lineages of Black, Muslim, and Texan writers. Narrating the trajectory of her artistic journey, Mubashshir names a variety of queer and Black women who have informed her and the form in which she writes: debbie tucker green, Robbie McCauley, Nell Irvin Painter, Suzan-Lori Parks, and Lynn Nottage. Reflecting on her role as a Texan writer, she asserts, "In my work, I've always been three floors underneath the basement of the world ... and the question is: how do I climb out of these burying systems to get to fresh air?" She acknowledges the influence that the Houston art scene had on her practice by saying, "Everyone there was working underneath systems that had rejected them from the mainstream theatre. I learned from those who were also excluded, and I learned to make work without needing the validation of the mainstream."

Mubashshir's career has been prolific and celebrated by commercial (primarily white) theatre venues, as well as a variety of independent spaces. She has been a MacDowell Fellow (2017), a Women's Project Theater Lab Fellow (2020–2022), and was awarded the 2021 PlayCo Residency for Black Women Theatre Makers and the 2021 Helen Merrill Award for Playwriting. Several of her plays have been published, including *Come with Me—Solve for X* (2018), *Molasses and a Blue Coat* (2019), and *The Zero Loop* (2019). She collaborated with choreographer Raja Feather Kelly, through Soho Rep's Writer Director Lab on *The Chronicles of Cardigan and Khente* (2019), a play from her Everyday Afroplay collection. She was also commissioned by the Guthrie Theater to write a one-act *Dining with the Ancestors*, which streamed online in March 2021.

Despite these successes, Mubashshir still feels trepidation as she speaks of the honors she has accumulated over the years. When she reflects on how her emerging practice in the queer theatre scene in Houston took her to the School of the Art Institute of Chicago, where she earned the Presidential Scholarship, she becomes emotional: "I went in and made work and I got accolades and I thought, 'I don't understand'." As a queer, Black, Muslim woman, at that point in her life Mubashshir believed she was "built to self-hate" and that she could not have meaningful contributions as an artist. Like *The Immeasurable Want of Light*, much of Mubashshir's work is queer in how it destabilizes assumptions about her lived experience; her work asserts that her perspective is ever-shifting and thus cannot be easily digested or integrated into the commercial/white, cultural mainstream. In doing so, her writing inherently rejects essentialization. When asked what she sees as lacking in US theatre and, more specifically, queer US theatre, Mubashshir reflexively turns the question inward, speaking of her own practice and the upcoming plays she aims to create:

> I want to examine and take responsibility for the instances where I may be perpetuating oppressive ideologies on myself and in my communities. As I am drawn to making dangerous work, it is important that I put myself on the line, to embody the courage that I need from other people. It is the only way for me to earn the audience's trust. I must recognize and own that I was born, built, and shaped by harmful systems. Only with that awareness will I be able to effectively push these conversations forward.

NOTES

1 All of Mubashshir's quotes are from interviews with the author on May 22 and 29, 2021.
2 Rachel Valinsky, "Daaimah Mubashshir's *The Immeasurable Want of Light*," *BOMB Magazine*, September 18, 2018. https://bombmagazine.org/articles/daaimah-mubashshirs-the-immeasurable-want-of-light/
3 Ibid.

FURTHER READING

Mubashshir, Daaimah. "*Molasses and a Blue Coat*," in *Kenyon Review*, May/June 2019. https://kenyonreview.org/kr-online-issue/2019-mayjune/selections/daaimah-mubashshir-373633

Mubashshir, Daaimah. "*The Zero Loop*," in *No Tokens Journal*, November 27, 2019. https://notokensjournal.com/fiction/the-zero-loop

THE NEA FOUR: KAREN FINLEY, JOHN FLECK, HOLLY HUGHES, AND TIM MILLER
Jimmy A. Noriega and Jordan Schildcrout

"So," asks Holly Hughes in her 1999 solo performance, *Preaching to the Perverted*, "you hear the one about the lesbian, the feminist, and a couple of fags who go to the Supreme Court?" She is referring to herself, Karen Finley, John Fleck, and Tim Miller, who were collectively known as the "NEA Four." In 1990, these performance artists had their grants from the National Endowment for the Arts rescinded because of pressure from right-wing politicians who deemed their work "indecent." The foursome subsequently sued the NEA, and the case (*National Endowment for the Arts v. Finley et al.*) went all the way to the Supreme Court, which decided that the government had not engaged in "viewpoint discrimination" by denying grants to work that they considered outside "general standards of decency."

Homophobia was a key factor in the brouhaha surrounding the case, which landed queer performance artists on the front page of newspapers around the country. In rejecting the grants recommended by his own theatre panel, NEA Chairman John E. Frohnmayer observed, "Holly Hughes is a lesbian and her work is very heavily of that genre."[1] David Gergen, fuming in the pages of the *US News and World Report*, quoted an innocuous description of Tim Miller's work ("As a member of the gay community, his work presents this vantage of the world to encourage education, understanding, and eventual acceptance"), which was seemingly all the evidence he needed to assail these artists as "pornographers" who "want to engage in the wanton destruction of a nation's values."[2] Looking back on the attacks, John Fleck commented, "I was the sort of avant-garde freak and was made to feel like a disgusting pervert leeching on the taxpayers' money."[3]

Newspapers at the time reported that Frohnmayer had vetoed the grants under political pressure from the White House of George H. W. Bush and Congressional Republicans led by Senator Jesse Helms. The politicians fomenting this "culture war" were explicit about their homophobia and their desire to defund "liberal" programs like the NEA. The ongoing AIDS crisis further drove the right-wing narrative that queer people were "sick," a threat, and anathema to the values of "tax-paying Americans." This rhetoric, which resulted in death threats against the performance artists, also fueled the agenda of a federal government passing homophobic laws regarding military service ("Don't Ask, Don't Tell," 1994) and same-sex marriage (Defense of Marriage Act, 1996).

The case of the NEA Four was a crucial flashpoint in the culture wars of the 1990s, but the three queer members of the quartet should also be regarded as key figures for their long and vibrant artistic careers and impact on the field of queer performance. As David Román has noted, "queer solo performers are often at the frontiers of new social identities and more inclusive community formations."[4] In this, Fleck, Hughes, and Miller were, of course, not alone in the 1990s, but part of a thriving scene that included Luis Alfaro, Ron Athey, David Cale, Marga Gomez, Craig Hickman, Michael Kearns, Jeff McMahon, Susan Miller, Paul Outlaw, Pomo Afro Homos (Eric Gupton, Brian Freeman, and Djola Branner), Reno, Annie Sprinkle, Carmelita Tropicana, Danitra Vance, and Ron Vawter.

John Fleck has had an extensive career as an actor, starring in Los Angeles theatre productions of Charles Ludlam's *The Mystery of Irma Vep* (1998), Tennessee Williams's *Small Craft Warnings* (2003), and David Greenspan's plays *She Stoops to Comedy* (2005) and *Go Back to Where You Are* (2016). He acknowledges that his work as a character actor on television and in film—including the queer indie movies *Grief* (1993) and *Alaska is a Drag* (2017)—supports his ability to create "not-necessarily-for-profit experimental theater."[5] *Blessed Are All the Little Fishes* (1989), directed by frequent collaborator David Schweizer, offended conservative politicians with its exploration of alcoholism and Catholicism, which included a toilet turned into an altar and on-stage urination. But Fleck won numerous awards for his 1992 production of *A Snowball's Chance in Hell*, playing multiple characters inundated by the inanities of mass media. Other lauded solo performances include *Mad Woman* (2012), *Black Top Highway* (2015), and *it's alive, IT'S ALIVE!* (2021), and he is the subject of Kevin Duffy's 2019 documentary, *John Fleck is Who You Want Him to Be*.

Holly Hughes was integral to the formative years of the WOW Café, writing outrageously comic and unapologetically sexy plays like the lesbian pulp/soap opera parody *The Well of Horniness* (1983) and the "dyke noir" *Lady Dick* (1985). She collaborated with the lesbian performance duo Split Britches on *Dress Suits to Hire* (1987), but Hughes became best known for her solo performances, including *World Without End* (1989). The show, which includes her childhood memories of her mother's sexuality, as well as stories of her own lesbian sexuality, caused outrage among culture warriors who flagrantly misrepresented the piece, claiming it included mother-daughter incest and the performer "placing her hand up her vagina."[6] More honest critics lauded Hughes's combination of "surrealistic autobiography, feminist polemics and comic asides" delivered with "verbal energy and a disarming humor."[7] In a *New York Times* op-ed in 1990, and later in her solo performance *Preaching to the Perverted* (1999), Hughes placed her experience of the NEA saga within the larger context of American homophobia, misogyny, and racism, asking, "How does the government decide who is decent?"[8]

In addition to other solo performances such as *Clit Notes* (1996) and *The Dog and Pony Show (Bring Your Own Pony)* (2010), Hughes has also collaborated with scholars on publications that have made important contributions to theatre and performance studies. These include *O Solo Homo: The New Queer Performance* (1998), co-edited with David Román, and *Memories of the Revolution: The First Ten Years of the WOW Café Theater* (2015), co-edited with Carmelita Tropicana and Jill Dolan. A native of Michigan, she has been a professor at the Stamps School of Art & Design at the University of Michigan since 2001, influencing a generation of artists, including protégés in queer performance like Joseph Keckler and Erin Markey. Hughes continues to create performance as a form both of personal expression and political intervention, as seen in her most recent piece, *Indelible* (2021), which views Anita Hill and Christine Blasey Ford through the lens of feminist performance art.

Very early in his career, Tim Miller was a co-founder of P.S. 122 in New York and Highways Performance Space in Los Angeles. His autobiographical solo performances (which number over a dozen) combine the deeply personal with the radically political, are equally funny, sexy, and angry, and often present his naked body as a site of emotional and sexual liberation. During the height of the AIDS crisis, Miller was an active member of the protest group ACT UP, and this experience influenced the creation of *Civil Disobedience Weekend* (1989), in which he imagines a jailhouse orgy among imprisoned activists bringing about the downfall of the Bush White House. As one of the NEA Four, his performances around the country were met with protests and bomb threats, but he persisted with works such as *My Queer Body* (1992), which follows his trajectory from "swimming upstream as a queer spermlet" to coming of age as a gay man in a homophobic world. In *Glory Box* (1999), Miller advocated for marriage equality as a matter of international human rights, focusing on his struggles to remain with his Australian life partner (and now husband), Alistair McCartney.

Through much of his career, Miller has maintained an extensive touring schedule, traveling around the US to communities large and small, describing himself as a "queer Johnny Appleseed," and sharing a Whitman-esque view of the nation in works like *Lay of the Land* (2010). The University of Wisconsin Press has published his performance texts and other writings in the collections *Body Blows* (2002), *1001 Beds* (2006), and *A Body in the O* (2019). As a teaching artist, Miller has inspired numerous participants in his performance workshops—largely conducted at community centers and colleges—by empowering individuals, creating community, and envisioning social change through performance.

In 2013, the New Museum "reunited" the NEA Four, hosting residencies for Finley, Fleck, Hughes, and Miller with the goal of "tackling contemporary issues surrounding funding for performance art today in light of the culture wars of the early '90s."[9] The NEA no longer gives grants to individual artists, contributing to the further "institutionalization" of the arts in the US, and many alternative performance venues have failed to survive. While these shifts have presented challenges to queer solo performers, the members of the NEA Four continue to produce new work, and their public stand against anti-queer governmental policies paved the way for new generations of artists exploring diverse queer identities through performance, including Heather María Ács, Becca Blackwell, Maybe Burke, Nao Bustamante, Stacyann Chin, Xandra Nur Clark, D'Lo, Tina D'Elia, Cecilia Gentili, Ryan J. Haddad, Xandra Ibarra, Daniel Alexander Jones, Justin Elizabeth Sayre, Pandora Scooter, and Dane Terry.

NOTES

1 Kim Masters, "Politics of Arts Grants Questioned; NEA Papers Released In Artists' Lawsuit," *Washington Post* (September 18, 1991), B1.
2 David Gergen, "Who Should Pay for Porn?" *US News and World Report* (July 30, 1990), in *Culture Wars: Documents from the Recent Controversies in the Arts*, ed. Richard Bolton (New York: New Press, 1992), 256.

3 William Harris, "The NEA Four: Life After Symbolhood," *New York Times* (June 5, 1994), B1.
4 Holly Hughes and David Román, "An Introductory Conversation," in *O Solo Homo* (New York: Grove Press, 1998), 6.
5 "Biography," John Fleck website, accessed October 1, 2021, http://johnfleck.net/
6 Gergen, 256.
7 Stephen Holden, "When the Garden of Eden is on the Lower East Side," *New York Times* (October 6, 1990), L11.
8 Holly Hughes and Richard Elovich, "Homophobia at the NEA," *New York Times* (July 28, 1990), 21.
9 "NEA 4 in Residence: May–June 2013," New Museum website, accessed October 1, 2021, www.newmuseum.org/pages/view/residence-2

FURTHER READING

Meyer, Richard. "'Have You Heard the One About the Lesbian Who Goes to the Supreme Court?' Holly Hughes and the Case Against Censorship," *Theatre Journal* 52:4 (December 2000), 543–552.

Miller, Tim, and Román, David. "Preaching to the Converted," *Theatre Journal* 47:2 (May 1995), 169–188.

ROBERT O'HARA
(Cincinnati, Ohio, 1970–)
Faedra Chatard Carpenter

When measuring an artist's significance, there is no better barometer than evidence that reveals both "micro- and macro-waves" of influence. In the case of director-playwright Robert O'Hara, these waves of influence are multidirectional and plentiful, not only exhibited by the successes that speedily catapulted O'Hara into the ranks of our most celebrated and sought-after theatre practitioners, but also demonstrable through a career that was cultivated by—and altruistically caters to—some of the hottest artists of our contemporary moment. While centered within an impressive network of theatrical innovators, shape shifters, and playmakers, O'Hara has earned his many accolades from being decidedly *off*-center; his career is punctuated with daring irreverence and a liberating refusal of the status quo.

Born in 1970 in Cincinnati, Ohio (whence he often says he "escaped" at the age of 18), O'Hara was drawn to the magnetic qualities of deftly utilized language and embodied performance from a young age—an appreciation that was routinely expressed through the writing and staging of stories performed by his family members and childhood friends.[1] While he always understood his own creativity, it wasn't until O'Hara was an undergraduate at Tufts University that he fully acknowledged and embraced his identity as a gay Black man—a coming-out journey that was propelled by the dramatic compositions he created in his capacity as founding director and playwright of Tufts' Black Theater Company.[2] Following graduation, O'Hara continued to write while earning his MFA in Directing from Columbia University and earning invaluable work experience with Shakespeare in the Park, the Manhattan Theatre Club, and Joseph Papp's Public Theater—the latter being particularly bountiful in that it granted him the chance to learn under the auspices of its artistic director, George C. Wolfe, a fellow director-playwright whose work O'Hara had long admired. Notably, it would be under Wolfe's helm that O'Hara's groundbreaking play, *Insurrection: Holding History*, would be produced at the Public in 1996—marking O'Hara's first major New York City production as both a playwright *and* director.

When asked which he prefers more—playwrighting or directing—O'Hara answers with pragmatic clarity: "One takes place in solitude and the other takes place in front of others. When I get tired of one, I have the other."[3] This inspired pragmatism extends to when he is taking on *both* tasks for a singular production (a challenge that many a writer would avoid, and many a critic would admonish): "Sometimes I direct my plays in order to better understand them."[4] This pursuit of nuance and self-reflexivity affords O'Hara a creative purpose that aids in repelling the inevitable stings of criticism. To this point, when prompted by an interviewer to finish the phrase, "It isn't theatre unless …," O'Hara responded: "People walk out. It's the only real live moment in a live event. The people on stage have rehearsed what they're doing, but the person walking out has not."[5] Nonplussed by the occasional walkout or disparaging rant (like when critic Rex Reed sorely lamented that Playwrights Horizons 2014 production of *Bootycandy* "sets back the cause of humanity at least 50 years"),[6] O'Hara masterfully uses these sporadic expressions of discord to his own advantage (as he did when he offered a dramatic reading of Reed's review, in tandem with his own personal commentary, while delivering the opening remarks for Theatre Communications Group's 2014 Fall Forum on "Governance: Cash and Culture"). Recognizing that fearless art making is not without its detractors, O'Hara remains dedicated to crafting theatre that—through its fantastical scenarios, cutting-edge humor, poetic lyricism, and unabashed rawness—engenders both a generative discomfort and a welcomed respite from the ubiquitous and "everyday."

A quick perusal of O'Hara's playwriting career will reveal the formal recognition of at least a dozen plays—and counting. Within this growing litany are several notable and widely celebrated works, among them *Insurrection: Holding History* (1996), *Antebellum* (2009), *Bootycandy* (2011), and *Barbecue* (2015). *Insurrection* chronicles the time-traveling and life-altering adventure of its protagonist, Ron—a young, Black, gay, graduate student who is not only transported to the time and place of Nat Turner's rebellion, but also finds love with a devotee of the uprising. Following this impressive debut, Woolly Mammoth's 2009 world premiere of *Antebellum*, directed by gay, Chinese American playwright-director Chay Yew, introduced audiences to another history-inspired piece from the imaginative annals of O'Hara. Taking audiences to and between the eras and events of Germany's Holocaust and America's Jim Crow,

Antebellum, like *Insurrection*, underscores the truths and queer possibilities that reveal what has been erased, silenced, and obscured within our historical narratives.

O'Hara returned to Woolly Mammoth in 2011, as both playwright and director of *Bootycandy*, which went on to win the Lambda Literary Award for Best LGBT Drama of 2014–2015. Through a series of vignettes, *Bootycandy* traipses through two decades, the 1970s and 1980s, to offer a bevy of incidents and instances as part of the larger coming-of-age (and coming-out) story of its protagonist, Sutter. Notably, the structure of *Bootycandy*—a series of mini-scenes—has drawn understandable comparisons to George C. Wolfe's similarly structured play, *The Colored Museum* (1986). As theatre and performance scholar Isaiah P. Wooden observes: "Like *The Colored Museum*, *Bootycandy* takes as its object of satirization certain tropes within African American culture. And, like Wolfe's before him, O'Hara's incisive, insightful critiques are decidedly queer."[7] While *Bootycandy* is wholly distinctive in what it addresses, the play's form pays appropriate homage to Wolfe, a Black and openly gay theatre artist whose direct and unapologetic treatment of race and sexuality served as a model of inspiration for a young O'Hara to be equally forthright and courageous in his own work. O'Hara's now-signature boldness, novel dramaturgy, and perennial riffing on identity continues to be ever-present in his work. In *Barbecue*, O'Hara creates a scenario that casts, then *re*casts, the perceived racial identities of its characters and, in doing so, demands that audience members wrestle with how racial bias and stereotypes simultaneously propel and corrupt media, entertainment, and popular culture.

Reflecting on his oeuvre, O'Hara says:

> just being who I am—an out homosexual, someone who is proud to be black, and an artist who speaks his mind freely—makes me political in some way ... and I do believe in political consciousness raising, although that's not why I write. I write because I think everybody has stories of significance that they need to tell.[8]

One measure of his own artistic endeavors, however, is O'Hara's ability to activate what he calls the "Theatre of Choke." Contrary to creating escapist entertainment, O'Hara wants his audience members to "choke" on the material he sets before them. "I don't want them to easily digest the play and then go home and forget it," he asserts. "I want them to remember the sensation of the play just how everyone knows what it feels like to choke."[9]

As an eclectic artist whose motivations come from diverse and varied sources, O'Hara readily credits a number of inspirations and inspirers. In addition to George C. Wolfe, O'Hara honors queer writers and artisans such as James Baldwin, Audre Lorde, Essex Hemphill, Anne Bogart, and Paula Vogel, as well as other theatre luminaries such as Douglas Turner Ward and Adrienne Kennedy. Just as O'Hara pays tribute to those who have informed his work, his own genealogy continues to proliferate as he helps to shape and propel the careers of younger artists.

In 2005, O'Hara directed Primary Stages' world premiere of the Obie Award-winning and Pulitzer Prize-nominated *In the Continuum,* written and performed by Danai Gurira and Nikkole Salter. A beautifully crafted two-person play, *In the Continuum* delivers audiences a stark, yet lyrical reminder of the continuing havoc and devastating effect that HIV/AIDS has on Black women within the United States and Africa. And, 15 years later, O'Hara made his Broadway directorial debut as a part of another celebrated collaboration: working with fellow Black queer playwright—and his former student—Jeremy O. Harris. Harris is the author of the much-buzzed-about, break-out drama *Slave Play*—which received 12 Tony nominations in 2020, including O'Hara's nomination for Best Director, thereby granting *Slave Play,* at the time of this writing, the most Tony nominations for a nonmusical play. According to Harris, one of the greatest gifts O'Hara bestowed upon him during their rehearsal process for *Slave Play* was a genuine granting of support, protection, and respect.[10] For O'Hara, however, the gift of mentorship is always a mutual one: "Mentoring helps the mentee as well as the mentor. For the mentor, it allows your voice to be heard in other spaces, and the legacy of your work as the mentor gets transmitted through the work of the mentee."[11]

NOTES

1 Johnny Woodnal, "Robert O'Hara," *African American Dramatists: An A-to-Z Guide*, ed. Emmanuel S. Nelson (Westport, CT: Greenwood Press, 2004), 321.
2 Ibid., 322.
3 "20 Questions: Robert O'Hara," *American Theatre*, vol. 28, issue 5 (May 2011), 96.
4 Mervyn Rothstein, "Stage Directions: How Writer-Director Robert O'Hara Decides Which Plays to Direct and Which to Hand Over," *Playbill*, December 30, 2018, www.playbill.com/article/stage-directions-how-writer-director-robert-ohara-decides-which-plays-to-direct-and-which-to-hand-over

5 "20 Questions."
6 Rex Reed, "'Bootycandy' is a Tasteless Mish-Mash of Ugly Stereotypes Verging on Racism," *Observer*, September 17, 2014, https://observer.com/2014/09/bootycandy-is-a-tasteless-mish-mash-of-ugly-stereotypes-verging-on-racism
7 Isaiah Wooden, "Bootycandy," performance review, *Theatre Journal*, vol. 64, issue 2 (2012), 282.
8 Jessica Werner, "A Love Affair with History," ACT stagebill (January 1998), 25.
9 Isaiah Wooden, "Robert O'Hara's Defamiliarizing Dramaturgy," *The Routledge Companion to African American Theatre and Performance*, ed. Kathy A. Perkins et al. (New York: Routledge, 2020), 289.
10 Janice C. Simpson, "Shutdown Spotlight: Jeremy O. Harris & Robert O'Hara on *Slave Play*," *BroadwayDirect*, January 26, 2021, https://broadwaydirect.com/jeremy-o-harris-and-robert-ohara-in-conversation-about-slave-play
11 Anthony Myers, "Robert O'Hara: Finding the Beauty in the Horror," *Clyde Fitch Report*, November 3, 2019, www.clydefitchreport.com/2019/11/robert-ohara-slave-play

FURTHER READING

"Artist Interview with Robert O'Hara," Playwrightshorizons.org, October 21, 2024. Accessed June 5, 2021. www.playwrightshorizons.org/shows/trailers/artist-interview-robert-ohara/

Wooden, Isaiah. "Robert O'Hara's Defamiliarizing Dramaturgy," *The Routledge Companion to African American Theatre and Performance*, ed. Kathy A. Perkins et al. New York: Routledge, 2020 (287–290).

MONICA PALACIOS
(San Jose, California, 1959–)
Marci R. McMahon

Throughout her 40-year career, Monica Palacios's comedic solo performances, plays, and publications have amplified Chicana lesbian sexuality in theatre and academic spaces across the US. Grounded in Chicana feminism and queer women of color critique, Palacios's body of work counters homophobic and nationalist scripts of family in both Chicanx and US culture. As a writer, her works have been published in numerous queer and Latinx anthologies and her contributions in performance, playwriting, and activism have made audible and visible Latina lesbian sexuality and its call for social justice.

Palacios began her career as a stand-up comic in San Francisco in the 1980s, where she found a home in the city's well-known queer-friendly comedy club Valencia Rose Cabaret in the Mission District, the first of its kind in the nation.[1] There, Palacios, along with Marga Gomez, found support to express Latina lesbian identities through stand-up, in stark contrast to the white homophobia they experienced in mainstream comedy clubs. Palacios recounts such experiences:

> When I started doing standup comedy … I would get questioned by various people wanting to know why I had to talk about being a lesbian … Yet these same people had no problem listening to straight comics talk about their personal lives … And I would tell them, "If you want me to stop talking about my personal life, that would be like asking [me] to stop breathing. Can't do it."[2]

Palacios and Gomez collaborated as Gomez & Palacios: The Only Latin Female Comedy Duo in The Universe from 1982 to 1986, performing across the San Francisco Bay Area and nationally. Both performers also contributed their comedic skills as original ensemble members of the satirical Chicanx theatre troupe Culture Clash in 1984—the group formed at Galería de la Raza in San Francisco's Mission District during the height of the Chicanx visual arts and performance renaissance in the city. Palacios and Gomez left Culture Clash a year later due to the troupe's elision of Latina lesbian sexuality in the collective's storytelling. While Gomez stayed in San Francisco to pursue a career in stand-up, Palacios, after a short time in New York City, moved to Los Angeles to continue stand-up, but with a focus on solo performance that enabled her to find an activist queer and Latinx audience.

Amidst a renaissance of Chicana feminist and queer production throughout the 1980s and 1990s, Palacios developed her one-woman shows that enabled her to express her intersectional identities. She explains: "My work is bicultural because I create it from a Chicana lesbian perspective. I am never one without the other."[3] Defined by a mixture of stand-up comedy, physical movement, queer gesture, and music, some of Palacios's one-woman shows from this period include *Latin Lezbo Comic* (1991), *Confessions: A Sexplosion of Tantalizing Tales* (1994), and *Greetings from a Queer Señorita* (1994), which combines aspects of the two previous shows. These performances were supported, not by theatre spaces or academic theatre programs, but by Women and Gender Studies programs, LGBTQ communities, and queer-friendly Chicanx studies organizations.

Greetings from a Queer Señorita uses digital projections, song, and physical movement to centralize Chicana lesbian desire in her childhood, highlighting the queerness of everyday Chicanx life. In one iconic scene, Palacios recounts the visits of Lala and Trini, her parents' comadres, whose belting of the iconic ranchera "La Paloma," with their intimate bodies and lips, registered a lesbian sexuality that was always present in her family's gatherings. *Greetings* is one of Palacio's most produced performances and she updated the show throughout its 1994–2011 production history to reflect timely topics, including the conservative backlash against same-sex marriage with California's Proposition 8 in 2008. Notable productions of *Greetings* include a four-week run at the Breath of Fire Latina Theater Ensemble in Santa Ana, California (2008), and an international performance at the Association of Inter-American Studies Conference at the University of Duisburg-Essen, Germany (2010).[4]

In recent years, Palacios used the one-woman show to address Latina lesbian experiences with aging and body image. These works include her thirty-year retrospective, *Queer Chicana Soul* (2013), performed at Highways Performance Space, as well as *Queer Latina Love & Revolution* (2013), which was performed at universities across the US. In her solo performance, *San Francisco, Mi Amor!* (2015), which premiered at San Francisco's Galeria de la Raza, Palacios narrates the fraught history and love that she has for San Francisco. Throughout the 1990s and early aughts, Palacios expanded her performance portfolio with full-length plays, responding to the lack of productions about Chicana queer experiences. Her most well-known plays feature Chicana lesbian characters and families beyond biological kinships, including *Prom* (2013), *Clock* (2014), and *I Kissed Chavela Vargas* (2017). *Prom*—produced at the 2013 Brown and Out Theater Festival at CASA 0101 in Boyle Heights, California—follows a Chicana lesbian high school student who challenges her school's ban on same-sex couples and invites audiences to join her protest. *Clock*, commissioned by the Latinx Theater Initiative at the Mark Taper in Los Angeles with a world premiere at Teatro Bravo in Phoenix, Arizona, centers a Latina lesbian couple navigating motherhood. *I Kissed Chavela Vargas*, a memory play that follows Rosa, a 70-year-old former cabaret singer, counters stereotypical images of Chicana sexuality by tackling Chicanx aging and female sexuality with a cast of multigenerational female performers. For this work, Palacios received the Nancy Dean Lesbian Playwriting Award sponsored by Open Meadows Foundation (2021).

During the turbulent years of the Trump era—especially for Latinx and queer communities—Palacios created performances that captured the rage and anger of living amidst white supremacist violence. Her storytelling during this period is defined by a more sobering slant beyond her usual comedy, especially as it confronts the onslaught of racial injustices and violence experienced by queer communities of color. *Say Their Names* (2016), a tribute to the victims of the Orlando Pulse Nightclub shooting, was developed as part of the Maria Irene Fornés Playwriting Workshop in Chicago. It was subsequently performed internationally in *After Orlando*, a global theatre action honoring the victims of the shootings. Palacios also created *BROWNER QUEERER LOUDER PROUDER* (2017), which tackles racism and homophobia with direct commentary and calls for social action. It was performed at several theatre festivals and academic spaces.

Palacios's career-long focus on Latinx queer identity is guided by a responsibility to LGBTQ activist communities. In the spaces she has lived and performed, LGBTQ communities have asked Palacios to take leadership roles in queer activism. From 1992 to 2000, she was the founding executive director of VIVA, a nonprofit queer arts collective in Los Angeles, where she promoted and empowered many emerging Latinx LGBTQ artists. She also helped to develop Teatro VIVA, which comprised a trio of actors who performed comedy skits to educate audiences about HIV/AIDS prevention. Palacios was recognized by the City of Los Angeles twice: in 2012, Mayor Antonio Villaraigosa honored her groundbreaking work as a Chicana lesbian performer with "Palacios Day" on October 12; and, in March 2017, she was given the Latinx LGBTQ Trailblazer Award for her activist work. She has also taught at numerous academic institutions and was selected as the playwriting faculty for the 2021 Writers Retreat for Emerging LGBTQ Voices, a program of Lambda Literary. Without a doubt—and despite the homophobia of elite theatre spaces and academic theatre programs—Palacios's work has been persistent and groundbreaking. Her legacy is represented by the prestigious awards she has received, the many entities that have supported her, and the many people she has mentored in education, theatre, and performance.

NOTES

1 See *Stand Up, Stand Out: The Making of a Comedy Movement*, directed by David Pavlosky, a documentary that features Palacios reflecting on the role of gay comedy at Valencia Rose during 1980s conservative politics.
2 From *Out of the Fringe: Contemporary Latina/Latino Theatre and Performance*, ed. Caridad Svich and Teresa Marrero. New York: Theatre Communications Group, 2000, 367.
3 Ibid.
4 *Greetings* was first developed at Josie's Cabaret in San Francisco in 1994, and early shows include performances at the "Fierce Tongues Women of Fire Latina Festival" at Highways Performance Space in Santa Monica, California (1994), the One In Ten Theatre Company in Tucson, Arizona (1995), and "Out On The Edge: Festival of Lesbian & Gay Theater" at The Theater Offensive in Boston, Massachusetts (1999).

FURTHER READING

Arrizón, Alicia. "Monica Palacios: Coming Out as a Latin Lezbo Comic." In *Latina Performance: Traversing the Stage*. Bloomington, IN: Indiana University Press, 1999, pp. 139–150.
Danielson, Marivel T. "Loving Revolution: Same Sex Marriage and Queer Resistance in Monica Palacios's *Amor y Revolucion*." In *Performing the US Latina and Latino Borderlands*, ed. Arturo J. Aldama, Chela Sandoval, and Peter Garcia. Bloomington, IN: Indiana University Press, 2012, pp. 309–327.
Danielson, Marivel T. "Performing the Erotics of Home: Monica Palacios, Marga Gomez, and Carmelita Tropicana." In *Homecoming Queers: Desire and Difference in Chicana Latina Cultural Production*. New Brunswick, NJ: Rutgers University Press, 2009, pp. 121–143.

MIGUEL PIÑERO
(Gurabo, Puerto Rico, 1946–1988)
Karen Jaime

Poet, playwright, actor, and screenwriter Miguel Piñero was born in Puerto Rico, raised in the Lower East Side of New York City, and died of cirrhosis of the liver. In 1973, alongside poet Miguel Algarín, Piñero established the Nuyorican Poets Cafe, a community performance space for marginalized writers to share work that rejected constructions of what constituted "proper" writing, specifically through their inclusion of Spanglish and their employment of an urban vernacular. While often historicized within a heterosexist framework, queer politics—in terms of the sexuality of Algarín, Piñero, and others, and the formative countercultural performance practices—inform the founding and maintenance of the space.

Piñero spent almost a third of his life in prison and, at 25 years old, while at Ossining Correctional Facility ("Sing Sing"), he met Marvin Felix Camillo, who, along with Clay Stevenson, led a writing workshop for inmates.[1] Camillo also founded the Family, a theatre workshop comprising formerly incarcerated people from Bedford Hills Correctional Facility that Piñero joined before eventually starting his own collective, the Young Family, a group comprising at-risk youth.

Initially, Piñero achieved success as a poet who wrote about Nuyorican identity, drug use and abuse, and Puerto Rican liberation. Alongside poetry, Piñero also wrote plays and went on to win several awards, including a prestigious Guggenheim Fellowship in 1982 in Drama and Performance Art. He won the 1973–1974 New York Drama Critics' Circle Award for Best American Play, as well as two Obie Awards, for his canonical play *Short Eyes*, which was directed by Camillo. *Short Eyes* is set in jail and follows an alleged child molester who is found innocent only after he is murdered by other inmates. Originally staged at the Theatre of the Riverside Church, where Piñero was a playwright in residence, it was then produced off-Broadway by Joseph Papp in March 1974 at The Public

Theater, followed by a two-week run at the Annenberg Center of Performing Arts. It eventually opened on Broadway as part of the New York Shakespeare Festival at the Vivian Beaumont Theatre in Lincoln Center. Later adapted as a film in 1977, directed by Robert M. Young, *Short Eyes* also contains a queer libidinal narrative staged between two Puerto Rican inmates, Cupcakes and Paco. Paco's desire for Cupcakes, both romantic and violent, is akin to the same-sex desire expressed by other characters in Piñero's oeuvre. For example, *The Sun Always Shines for the Cool* (1975) is set in a bar frequented by pimps, young hookers, and hustlers; *Cold Beer* (1979) is a play about a writer in Los Angeles who is offered oral sex by a stranger walking by his house; and, in *The Paper Toilet* (1979), the characters cruise and masturbate in a public restroom. Other Piñero plays include *All Junkies* (1973), *Straight from the Ghetto* (1973), *Sideshow* (1974), *The Guntower* (1976), *Eulogy for a Small Time Thief* (1977), *NuYorican Nights at the Stanton Street Social* (1980), and *Playland Blues* (1980).

None of these narratives conform to, nor contain, the hallmarks and references of the (white) gay theatre of their time. While often hilarious, they do not engage in camp, and there are few characters who identify as gay or with the gay community or political movement. The sexuality of Piñero's Black American and Puerto Rican characters is complex, fraught, and coterminous with the racism, poverty, and imprisonment they experience. The pleasure and profit they seek and find in same-sex acts are often framed as negative by society. Yet, rather than refuse such abjection and form a collective identity around empowerment and social justice, Piñero's characters both revel in and reject their (un)desirability, refusing to construct a world wherein faggots, fairies, junkies, cons, and hookers would be displaced and erased.[2] Additionally, Piñero's characters often code-switch, or move between English and Spanish, in order to highlight a bicultural, bilingual Nuyorican experience.

For example, in a prison shower scene from *Short Eyes*, Piñero stages an interaction between Paco and Cupcakes. Paco sneaks up on Cupcakes and proceeds to embrace and kiss him on the neck. Cupcakes rejects Paco, advising him that he doesn't engage in "that faggot shit," to which Paco responds, "Man, cause I kiss you doesn't mean you're a faggot." Cupcakes then retorts, "it means you're a faggot ... don't do it again."[3] This exchange denotes physical and emotional expression and rejection of same-sex desire, a homosexuality produced and contextualized by the compulsory homosociality of incarceration. While Cupcakes attempts to establish firm boundaries, telling Paco, "que me deje quieto … yo no soy maricon" ("Leave me alone … I'm not a faggot"), Paco seemingly embraces sexuality as fluid, responding with "Papisito, yo no estoy diciendo que tú ere maricon … Yo no pienso así" ("Papasoito, I'm not saying that you're a faggot … I don't think like that").[4] Cupcakes' demands to be left alone because he is not gay are met with Paco's insistence that he (Paco) does not consider Cupcakes a homosexual, as he does not think in those terms. For Paco, it is about his love for Cupcakes. His emotional and sexual desire demands reciprocity, even if it necessitates taking it by force, as evidenced by his telling Cupcakes that, if "push comes to shove, I'll take you. But I don't wanna do that cause I know I'm gonna have to hurt you in the doing."[5] Throughout the play, Paco refuses a binaristic framing of his sexuality as either gay or straight, or even bisexual, although he does express a willingness to "go both ways with [Cupcakes]."[6]

Piñero's challenge of fixed identitarian categories continues in later works such as *Cold Beer*, wherein he describes a series of conversations between the protagonist Mike, a writer living in Los Angeles with his girlfriend, and passersby. One of the exchanges involves a man who asks Mike if he "would like a dynamite blowjob," which Mike declines by telling him, "sorry … I'm creating."[7] Another involves two young, blond, tanned teenage boys known as Smiles and Legs, who ask Mike for cigarettes and beer, before Mike turns to Legs and tells him that he's "got nice legs." Smiles then asks Mike what he does for a living. Mike's answer—that he is a poet—is met with Smiles' snide comment, "oh, sweet Jesus, another fairy."[8] Mike refuses Smiles' queering, letting Smiles know that, unless he is willing to fight him, he will refer to him as a poet, rather than as a "fairy." In these plays, Piñero creates a queer theatre that is intergenerational and intra- and interracial. It is also sexually charged, fixed, and fluid, as well as equal parts romantic and violent.

Much of Piñero's writing is informed by his frequent incarceration, his drug use, and his fluid sexuality. Themes for his plays also include immigration, colonialism, Puerto Rican identity, intergenerational relationships, incest, rape, cruising, drug dealing, hustling, and same-sex desire and practice. Located in jails, bars, public restrooms, and urban neighborhoods, his characters utilize bilingualism and a raced urban vernacular as ways to highlight their ethnicity and social, political, and economic marginality. Also evident throughout Piñero's plays is his employment of an outlaw aesthetic, what Miguel Algarín defines as "a social and political aesthetic" that challenges "unjust authority" either individually or collectively.[9]

Importantly, Piñero's writing offers readers and audiences a multilayered vision and articulation of raced and criminalized sexuality, without sanitization. His artistic voice is part of a lineage that includes other poets-turned-playwrights who emerged from the Nuyorican Poets Café, such as Ntozake Shange, Pedro Pietri, and Ishmael Reed, while his influence is most notably evidenced in the works of his protégé and lover, the late Reinaldo Povod.[10] Piñero's legacy is further evidenced in his poetry collections, a 2001 biopic starring Benjamin Bratt, and his continued influence on contemporary poets who cite his work, while often mimicking his verbal delivery and cadence as they perform poems challenging definitions of high versus low art.

NOTES

1 Marvin Felix Camillo, "Introduction," in Miguel Piñero, *Short Eyes* (New York: Hill and Wang, 1975), vii.
2 Only in *Irving*, a play about a young Jewish man sleeping with his sister's boyfriend who then invites his family to his apartment in order to "come out," does Piñero portray homosexuality within a dominant framework recognizable to mainstream audiences.
3 Piñero, *Short Eyes*, 67.
4 Ibid., 68.
5 Ibid., 70.
6 Ibid.
7 Miguel Piñero, *Outrageous: One Act Plays* (Houston: Arte Público Press, 1986), 43.
8 Ibid., 44.
9 Miguel Algarín, "Part I: Outlaw Poetry," in *Nuyorican Poetry: An Anthology of Words and Feelings*, ed. Miguel Algarín and Miguel Piñero (New York: William Morrow and Company, 1975), 26–27.
10 Before his death in 1994 from tuberculosis, Povod authored two plays, *Cuba and His Teddy Bear* (1986) and *La Puta Trilogy* (1988). *Cuba and His Teddy Bear*, a play about a small-time Cuban drug dealer and his son in the Lower East Side, proved to be Povod's most successful, and was first produced by Joseph Papp at The Public Theater in 1986 before later enjoying a run on Broadway in 1988.

FURTHER READING

Jaime, Karen. *The Queer Nuyorican: Racialized Sexualities and Aesthetics in Loisaida*. New York: New York University Press, 2021.
Piñero, Miguel. *La Bodega Sold Dreams*. Houston: Arte Público Press, 1985.
Piñero, Miguel. *The Sun Always Shines for the Cool; A Midnight Moon at the Greasy Spoon; Eulogy for a Small Time Thief*. Houston: Arte Público Press, 1984.

BILLY PORTER
(Pittsburgh, Pennsylvania, 1969–)
Eric M. Glover

Billy Porter, also known as "The Voice," was born and raised in Pittsburgh's Hill District, where his singing voice earned him early childhood acclaim. Growing up in a Black Pentecostal church and singing in a choir where members called him "little preacher man," Porter thought that he was destined to become a minister in his adulthood. He played Gus Fielding in a middle school production of the 1937 Richard Rodgers-Lorenz Hart musical *Babes in Arms*, but it did not occur to him to pursue a career in acting. Porter watched the 1982 Tony Awards broadcast while he washed dishes, seeing and hearing the *Dreamgirls* cast participating and performing "It's All Over"/"And I Am Telling You (I'm Not Going)." Jennifer Holliday's performance was the first time that a young Porter heard a Black performer sing in a musical how people sang in church.

Porter, library card in hand, checked out available original Broadway cast recordings from the Carnegie Library of Pittsburgh to learn more about his calling. One day, "the queen, uh, who was the librarian" provided Porter with James Lapine and Stephen Sondheim's *Sunday in the Park with George*, triggering his love affair with Lapine and Sondheim's musical.[1] Training in the fine arts as an actor, dancer, and singer, Porter attended Pittsburgh Creative and Performing Arts School before attending Carnegie Mellon University, where he graduated with a BFA in acting in 1991. Porter saw a casting call announcing the original Broadway production of *Miss Saigon* in *Backstage*, auditioned, and made his Broadway debut in the ensemble.

Three-time Tony Award-winner for acting Hinton Battle, who also appeared in *Miss Saigon*, secured Porter an audition for the television talent competition *Star Search*. In the period of a week, and on his days off from *Miss Saigon* in 1992, Porter was crowned the $100,000 male vocalist grand champion in front of a studio audience. Porter's next act was Teen Angel in the 1994 revival of *Grease* (1971), directed by Tommy Tune; he arranged and sang "Beauty School Dropout" in the style of Black gospel music. Porter hated his role initially because *Grease* was his least favorite musical, and he hated wearing the character's space suit costume and wig, a bouffant 14 inches high. He longed to do Tony Kushner's *Angels in America* (1993), seeing and hearing in Belize his identity as a gay Black man in the US.

Porter alighted Broadway, performing off-Broadway and embarking on a music career as a recording artist against the backdrop of his disappointment with the ways of the world. He appeared in the WPA Theatre's original off-Broadway production of Jason Robert Brown's song cycle *Songs for a New World* (1995), singing contemporary musical theatre songs such as "King of the World." (Ty Taylor replaced Porter and performed his role on the original off-Broadway cast recording because of Porter's contract with A&M Records at the time.) Porter played James Thunder Early opposite Heather Headley, Audra McDonald, Tamara Tunie, and Lillias White in a "one-night-only" concert of *Dreamgirls* two weeks after 9/11, benefiting the Actors Fund of America. In 2010, he finally played Belize in the Signature Theatre Company 20th-anniversary production of *Angels in America*, working with Kushner and director Michael Grief.

The 2002 Broadway revival of Lapine and Sondheim's *Into the Woods* brought Porter one step closer to resuming his Broadway career after an absence. He auditioned for the role of the Baker, only for Sondheim to inform him that he had "a little too much pizzazz" for the character.[2] Instead, Sondheim encouraged Porter to audition for the Witch—a role that Porter claims he did not need to prepare for, since he knew the Witch's eleven o'clock number "Last Midnight" by heart. Porter believes that the 9/11 attacks convinced the producers to put on a more traditional production of the show, and Vanessa Williams went on to play the Witch to rave reviews. Nevertheless, Porter's soaring rendition of "Last Midnight" was eventually captured on his 2005 album, *At the Corner of Broadway and Soul*.

Porter started to try his hand as a playwright and director by writing and telling stories, especially autobiographical ones, of Blackness and queerness. He directed a gender-bending production of Sondheim's *Company* (1970) at his undergraduate alma mater in 2002, and he wrote and performed his autobiographical one-man show *Ghetto Superstar: The Man That I Am* (2005) at both Joe's Pub and Pittsburgh Public Theatre. Porter also conceived and directed *Being Alive: A New Musical Celebration* (2007), setting Sondheim's songs to Black vernacular music to tell his story of Black people's past and present across America. Porter's play *While I Yet Live* (2014) picked up where his *Ghetto Superstar* left off, looking at childhood sexual abuse and delving into homophobia. He also directed a 2015 Boston production of George C. Wolfe's *The Colored Museum* (1986), which featured a Black trans woman character.

Porter came home to Broadway at last playing Lola in Harvey Fierstein and Cyndi Lauper's *Kinky Boots* (2013), a musical about drag queens rallying to rescue shoe-factory workers. Written and composed with him in mind, Lola is a character worthy of Porter's prodigious talents. His Act 1 duet with costar Stark Sands, "I'm Not My Father's Son," was cathartic for Porter, helping him address and heal past trauma. Porter won the 2013 Drama Desk Award and Tony Award for Best Actor in a Musical, which made him the first openly gay Black musical theatre male lead to be so honored. Porter's music career was foiled by bigotry so his winning, as a principal soloist, the Best Musical Theatre Album Grammy Award was also meaningful.

Porter and playwright-director Wolfe reunited in 2016, working on *Shuffle Along or the Making of the Musical Sensation of 1921 and All That Followed*. Based on the greatest story never told, the history of the musical *Shuffle Along*, Brian Stokes Mitchell and Porter played the writers and stars F.E. Miller and Aubrey Lyles, respectively, reviving vaudeville's Miller & Lyles. Porter's Act 2 solo "Low Down Blues" was him doing what he did best as he resided at the corner of Broadway and soul. Even though he, a homosexual, played Lyles, a heterosexual, in Act 2, Porter broke the fourth wall to directly address his audience and exclaimed, "Yes, I had a wife," to knowing smiles. Porter's next major role brought him to television audiences in his Emmy Award-winning turn as drag ball emcee and mentor Pray Tell on FX Networks' *Pose* (2018–2021).

Belize, the character Porter played in *Angels in America*, uses the metaphor of singing to argue that freedom for marginalized people has remained out of reach:

> The white cracker who wrote the National Anthem knew what he was doing. He set the word "free" to a note so high nobody can reach it. That was deliberate. Nothing on earth sounds less like freedom to me.[3]

But, as Porter sings out, freedom for marginalized people becomes more of a possibility than a limit. Porter's singing voice claims and occupies both space and time not intended for him as a gay, Black, and proud man living with HIV. He has become an icon of men's and women's fashions, stepping onto the 2019 Academy Awards red carpet wearing his tailor-made Christian Siriano velvet black tuxedo jacket and full-length ballgown, reconciling his twoness. He has also used his voice to take political stands, covering Stephen Stills' "For What It's Worth" in a taped performance for the 2020 Democratic National Convention to draw attention to nationwide racial and social injustice protests. Porter has also supported emerging artists, appearing in a cameo for Lil Nas X's "That's What I Want" music video (2021) as a minister who bestows upon the rapper an electric guitar that divines music stardom. Porter busted doors wide open for Lil Nas X and other inheritors to come out of the proverbial glass closet, unapologetically Black and queer.

NOTES

1 Billy Porter, *At the Corner of Broadway and Soul (Live)*, Ghostlight Records, 2005. www.youtube.com/playlist?list=OLAK5uy_lMYUlVGe HR7J8isBq6sA--RgnqedsikCI
2 Ibid.
3 Tony Kushner, *Angels in America: A Gay Fantasia on National Themes*, New York: Theater Communications Group, 2013, 230.

FURTHER READING

Kheraj, Alim. "Billy Porter: For Me as a Black Queer Man, Having an EGOT Would Crack Open Spaces." *GQ*. October 8, 2021. www.gq-magazine.co.uk/culture/article/billy-porter-interview

Porter, Billy. *Unprotected: A Memoir*. New York: Abrams Press, 2021.

CLINT RAMOS
(Cebu, Philippines, 1974–)
Jimmy A. Noriega

Clint Ramos is an award-winning costume and set designer who proudly identifies as an immigrant and Filipino American. He earned his BA in Theatre at the University of the Philippines and moved to New York City in the mid-1990s. He received an MFA in Design for Stage and Film from New York University in 1997 and upon graduation worked off-Broadway and in television. In 2013, he received an Obie Award for Sustained Achievement in Design for his body of work. Ramos holds the distinction of being the first BIPOC person to win a Tony Award for Best Costume Design in a Play (*Eclipsed*, 2016) and was subsequently nominated for four additional Tony Awards: three for costume design (*Once on This Island*, 2017; *Torch Song*, 2018; and *The Rose Tattoo*, 2019) and one for set design (*Slave Play*, 2019). His designs have appeared in productions across the US, as well as in the Philippines, UK, Russia, Romania, and Israel, and he has twice been awarded the Ani ng Dangal Presidential Medal for Dramatic Arts from the President of the Philippines.

His first encounter with theatre occurred when he was in boarding school in Manila. The young Ramos was part of a drama troupe, and his teacher, who he credits as being one of his earliest influences, took him to witness theatre of protest and street theatre. Ramos says,

> That's how I discovered the power of theatre and performance and how it truly could change the way we think of and the way we conceive of art. And the way that art can be a catalyst for thought and for change.[1]

This occurred during the popular demonstrations known as the People Power Revolution, which brought an end to the presidency of Ferdinand Marcos, who ruled over the Philippines as a dictator for over 20 years. Ramos recalls, "Activists and artists were making street theatre throughout the Philippines as part of the revolution and seeking to contribute to the social movement. I remember all of that."

Ramos got his big break when he was hired by George C. Wolfe, who was artistic director of the Public Theater, to design costumes for the production of José Rivera's *References to Salvador Dalí Make Me Hot* (2001). Prior to this, Ramos said, "Nobody hired me." Most of his contemporaries from graduate school were advancing in their film and theatre careers and he felt like he "stayed in a rut." He continues,

> I didn't put two and two together. When you immigrate to the United States and you are a person of color, nobody teaches you what the system is out of school, both the social system and theatrical system. It took me a long time to get my feet off the ground.

Ramos credits Wolfe for giving him an "artistic home" at the Public, which allowed him to work alongside other BIPOC artists that eventually became a network of close collaborators. He has designed sets and costumes for 23 productions at the Public, including a number of shows authored by queer playwrights, such as Colman Domingo's *Wild with Happy* (2012), Robert O'Hara's *Barbecue* (2015), Sara Burgess's *Dry Powder* (2016), and Hansol Jung's *Wild Goose Dreams* (2018).

Throughout his career, Ramos has collaborated with a number of queer directors. Most notably, he has designed sets and costumes for several productions with Robert O'Hara, including: *Wild with Happy*, *Bootycandy* (2014), *Marie Antoinette* (2015), *Bella: An American Tall Tale* (2017), *Mankind* (2018), *BLKS* (2019), and *Slave Play*. Ramos notes that his working relationship with O'Hara is rooted in their "queerness and POCness." His design work with Leigh Silverman includes *Violet* (2014), *The Heidi Chronicles* (2014), *Wild Party* (2015), *Sweet Charity* (2016), *Wild Goose Dreams*, and *Grand Horizons* (2019). He has also designed under the direction of Moisés Kaufman for *The Common Pursuit* (2012), *The Tallest Tree in the Forest* (2013), and *Torch Song*, and Billy Porter in *The Colored Museum* (2015) and *Topdog/Underdog* (2017). Ramos views strong networks of collaboration as the key to a successful production. "I think a lot of folks in the theatre think of collaboration as everybody doing their own separate jobs and staying in their lanes and going at it side-by-side and arriving at one destination," he says. "For me, part of how I define collaboration is that we all have this common experience." For Ramos, living on multiple margins of society has also marked his and his collaborators' understanding of life and their approach to making art. He is inspired by a number of other designers and, in particular, credits queer designers

Rachel Hauck and David Zinn as inspirations and comrades. He says, "because we orbit the same circles, I am influenced not only by their work, but by the way they actually view things."

In March 2020, *Town & Country* magazine published an article titled "Clint Ramos is the Man Behind the Most Talked About Set on Broadway," which featured a discussion of his design for *Slave Play*.[2] The Jeremy O. Harris script is an intricate portrayal of sexuality, desire, trauma, and race relations in the US. Under the direction of O'Hara, the production concept merged modern-day discussions of Black and non-Black identity and space with images of the antebellum South. Throughout the play, interracial couples undergo sex therapy sessions as they role-play various identities, which spurred Ramos to research the themes of sex, voyeurism, and intimacy. "I was inspired by those glass windows in Amsterdam, stills of pornography, and what couples do when in their private bedrooms with mirrors on the ceilings," he explains.

> The genius of the mirrors was watching a sexual act being performed and observed. For me, it clicked. Let's just do a whole wall of mirrors that face the audience and the audience can watch the actors and watch themselves—it's a reflection in so many ways.[3]

Harris includes Rihanna's "Work" as the initial sound heard at beginning of the script, which prompted Ramos to expand on the role the song could play in the production—across the top of the stage in neon are the lyrics "nuh body touch me you nuh righteous."

In addition to his work as a designer, Ramos is Head of Design and Production at Fordham University and helps to mentor emerging theatre designers. His impact within the industry is further marked through his advocacy work. As he explains,

> The last twelve years of my practice has really been about unlearning what I had signed on to learn in terms of the oppressor's techniques and oppressor's way of designing and oppressor's way of practicing. So a lot of what I do right now is deeply invested in a decolonized system of practice.

He intentionally advocates for rising BIPOC designers and technicians in theatre and film, and he employs only women and people of color in his studio.[4]

In June 2021, Ramos joined the "community-based, decentralized inter-generational" group Design Action in releasing a 30-page document that outlines its "Five Guiding Principles," which are: Anti-Racist Codes of Conduct, Harm Reduction, Cultural Competency, Equitable Representation, and BIPOC Advocacy.[5] Design Action is a "coalition of BIPOC and white designers working to end racial inequities in the North American Theater by confronting racism in [the] workplace and forging new pathways into the industry for rising designers of color."[6] Ramos, Hauck, and Zinn were among 18 designers who formed the 5 Principles Committee. Ramos is also on the advisory board of the American Theatre Wing and proudly takes part in several of its initiatives, including "Springboard to Design," a free program for high school students that introduces them to design for theatre and film. His other advocacy work includes involvement in the Broadway Advocacy Coalition and Asian American Advocacy Coalition. Ramos maintains a fervent commitment to making the theatrical world more equitable and accessible to those historically underrepresented in the profession. When asked what advice he would give to young artists, he says,

> If you are a young queer person, particularly if you are a queer person of color, who wants to practice, my advice is go find your people. That's what I did and they saved me. When people wouldn't hire me, it was people of my kind, my kind of people, that gave me a home.

NOTES

1. Personal interview with author, July 7, 2021. All of Ramos's quotes are from this interview, unless specified otherwise.
2. Stellene Vollandes, "Clint Ramos is the Man Behind the Most Talked About Set on Broadway," *Town & Country*, March 12, 2021. www.townandcountrymag.com/leisure/arts-and-culture/a35813948/clint-ramos-slave-play-tony-awards-interview
3. Quoted in Josh Ferri, "Slave Play Tony Award Winner Clint Ramos Reveals How Sex and Race Inspired the Famed Mirror Wall Set," *BroadwayBox*, November 21, 2019. www.broadwaybox.com/daily-scoop/clint-ramos-reveals-his-inspirations-for-the-slave-play-set
4. "Clint Ramos: We Design Online Exhibition," *Design Museum Everywhere*. https://designmuseumfoundation.org/we-design-online-exhibition/clint-ramos
5. Design Action, "Activating Design Action's Five Guiding Principles," June 2021. www.design-action.com/new-page-1
6. Design Action. www.design-action.com/about-us

FURTHER READING

Macias, Ernesto. "Rihanna, Mirrors, and America: Processing *Slave Play*'s Set Design," *Interview Magazine*, November 19, 2019. www.interviewmagazine.com/art/rihanna-mirrors-and-america-processing-slave-plays-set-design

Rabinowitz, Chloe. "Clint Ramos Talks SLAVE PLAY's Set Design, THE ROSE TATTOO's Costume Design, Racial Equity in Theatre & More," *BroadwayWorld*, March 13, 2021. www.broadwayworld.com/article/BWW-Interview-Clint-Ramos-Talks-SLAVE-PLAYs-Set-Design-THE-ROSE-TATTOOs-Costume-Design-Racial-Equity-in-Theatre-More-20210313

GUILLERMO REYES
(Santiago, Chile, 1962–)
Jimmy A. Noriega

Guillermo Reyes is a playwright, director, producer, author, and educator. He moved to the United States with his mother at age nine and they lived in the Washington, DC area until settling in Los Angeles when he was a teenager. As he explains, "My mother was the immigrant, I was her child and I was tagging along. I didn't know any better."[1] Reyes chronicles his mother's experiences in the US, as well as his own coming to terms with his sexual identity, in the book *Madre and I: A Memoir of Our Immigrant Lives* (2010). He has won several awards, including the 1997 National Hispanic Playwrights Contest for *A Southern Christmas*. His plays have been staged across the US, including *Chilean Holiday* (1996) and *Saints at the Rave* (2001), which were produced at Actors Theatre of Louisville. Reyes is noted for his ability to create complex queer and Latinx characters that are grounded in sociopolitical circumstances often tied to racialized desire, queer shame, body image, sexual repression, and immigration. This is especially significant since many of his works were staged at a time when queer Latinx characters were nothing more than stereotypical representations in cinema and television.

One of his earliest memories of wanting to be a playwright occurred after he watched the 1968 film version of *Romeo and Juliet*. As he recalls, the naked image of the actor playing Romeo "awakened me to the experience of make believe by appealing to eros" and he wanted to write a script for his cousins to perform their own version of the story in their backyard. His interest in writing continued throughout high school and into college. He studied Italian Literature at University of California, Los Angeles and earned an MFA in Playwriting from University of California San Diego (UCSD), where he also studied Chicanx/Latinx theatre with Jorge Huerta. While at UCSD, he developed a newfound freedom to write about his own Latinx and immigrant identity and was encouraged to pen stories with LGBTQ characters and themes.

His most successful play is *Men on the Verge of a His-panic Breakdown*, which premiered at Celebration Theatre in Los Angeles in June 1994. The show consists of a series of comedic monologues and tells the stories of seven gay Latino immigrants, including: Federico, "The Gay Little Immigrant That Could"; Vinnie, one of the "Aging Kept Boys of West Hollywood" who is abandoned by his sugar daddy after turning 30; Paco, who was formerly incarcerated in an anti-gay detention camp in Cuba; and La Gitana, a flamenco drag performer dying of AIDS. The production featured gay Latino actor Felix A. Pire and was originally presented on the theatre's "off" nights until rave reviews led to an expanded run. A critic for the *Los Angeles Times* wrote, "Pire is a human buzz saw whose over-the-top, comic gusto complements Reyes' flamboyant artistry."[2] Reyes won the LA Ovation Award for Best Original Play, and Theatre Rhinoceros went on to produce it in San Francisco only three months after its debut. In 1997, the Los Angeles creative team restaged the production off-Broadway at 47th Street Theatre, with Pire winning an Outer Critics Circle Award for Best Solo Performance. Over the years, the play has continued to be staged around the country, including revivals at the Apollo Studio Theater in Chicago (2015) and Teatro Audaz in San Antonio (2021).

Reyes describes *Deporting the Divas* as "a love story trapped in a Ridiculous Theater travesty of a play." It was first staged at Celebration Theatre in 1996 and, after rewrites and a new cast, premiered at Theatre Rhinoceros in a co-production with Teatro de la Esperanza that same year (both versions were directed by Huerta). The play is a collision of gender, machismo, sexuality, immigration status, and forbidden desire. It centers on Michael González, a married Latino Border Patrol agent, who has an affair with Sedicio, a gay and undocumented Mexican immigrant. The play employs drag, disguise, and fantasy sequences to reveal the parallels between hiding one's sexual identity "in the closet" and hiding one's undocumented immigrant status as a means of survival. As Huerta notes,

> In a clever reversal of sexual borders, it is the undocumented Mexican who can be openly comfortable with his sexuality, while the citizen must hide his ... [As] an undocumented gay immigrant, Sedicio represents everything Michael has been taught and trained to fear and to reject.[3]

Throughout the play, Michael also interacts with and falls in love with a fantasy character, Sirena, who dresses in drag and dances the tango.

Reyes further developed this character in the play *Sirena, Queen of the Tango*, which was staged at Theatre Rhinoceros in 2001. It mixes elements of film noir and telenovela to tell the story of Sirena and the hunk cop who is investigating the deaths of her many husbands. In typical Reyes fashion, these mismatched characters fall in love through a series of twists and turns.

Reyes says that he had three major influences while writing *Men on the Verge* and *Deporting the Divas*: Charles Ludlum, Charles Busch, and John Leguizamo. He says:

> When I read John Leguizamo's plays (without yet watching his HBO specials), I recognized the sense of humor and saw what he could do with the monologues. Ludlum and Busch were excellent models of the type of work you can do with drag. Busch seemed more bound to have fun and was more spoofy than Ludlum.

In addition to drag and camp, Reyes also plays with various themes, forms, and aesthetics, and he does not shy away from political and social issues, including gun violence. *They Call Me a Hero*, later published under the title *That Day in Tucson*, premiered at Borderlands Theatre in Tucson, Arizona in 2014. It depicts the events that led to the 2011 shooting of congresswoman Gabrielle Giffords and is based on the memoir by Daniel Hernández Jr., the gay Mexican American intern who is credited with saving her life. Additionally, his play for younger audiences, *Q-Kid Rap* (2017), employs rap to explore the issue of attempted teen suicide through the eyes of a queer Latino youth.

In 2000, Reyes co-founded Teatro Bravo, a bilingual theatre company, with Daniel Enrique Pérez and Trino Sandoval. The three gay men set out to transform the Phoenix arts scene by promoting Latinx and Latin American culture through the theatre, and Reyes served as its artistic director for ten years. During that time, he wrote and directed *Places to Touch Him* (2002), which became the first gay-themed play that the company produced.

> It was a hit and it was also rather sexy ... I made sure that actors actually touched and made out and did a three-way, I mean, with a title like that. But it was also the problem with Latino theater, some audiences stayed away because of the subject matter and considered us suspect when we did plays with LGTBQ themes. We did not become a reliably safe, family friendly theater—and

we really didn't want to. It wasn't part of our mission, but let's face it, corporate funders would prefer to finance a "cultural heritage" type of theater, not the edgy types like us.

For Teatro Bravo, artistic freedom and a desire to present queer lives on stage meant instability and underfunding. Although his plays had found great success in Los Angeles, San Francisco, and New York, Reyes was ahead of his time in the politically and socially conservative climate of Arizona.

In addition to his regional impact as an artistic director and producer, Reyes is also head of the playwriting program at Arizona State University. He has taught many theatre artists and writers, most notably queer Chicano playwright and performer Carlos-Manuel, who is best known for his solo plays *La Vida Loca* (2005) and *Joto! Confessions of a Mexican Outcast* (2016), as well as the full-length play *Vaqueeros* (2006). Reyes has always understood the importance of mentorship and support, as well as challenging the limits placed on writers because of their identities. In 1997, he wrote an essay that advocated for Latinx, Latin American, immigrant, and queer voices in the US theatre. Writing about his work, he said,

> I am proud of my bilingualism as a form of power, a cross-generational, cross-national communication. I'm not interested in separateness and shielding myself from the majority. I'm interested in seeing Hispanics contribute to the majority culture without having to sacrifice any form of uniqueness.[4]

Without a doubt, Reyes has brought his unique lens to the US theatre, merging queer and Latinx identities in the most fabulous, insightful, and hilarious ways.

NOTES

1 Personal interview with the author, January 30, 2022. All of Reyes' quotes are from this interview, unless specified otherwise.
2 Kathleen F. Foley, "'His-Panic Breakdown' a Sensitive Romp," *Los Angeles Times* (June 10, 1994), F16.
3 Jorge Huerta, *Chicano Drama: Performance, Society, and Myth* (Cambridge: Cambridge University Press, 2000), 175.
4 Guillermo Reyes, "The Latin American Writer: Writing in English," *Latin American Theatre Review*, 31, 1 (Fall 1997), 115.

FURTHER READING

Cortez, Beatriz. "Hybrid Identities and the Emergence of Dislocated Consciousness: *Deporting the Divas* by Guillermo Reyes." In *Chicano/Latino Homoerotic Identities*, ed. David William Foster. New York: Routledge, 2013, 131–146.

Fitch Lockhart, Melissa. "Queer Representations in Latino Theatre," *Latin American Theatre Review*, 31, 2 (Spring 1998): 67–78.

Reyes, Guillermo. *Madre and I: A Memoir of Our Immigrant Lives*. Madison: University of Wisconsin Press, 2010.

EDWIN SÁNCHEZ
(Arecibo, Puerto Rico, 1955–)
Analola Santana

Edwin Sánchez is an award-winning and internationally produced playwright and novelist; he has written 11 full-length plays and over a dozen short theatrical pieces. He was born in Puerto Rico and moved to New York City when he was two years old. Sánchez began his studies in playwriting at Circle Rep Theater Lab (now the New Circle Theater Company) in New York City, a company of actors, writers, and directors known for their nourishing and fostering of new American theatre. This experience gave Sánchez an opportunity to perfect the writing he had been doing on his own, also catching the eye of playwright Milan Stitt, who was part of the company and director of playwriting at Yale. Following Stitt's suggestion to pursue a degree in playwriting (even though he did not have an undergraduate degree), Sánchez graduated in 1994 with an MFA from the Yale School of Drama. He is the recipient of prestigious awards such as the National Latino Playwright Award, the Princess Grace Playwriting Award, the Kennedy Center Fund for New American Plays (among many others), and his work has been selected by the Eugene O'Neill Playwrights Conference to represent the National Playwrights Conference at the Schelykovo Playwrights Seminar in Russia. Sánchez's theatre has been translated into multiple languages and produced in stages from Brazil to Switzerland, demonstrating the capacity of his work to break boundaries that cross genres, media, languages, and nations.

It is important to note that Sánchez was a playwright before he entered the Yale School of Drama. He had already written one of his best-known plays, *Trafficking in Broken Hearts*, which, as Sánchez has said, was being read by many but had not yet been produced. This first play—a love story between a Nuyorican street hustler, a timid lawyer from the Midwest, and a young runaway who is the victim of sexual abuse—was considered too risqué for most theatres and was finally produced in 1994 as a staged reading by the Atlantic Theater in New York City. While at Yale, he wrote some of his best-known works, including *The Road* (1998), a play about a young man with AIDS who hitchhikes in search of the perfect beach on which to die while dealing with his extreme anger towards his parents. Typical of his theatre, in this play Sánchez articulates a new politics of representation and difference in US Latinx theatre as he distances himself from both realist theatre and the Nuyorican theatre of the 1970s and 1980s (which concentrated on barrio life, the crisis of patriarchy, the dysfunctionality of the family after migration, and the transcultural condition of the second generation). Instead, Sánchez creates characters who are out of the norm, uncanny, and extremely abject in their exploration of a queer identity that is often explored through the prism of traditional love stories, but always with a twist.

The characters in his plays are often outsiders struggling for any semblance of respect in their lives, and it so happens that many are also gay characters. A good example of this is found in the play *Clean* (1995), which weaves together a series of stories about impossible loves. The play centers on a sweet-natured boy named Gustavito from the ages of 7 to 15. The young boy has a troubling relationship with his brother Junior, who pines for an unattainable girl next door, and with Kiko, their volatile father, who has been married to all three of the Gomez sisters. The boys' stepmother, Mercy, is a sad seamstress who forges a special relationship with Norry, a drag queen in need of a wedding dress. Most important of all, though, is a priest identified only as Father, with whom Gustavito falls in love. The play is not about pedophilia in any way; it is about love and acceptance of your own self, regardless of what the world around you thinks. Sánchez explains, "Queer identity is the journey towards self-respect and self-acceptance. Accepting every part of you,"[1] and this is Gustavito's journey in the play, culminating with a final encounter with the priest that allows both to come to terms with their own sexuality.

Sánchez creates stories and characters who expose their divergent ways of being to engage spectators in unexpected situations in which bodies, images, and actions surprise, trouble, shock, disturb, scandalize, and capture audiences. Nevertheless, it is all encapsulated within love stories that explore characters who feel vulnerable and unworthy of love. As Peter Marks explains in his review of *Barefoot Boy with Shoes On* (1999), a play about a tough window washer willing to let a gay customer smell his sweat for money, Sánchez's efficacy lies in his ability to "examine the corruptibility of the flesh in novel, eccentric, or downright creepy ways."[2] Without questioning or judging the eccentricities of his protagonists, Sánchez makes spectators (on their own and stepping outside their comfort zone) face difficult issues such as victimization, exploitation, and marginalization; he does so with a great capacity for poetic beauty in representing a world out of joint and spinning in fractured memories and broken dreams.

Theatre allows Sánchez to explore taboo subjects, especially those related to queer eroticism. Through his characters and their actions, he explores "illicit" territories that include incest, masturbation, nudity, sexual fetishes, and homoeroticism, to question the limits of what is acceptable on stage and on the page through impactful visual and linguistic images. For example, in *Unmerciful Good Fortune* (1996) we follow Maritza, a successful assistant district attorney, through her encounters with Fatima, who can read the life of whoever holds her hand and is now jailed after deciding to poison and kill as many people as she could to put them out of their misery. Their relationship evolves into repressed desire and manipulation as Maritza searches for a solution to her mother's sickness and deals with Fatima's unyielding demand to touch her and, thus, force her to face her own misery. Through the warped desire turned love story between these two women, Sánchez can seamlessly explore issues of class, race, gender, family, friendship, personal worth, and the ethics of euthanasia.

Sánchez's unique theatrical language allows his audience to find beauty in what is often deemed ugly or disturbing. He writes with an open and fragmented structure, though still following a linear chronology that can extend for as long as necessary, allowing us to see an evolution beyond the present moment. Each character speaks their own lyrical idiolect of English, which signals their social position and age group. The play *I'll Take Romance* (2009), a story reminiscent of Hollywood romantic comedies, focuses on the attempts of four gay men from very different places to find love: Angel, a gorgeous gold-digger who claims to only want a rich man; Dee, the loyal best friend who only cares about others' happiness; George, the recently out of the closet millionaire who falls for Angel; and Chi Chi, a complete stereotype of the Latinx gay man (who also turns out to be the most aware of them all). In this play, class and social status is clearly established through dialect above all else.

Though most of his characters have Spanish-sounding names and many of the stories come from the playwright's experiences, the force of his writing shows that Nuyorican/Latinx queer experiences are an American experience, a human experience. Reviews of his plays often underscore the complexity of antagonistic feelings that they elicit: funny and sad, familiar and foreign, erotic and repulsive, mysterious and mundane. Sánchez lets the audience see the effects of his characters' individual attempts to wrestle with self-acceptance and a search for love and family. His poetic realism creates imaginative works that break with theatrical structures as they question the very fabric of our contemporary societies. Even though the theatrical establishment may, at times, find his plays to be "risky," Sánchez's theatre continues to challenge the audience's cultural comfort zone, an important function of theatre that he takes on in order to make us feel more human.

NOTES

1 Edwin Sánchez, interview with author, May 1, 2021.
2 Peter Marks, "Three Plays Connected by Themes of Deviance," *New York Times*, October 22, 1999.

FURTHER READING

Lazú, Jacqueline. "'Til Death Do Us Part: Love and (Para)Normality in Edwin Sánchez's *Unmerciful Good Fortune*." *Ollantay Theater Journal* (2008): 96–107.

Reyes, Israel. Decolonizing Queer Camp in Edwin Sánchez's *Diary of a Puerto Rican Demigod*. *College Literature* 46.3 (2019): 517–541.

Sandoval-Sánchez, Alberto. "Nuyorican Fairy Tales: Allegories of Existence and Bare Survival in Migdalia Cruz and Eddie Sánchez's Theater." In Analola Santana and Sara Muñoz, eds, *Hispanic Issues Online: Freakish Encounters: Constructions of the Freak in Hispanic Cultures* 20 (2018).

LEIGH SILVERMAN
(Rockville, Maryland, 1974–)
Bess Rowen

When she was 11 years old, Leigh Silverman saw Lily Tomlin in *The Search for Signs of Intelligent Life in the Universe* (1985) at the Kennedy Center in Washington, DC. As she watched Tomlin on stage, she not only experienced some unspoken understanding and connection with Tomlin's presence, but also a realization that theatre could be "like this."[1] The "this" in that sentence—both in terms of queerness and storytelling—is what Silverman has continued to explore throughout her directing career. She was born in 1974 in Rockville, Maryland, and grew up around Washington, DC, before attending Carnegie Mellon University, where she earned a BFA in Directing and an MA in Playwriting. She moved to New York City in 1996, and she still resides there today. Her directorial résumé includes not only a who's who of LGBTQ+ theatre artists, but also a series of mostly new plays that explore the marginalized, difficult stories that Silverman loves to usher through the production process. Silverman is an Obie Award winner for Sustained Excellence in Directing and has also been nominated for an Audelco Award for *Blue Door* (2007), a Drama Desk for *From Up Here* (2008), and a Tony for *Violet* (2014). Silverman's still-evolving career is characterized by her commitment to focusing on the experiences and stories of people whose lives do not usually take center stage. This trajectory includes her early success directing Lisa Kron's *Well* (2003), whose transfer in 2006 first led her to Broadway, and her helming of the first all-female Broadway design team for *The Lifespan of a Fact* (2018).

Silverman's drive stems from her own queer feelings of being an outsider to the heteronormative stories that often define the theatrical canon. Some of her earliest influences came from queer theatre makers like Lisa Kron, the Five Lesbian Brothers, Split Britches, Daniel Alexander Jones, Marga Gomez, David Cale, Carmelita Tropicana, David Greenspan, and Paula Vogel. Many of these artists are known for solo performance, and Silverman's interest in these narratives sprang from her connection and delight at Tomlin and Jane Wagner's storytelling in *Intelligent Life* and Kron's *2.5 Minute Ride*, another early influence. These performers and their stories spoke to a way of experiencing the world that she could connect with and understand. As Silverman explains, each of these queer artists:

> [comes] at the world as an outsider—and I certainly felt like I come to the world from that place ... In my experience of growing up feeling like you're a little bit on the other side of the looking glass, for one reason or another, then the work that you make has the reflection of that inside of it. It has that sense of being not in the center of the story, but looking at the center from another perspective, or making yourself the center.

Although queer voices are not the only stories that come from off-center, Silverman's directing began here. As a first-time director and high school senior, she chose Andy Kirby's *Compromised Immunity* (1986), a play about the AIDS epidemic that she had found in a drama bookshop in England. That early play choice is a part of her continual search for theatre artists talking about queerness. This continued once she was in New York, where she chose to frequent theatrical spaces like the WOW Café and intern at New York Theatre Workshop because both had connections to the Five Lesbian Brothers.

Kron's influence on Silverman has now evolved into one of the director's most sustained and well-known collaborations. The pair have worked together on Kron's solo works, but also on the Five Lesbian Brothers' *Oedipus at Palm Springs*, which Silverman directed at New York Theatre Workshop in 2005. In addition to *Well*, Silverman won an Obie Award in 2011 for her direction of Kron's *In the Wake* and David Greenspan's *Go Back to Where You Are*. *In the Wake* follows a group of friends and family through intense discussions about politics and personal choices over Thanksgiving dinner in 2000, when the outcome of that presidential election had not yet been decided. Despite having lesbian characters, the play's focus is not explicitly on LGBTQ+ issues, and yet Silverman and Kron show that queer theatre makers need not focus solely on this identity marker to represent aspects of the queer experience. Silverman clearly believes that the theatrical productions she realizes are important, but she is also deeply invested in the relationships that come with the vulnerability that attends the artistic process. For her,

> the thing that I have always cared the most about in my career is truly that the writers that I work with—because I work almost

exclusively on new plays and musicals—want to work with me again. To me, success is the repeated relationship. That's all I really care about, the depth of collaboration, the quality of the collaboration.

This commitment to mutual support among artists is evident in her attention to the role of directors within the theatrical ecosystem, and she has worked closely with the Stage Directors and Choreographers Society, serving for 13 years on the board and seven years as vice president. To Silverman, mentorship is part of the responsibility that comes with being a director. She says, "I care about leadership in some ways more than I care about directing, which is to say that I think about leadership all the time: what it means, how to do it, and how to do it better." As someone who identifies as Jewish and gay, she is acutely aware of both her privilege and marginalization, and is particularly concerned with the issues of equity and inclusion for BIPOC writers, especially BIPOC women. These are not new topics of interest for Silverman; her Audelco Award nomination resulted from her direction of queer, African American playwright Tanya Barfield's two-hander *Blue Door* (2006), which examines an African American math professor's complex relationship with his cultural history in the face of his decision not to attend the Million Man March. She also directed queer South Korean playwright and translator Hansol Jung's first play, *Cardboard Piano* (2016), followed by Jung's *Wild Goose Dreams* (2017).

Silverman's collaboration with David Henry Hwang on both *Chinglish* (2011) and the musical *Soft Power* (2019), co-written by Jeanine Tesori, shows her commitment to BIPOC writers is not limited to the LGBTQ+ community. But Silverman's connection with queer stories and playwrights also extends beyond her work with Kron and Greenspan. In 2007, she directed *The Beebo Brinker Chronicles*, a play co-authored by Linda S. Chapman and Kate Moira Ryan that dramatizes three books by lesbian pulp fiction author Ann Bannon. Another important collaborator is Madeleine George, who worked with Silverman on *The (curious case of the) Watson Intelligence* (2013) and *Hurricane Diane* (2019). The latter is George's version of *The Bacchae*, in which Dionysus takes the form of a butch lesbian gardener who sets her sights on a cul-de-sac in suburban New Jersey to acquire new Bacchantes by promoting permacultural backyards. *Hurricane Diane* was a Pulitzer Prize finalist, and starred queer, trans downtown performer Becca Blackwell, for whom the role was written.

Silverman is a seemingly indefatigable director—someone whose résumé continues to grow with work that challenges and provokes. Diep Tran notes that, not only is Silverman constantly working, but she approaches each play in a different way, meaning that "You can't pinpoint a Silverman 'style,' and she wouldn't call herself an auteur. Instead she's like Mary Poppins, reaching into her vast toolbox to find the best thing that will serve the play at hand."[2] Silverman's adaptability all goes along with her views on the function of theatre in our everyday lives. As she puts it: "I really care about theatre being a place for transformation, a place for justice, a place for rage, and a place for righteousness for everybody."

NOTES

1 Leigh Silverman, in discussion with author, April 9, 2021. Unless otherwise noted, all quotes attributed to Silverman are from this interview.
2 Diep Tran, "The Inexhaustible Leigh Silverman," *American Theatre*, February 1, 2019. www.americantheatre.org/2019/02/01/the-inexhaustible-leigh-silverman/

FURTHER READING

Miller, Winter. "All's Well That Ends in *Well*: Lisa Kron and Leigh Silverman." *Brooklyn Rail*, April 2006. https://brooklynrail.org/2006/04/theater/all-rsquo-s-well-that-ends-in-well-lisa-kron-and-leigh-silverman

Myers, Victoria. "The Once and Future Leigh Silverman: A Western." *The Interval*, July 5, 2016. www.theintervalny.com/interviews/2016/07/the-once-and-future-leigh-silverman-a-western/

ANA MARÍA SIMO
(Cienfuegos, Cuba, 1943–)
Virginia Baeta

Playwright and activist Ana María Simo is a Cuban exile who studied in Paris before settling in New York City and becoming an important contributor to American lesbian culture. Simo was 15 years old when revolutionaries led by Fidel Castro ousted the military dictatorship of President Fulgencio Batista; by age 18, Simo was deeply active as a journalist and creative writer in the Havana literary scene. The diverse, young community forming within *Ediciones El Puente*, a provocative outside-of-the-establishment project for underrepresented writers, drew the attention of an increasingly homophobic Cuban government. One night in 1964, Simo was taken from her home by Cuban State Security and, over the ensuing four and a half months, she was first interrogated by officials in prison and then subjected to a series of electric shock "treatments" in a psychiatric clinic. In both cases, the end goal seemed to be the same: to push Simo to reveal counterrevolutionaries and homosexuals within *Ediciones El Puente*. She did not consider herself a lesbian at the time, and she did not give any names. She wrote later that the experience made the world "a bleak place, with no playfulness anymore. It paralyzed me. I couldn't write again for 10 years."[1]

After being watched and harassed for another two years, Simo saw the 1968 Cultural Congress of Havana as a chance to escape Cuba. An exit permit that had eluded her for years suddenly appeared after she threatened to go public at the international gathering about her arrest and torture. In exile in France, she dove into an intellectually invigorating culture, immersing herself for two years in Roland Barthes's seminars on Balzac's novella *Sarrasine*. Her revolutionary, activist muscles engaged as she joined the Paris student revolution. Upon discovering her own lesbian identity, she attempted (unsuccessfully) to build an autonomous, activist lesbian community that could thrive in alliance with Paris's established gay and women's movements. As Simo puts it, her vision "didn't gain enough traction to overcome the violent hetero pushback, and the ambivalence of dykes ... By late 1972, I had given up on feminism as a home for lesbians, and vice versa."[2]

A transatlantic relocation to New York City gave Simo an opportunity to build a different kind of home for lesbians. In 1976, shortly after arriving in the United States, Simo and Magaly Alabau—Simo's girlfriend and fellow Cuban exile—founded the first lesbian theatre in New York City, Medusa's Revenge. Medusa's Revenge was born from Alabau's frustration with the lack of opportunity available for herself as a Latina artist. It was also an attempt to pull Simo out of a depression fueled by a mind-numbing day job and the drugs she took to cope with it.[3] Aiming for community impact over mainstream acceptance, Alabau and Simo described Medusa's Revenge as "an experimental ensemble of theatre women"[4] and "a theatrical outlet for a lesbian point of view and consciousness" driven by "sensibility."[5] They found Alabau's first cast by leafleting at local lesbian bars, and Alabau led over 60 newly recruited women artists through months-long improvisational workshops to find the company's artistic core as they developed their first production.

At the beginning, Simo was primarily responsible for managing the theatre, and she was cleaning the bathroom when Alabau asked her to help form a play out of the "voluminous transcripts" that grew from the improvisations.[6] Forcing her way through a decade of writer's block, Simo emerged with a play, *Going Slow*. She followed this in 1977 with an original play of her own, *Bayou*, which was the first Medusa's Revenge production at its 10 Bleecker Street home. "A fantasy play with music," *Bayou*'s publicity flyer announced it as "about a wild and mythical lesbian bar where anything can and does happen." Some members of the audience "walked out in a huff," possibly because of the representations of butch/femme identities (considered controversial at the time), and possibly because the creators made no attempt to cater to respectable, white, middle-class sensibilities.[7]

Over time, Medusa's Revenge grew to look more like Simo's vision for a lesbian community that would empower the multiverse of women who would come through its doors. Like many independent theatre spaces at the time, Medusa's Revenge didn't only serve up productions. Flyers and newsletters promoted a cornucopia of activities for women only (unless clearly indicated otherwise). Events included a recital of art songs (for soprano and piano), a weekly sound technician's course for women, an "ethnic dance" masterclass, films, lectures, multimedia performance, cabarets, and dances that lasted until dawn. Medusa's Revenge operated until it met the fate of many independent, women-run, community-funded establishments—they lost their lease. Simo says she felt relieved when they literally shifted the spotlight to the WOW Café Theater in 1981 by donating their lighting package to this new women's venture.[8]

Simo joined the playwriting lab at INTAR—New York's historic Latinx theatre company—working with María Irene Fornés, who directed Simo's next play, *Exiles*, for INTAR in 1982. After appearing from time to time on the WOW stage, Simo was granted a slot to direct her own play, *Pickaxe*, in 1986. Set in Mexico and featuring artist Frida Kahlo as a primary character, *Pickaxe* double-cast its three female actors as both male and female characters in a fictionalized retelling of the assassination of Leon Trotsky. In the same year, Simo directed her own play, *What Do You See?*, for Theater for the New City. A short play with music, *What Do You See?* traps a lesbian couple in an urban apartment—they shelter together from the filth and misogyny of the streets but watch as other desperate women fatally plunge past their window.[9] Simo's collaboration with Stephanie Skura and Company resulted in *The Bad Play* (1991), a dance theatre telenovela parody that elevates a storyline of lesbian sexual exploration over a wash of absurd heteronormativity.

In early 1992, Simo formed the Lesbian Avengers in collaboration with several other activist friends, including the renowned playwright Sarah Schulman, Anne-christine d'Adesky, Maxine Wolfe, Marie Honan, and Anne Maguire. Tired of lesbian invisibility within a movement that catered mostly to gay men, from the start the Lesbian Avengers was "a group totally focused on high-impact street activism, not on talking."[10] Employing elements of street performance more common in Europe and Latin America, the New York Lesbian Avengers made their direct actions memorable by making them theatrical. Notable actions included drawing a giant bed float (complete with lesbians cavorting) down 5th Avenue and fighting bigotry in the school system by distributing balloons instructing children to "Ask about lesbian lives." The Avengers spread across the country, with some chapters still designing actions today. In 1993, Simo joined forces with theatre producer Linda Chapman and filmmaker Mary Patierno to create Dyke TV, a public access, lesbian-focused program that ran for over a decade. When the internet boom began, Simo was there, too, with *The Gully* (2000–2006), an online magazine co-founded and co-edited with Kelly Cogswell, which offered "queer views on everything."

Where Ana María Simo didn't find community, she created it. And, as an immigrant lesbian woman of color, she designed artistic, literary, and cultural communities to be as diverse as her experience. At a theatre conference in 1995, Simo expressed misgivings about the term "queer," which she warned would entrench the dominant "mostly gay, mostly white" perspective as representative—erasing lesbian and BIPOC identities.[11] Her work as a theatre artist, author, and activist continues to play a crucial role in defying that homogenization.

NOTES

1 Tish Dace, "The Interrogation of Ana María Simo," *The Advocate*, July 10, 1984, 39.
2 Ana María Simo, interview in French by Stéphanie Delon, *Jeanne Magazine*, April 2021. English translation, accessed May 24, 2022, www.anamariasimo.com/about/interview.english.jeannemag.shtml
3 Don Shewey, "From the Invisible to the Ridiculous: The Emergence of an Out Theater Aesthetic," in *The Queerest Art*, ed. Alisa Solomon and Framji Minwalla (New York: New York University Press, 2002), 138–139.
4 Magaly Alabau, "Bowing on Bleecker St.," *New York Times*, April 29, 1977, C28.
5 Terry Helbing, "Gay Arts: There's No Such Thing But Everybody Loves It," *The Villager*, October 20, 1977, 11.
6 Shewey, "Invisible," 139.
7 Kate Davy, *Lady Dicks and Lesbian Brothers: Staging the Unimaginable at the WOW Café Theatre* (Ann Arbor, MI: University of Michigan Press, 2010), 41–42.
8 Shewey, "Invisible," 140.
9 Ana María Simo, "*What Do You See?*," in *Tough Acts to Follow: One-Act Plays on the Gay/Lesbian Experience*, ed. Noreen C. Barnes and Nicholas Deutsch (San Francisco, CA: Alamo Square Press, 1992), 112–120.
10 "An Incomplete History ..." Lesbian Avengers, accessed July 20, 2021, www.lesbianavengers.com/about/history.shtml
11 Shewey, "Invisible," 147.

FURTHER READING

Schulman, Sarah. *Stagestruck: Theater, AIDS, and the Marketing of Gay America*. Durham, NC: Duke University Press, 1998.

Simo, Ana María. *Pickaxe*, in *Memories of the Revolution: The First Ten Years of the WOW Café Theater*, ed. Holly Hughes, Carmelita Tropicana, and Jill Dolan. Ann Arbor, MI: University of Michigan Press, 2015, 107–132.

SPLIT BRITCHES: PEGGY SHAW, LOIS WEAVER, AND DEB MARGOLIN (New York City, 1980–)

Benjamin Gillespie

Split Britches is a New York City-based lesbian-feminist performance troupe that was founded in 1980 by Peggy Shaw, Lois Weaver, and Deb Margolin. The theatre company remains active today after more than four decades of trailblazing queer theatre. Split Britches is known for creating original works that deconstruct canonical "straight" plays and other texts such as Tennessee Williams's *A Streetcar Named Desire*; Louisa May Alcott's novel *Little Women*; popular comic duos of the 1950s and 1960s such as Elaine May/Mike Nichols and Sid Caesar/Imogene Coca; film noir; and, most recently, Stanley Kubrick's film *Dr. Strangelove* and the 2019 romantic drama *Marriage Story*. Split Britches' performances foreground the presence of queer desire through overt lesbian sexuality and butch/femme role play, thereby undermining heterosexual imperatives that exist both on and off stage.

Shaw and Weaver first met in New York City while Weaver was working with the primarily Indigenous women's performance troupe Spiderwoman Theater (founded by Muriel Miguel) and Shaw with the multi-gender drag troupe Hot Peaches (founded by Jimmy Camicia), with Shaw later joining Weaver in Spiderwoman. Recognizing a mutual desire to focus explicitly on gender and sexuality, drawn out of their off-stage romantic relationship, Shaw and Weaver began their own theatre company focused more prominently on issues and questions surrounding lesbian identity. They co-founded the Women's One World (WOW) Festival in New York, leading to the establishment of the WOW Café, a collectively run feminist performance space focusing on work by and for women, which also remains in operation today. Having a permanent space allowed for the open exploration of nonnormative desire on stage at a time when male voices dominated both the mainstream and the experimental margins in theatre.

Working with Margolin, who collaborated as both a playwright and performer, the trio staged their first theatre piece titled *Split Britches* in 1981. "Split Britches" is a reference to trousers worn by women while working in farm fields that allowed them to urinate without stopping their labor—a comment on their own working-class backgrounds and the unrecognized labor of theatre making itself. The enthusiastic response they received from audiences and participants, and their ongoing support and collaboration with other queer artists, including Carmelita Tropicana and Holly Hughes, quickly garnered them a coterie following that continues today and connects multiple generations of queer artists who credit Split Britches as their mentors. While Margolin played a major role in the early development of Split Britches, she is no longer an active member of the troupe, but has continued to write and perform as a solo artist, winning an Obie Award for Sustained Excellence in 2000 and the Kesselring Prize for Playwriting for her play *Three Seconds in the Key* (2005).

From the beginning, Split Britches has always embraced a makeshift aesthetic and do-it-yourself approach to theatre making which has defined their work (and the work of WOW), as the artists perform, direct, and produce their own work in collaboration with others in the community. As they write in their artistic statement,

> our work create[s] new forms by exploiting old conventions [and] borrows from classical texts and popular myths, but its true sources are the details of everyday life. We use popular culture as a mode of communication, like the vaudevillian comedy double act ... taking existing forms and cracking them open to queer and personalize them.[1]

Split Britches' performances do not rely on conventional plots or linear structures, instead reflecting a postmodern form by blending divergent theatrical styles including vaudeville, cabaret, slapstick comedy, and drag. Gender-bending role play is at the center of the company's earlier works, including *Beauty and the Beast* (1982), *Upwardly Mobile Home* (1984), *Dress Suits to Hire* (with Holly Hughes) (1987), *Little Women: The Tragedy* (1988), *Anniversary Waltz* (1990), *Belle Reprieve* (1991), and *Lesbians Who Kill* (1992), as well as solo works such as Weaver's *Faith and Dancing* (1996) and Shaw's *Menopausal Gentleman* (1996). While the troupe never garnered the mainstream success of their queer male contemporaries (such as Charles Ludlam or Charles Busch), the troupe has won countless awards and grants, including four Obie Awards as well as the Edwin Booth Award for lifetime achievement and contributions to New York City theatre. They have held countless residencies, including at the Barbican (London), Dixon Place (New York), and, most frequently, La MaMa Experimental Theatre Club (New York), where they have premiered multiple works and were strongly supported by the late founder, Ellen Stewart. Their work has functioned as a key subject for a generation of lesbian-feminist scholars in the fields of feminist, queer, and performance studies, including Sue-Ellen Case, Jill Dolan, and Alisa Solomon. In addition to Weaver's position as Professor of Contemporary Performance at Queen Mary University of London, the duo has taught in residencies at academic institutions across the US.

Working in a mode of what scholar Kate Davy describes as "lesbian camp," the company exaggerates and distorts masculinity, femininity, and gender binaries, making their work queer before *queer* was even recognized as a discipline or identity category.[2] In one of their most well-known performances, *Belle Reprieve*, based on *A Streetcar Named Desire*, the company queers Tennessee Williams's play, as well as the popular 1951 film version starring Marlon Brando and Vivien Leigh, by having Stanley played by "a butch lesbian" (Shaw) and Stella by a femme lesbian (Weaver) (or "a woman disguised as a woman," as the published script states). According to Sue-Ellen Case, Split Britches' butch/femme role play "eradicates the ruling powers of heterosexist realist modes" and "eras[es] the difference between theatre and real life, or actor and character, obliterating any kind of essentialist ontology."[3] Demonstrating gender as performative, Shaw and Weaver's semi-fictional roles blur the lines between self and character. As Weaver has often described it, the theatrical veneer of character is never too thick to see the performer beneath it.

Kate Davy observes that the challenges of understanding camp strategies for lesbian women and the difficulty of articulating a feminist subject position are a result of camp's erasure of women. With *Belle Reprieve*, Split Britches—in collaboration with Bette Bourne and Paul Shaw (aka Precious Pearl) of the UK-based male drag troupe Bloolips—expanded the gendered limitations of camp traditions by incorporating lesbian desire while also making the female body overtly visible. Neither Shaw nor Weaver performed in drag in *Belle Reprieve*, but instead made visible the queer desire between them as two women, thus avoiding the impersonation of heterosexual couplings, and mirroring their well-known off-stage relationship. The radical reversal of camp in *Belle Reprieve* is based on the presence of lesbian desire on stage, *not* drag as male impersonation, providing the ground for female representation outside of heterosexual culture.

More than four decades after its inception, Shaw and Weaver have continued working under the Split Britches moniker, creating duo and solo works that expand their queer aesthetic by considering the intersections of sexuality and gender with age and aging. This has been especially poignant following a stroke Shaw endured in 2011, leaving her unable to memorize new material, as captured in her solo work *Ruff* (2012/2013). Weaver has also continued to perform as her queer alter ego, Tammy WhyNot (based on country singer Tammy Wynette), in *What Tammy Needs to Know About Getting Old and Having Sex* (2012), co-created with older people in Croatia, New York, and the UK, and drawing upon their stories and experiences to undermine ageist tropes in culture and society through foregrounding queer desire across intergenerational lines. Their most recent co-performed works, *Unexploded Ordnances (UXO)* (2018) and *Last Gasp* (2020/2021), represent their largest-scale performances to date, indicating their ongoing creative vitality and capacity for experimentation and adaptation as they work into their seventies, thus challenging the cultural ideology of decline for older artists. In addition to being both a performer and director for Split Britches, Weaver has also spearheaded the development of "Public Address Systems," a series of public-facing projects centered on performance protocols (or "etiquettes") aimed at creating alternative spaces for hospitable and critical questioning and collective engagement for marginalized communities. These protocols include the Long Table, Porch Sitting, Care Café, and, most recently, the Situation Room.[4]

Through these and other projects, Split Britches has made an indelible mark on US theatre for more than 40 years. The impact of their engagement with audiences and artists continues to live on in their work and in the work of countless queer artists they have influenced across the US and beyond.

NOTES

1 Split Britches, accessed November 12, 2021. www.split-britches.com/about
2 Kate Davy, "Fe/male impersonation: The Discourse of Camp," in *The Politics and Poetics of Camp*, ed. Moe Meyer (London: Routledge, 1994): 130–148.
3 Sue-Ellen Case, "Fe/male Impersonation: The Discourse of Camp," in *Camp: Queer Aesthetics and the Performing Subject*, ed. Fabio Cleto (Ann Arbor: University of Michigan Press, 1999): 189, 196.

4 For more on Public Address Systems, see www.split-britches.com/public-address-systems

FURTHER READING

Dolan, Jill. "*Belle Reprieve*: LGBTQ Theory into Practice," in *Theatre & Sexuality*. New York: Palgrave Macmillan, 2010: 59–79.

Eschen, Nicole. "Pressing Back: Split Britches' *Lost Lounge* and the Retro Performativity of Lesbian Performance," *Journal of Lesbian Studies* 17.1 (2013): 56–71.

Gillespie, Benjamin. "Detonating Desire: Mining the Unexplored Potential of Ageing in Split Britches' *Unexploded Ordnances (UXO)*," *Performance Research* 24.3 (2019): 89–98.

PAULA VOGEL
(Washington, DC, 1951–)
Sara Warner

"The greater delayed, the greater delighted." This aphorism, a favorite of playwright Paula Vogel, speaks to the perverse pleasure of theatre, which is predicated upon deferred gratification—for characters, audiences, and artists alike. Plays take time to develop and produce. *Indecent*, Vogel's collaboration with Rebecca Taichman about the controversy surrounding Sholem Asch's *God of Vengeance*—a 1923 Yiddish drama of lesbian love, religious hypocrisy, and the transcendent power of art—took nearly a decade to go from page to stage, after incubating for twice that long. *Indecent* marked Vogel's long-awaited Broadway debut in 2017, at the age of 65. Her maxim about the dilatory progress of theatrical time speaks to the preternatural persistence of female play makers—especially those who identify as lesbian, transwomen, BIPOC, immigrant, impoverished, or differently abled. Minorities can labor their entire lives without seeing their scripts reach fruition. When their work is staged, it is typically in small venues with inadequate resources, limiting the impact of their voices. Vogel's oft-repeated adage acknowledges deeply entrenched inequities in the art world while focusing on the gay pleasures of theatre's world-making capacities, namely the joyful pursuit of what José Muñoz termed "the then and there" of queer futurities.[1]

Times do change, and Vogel has been instrumental in leveling the playing field. In 1974, when she staged her first play, *Meg,* only 16 percent of new works produced in this country had female authors. By the time *Indecent* garnered Tony Award nominations for Best Play and Best Direction, that number had more than doubled, to 35 percent.[2] Each play Vogel writes simultaneously chips away at theatre's glass ceiling, recasting the canon and dismantling historical barriers to human flourishing. *The Oldest Profession* (1981) and *Hot 'N' Throbbing* (1994) trouble the notion of obscenity (a lifelong obsession for Vogel) by challenging stereotypes about sex work.

The former offers a wry exploration of Reagan-era America and the economic realities of aging prostitutes. The latter wades into the second wave sex wars, distinguishing erotica (X-rated screenplays a single mom produces for a woman's production company) from pornography (her husband's misogynistic acts, violent gestures sanctioned by compulsory heterosexuality and the nuclear family). Critiques of domesticity also inform ribald comedies *And Baby Makes Seven* (1984) and *Desdemona, A Play About a Handkerchief* (1993), which celebrate promiscuity, queer kinships, and families of choice.

Vogel writes incendiary plays on taboo topics. At the same time, her work is deeply personal. *The Baltimore Waltz*, inspired by and dedicated to her brother Carl, who died of AIDS in 1988, is a memory play about events that didn't happen. Carl had invited his sister on a European vacation, but she, not knowing he was dying, took a rain check. This work underscores the unique ability of theatre to dramatize history, not only the way it was, but the way we want it to be. It highlights a primal function of performance: to serve as a living vessel through which the dead can speak. When *The Baltimore Waltz* is produced, the actors say the departed's name in the present tense: "Carl is going to Europe." Theatre queers time, resurrecting and reviving the deceased, enabling us to experience our ancestors in the present moment of life. Carl's likeness appears in other plays, including the mournful examination of unfulfilled desire, *The Long Christmas Ride Home* (2003), inspired by Thornton Wilder and Bunraku, with puppets by Basil Twist.

Whereas most "AIDS plays," especially ones written during the height of the pandemic, strike anxious or angry notes (e.g., William Hoffman's *As Is* and Larry Kramer's *The Normal Heart*), Vogel turned to the queerest mode of dramaturgy, camp, in penning *The Baltimore Waltz*, an absurdist fantasy about a hedonistic holiday with siblings, one of whom has a fatal disease. Vogel rose to prominence with the Circle Repertory Company's 1992 production (starring Cherry Jones, directed by Anne Bogart), earning an Obie Award and a Guggenheim Fellowship.

Vogel won the Pulitzer Prize for another memory play in 1998, becoming the first out lesbian to receive the award, for *How I Learned to Drive*, a waggish, deeply discomforting story of sexual abuse. Constructing the plot around driving lessons allows Vogel to time-travel (a recurring motif in her work), moving the action forward and in reverse. As this experiment in negative empathy unfolds, we see the protagonist get younger rather than mature, which enables Li'l Bit and pedophilic

Uncle Peck to take the audience for a ride they wouldn't necessarily consent to take, or even know they were taking, until the journey is well underway.

Controversial themes notwithstanding, Vogel's scripts are guided, not by issues, but by events that directly impact her life. Though an autobiographical dramatist, she bristles at the label "confessional author," with its negatively gendered associations. Vogel describes her process as writing backwards, moving from emotional circumstances and characters to plot and narrative structure; she often works on multiple scripts at once. She composed *How I Learned to Drive* in tandem with *The Mineola Twins* while an artist in residence at Perseverance Theatre in Alaska, with founding artistic director Molly Smith. *The Mineola Twins*, a comedy in six scenes, four dreams, and seven (bad) wigs, delivers a satirical jab at sexual stereotypes in three presidential administrations: Eisenhower, Nixon, and Bush. Vogel created the lead role—identical twins with polarizing political perspectives—for Lisa Kron of the Five Lesbian Brothers, but schedules conflicted and Swoosie Kurtz helmed the role, scoring an Obie Award for Best Actress (and a Drama Desk nomination) in the Roundabout Theatre's production.

The Signature Theater selected Vogel as the playwright in residence for their 2004–2005 season. On opening night, she wed her longtime partner, renowned biologist Anne Fausto Sterling. The two met at Brown, where Vogel taught from 1984 to 2009 as an endowed professor of creative writing and founding director of the MFA program in Playwriting. From there, Vogel moved to the Yale School of Drama, where she held the O'Neill Chair. Earlier in her career, she taught at McGill, the University of Alaska, and Cornell. No one has done more to cultivate and champion playwrights, except perhaps "La Maestra" María Irene Fornés. Vogel's students include Lynn Nottage, Nilo Cruz, Quiara Alegría Hudes, and Sarah Ruhl, and she has mentored hundreds of aspiring artists in her workshops and "Bake-Offs." These written exercises have an assigned theme with prescribed ingredients that participants cook up in 48 hours. They get their rise from reacting to other works of art or responding to another writer, ideally one who is centuries apart from themselves. Vogel led a Bake-Off on Joan of Arc at the Wilma Theater in Philadelphia with military veterans, whose experiences informed *Don Juan Comes Home from Iraq* (2014). Bake-Offs are foundational to the theatre workshop she founded for incarcerated women at a maximum security facility in Rhode Island.

Vogel's most recent initiative is Bard at the Gate. When the COVID-19 pandemic struck, shuttering theatres, the planned revival, and scandalously overdue Broadway premiere, of *How I Learned to Drive* was paused (it opened April 19, 2022 and received three Tony nominations). Seeing the COVID crisis as an opportunity for change, Vogel leaped into action, producing a virtual series of plays that have been neglected, overlooked, or ignored. To counter the obscenity of theatre's white supremacy, and to acknowledge the historical violence against Black bodies, conditions made newly urgent by George Floyd's murder and the Black Lives Matter movement, Bard at the Gate centers African American dramatists along with play makers of color, queers, and women.

In recognition of Vogel's many contributions to playwriting, multiple awards have been named in her honor: the Paula Vogel Award, given by the Kennedy Center American College Theater Festival; the Paula Vogel Award in Playwriting, granted by the Vineyard Theatre; and the Paula Vogel Mentorship Program, curated by Hudes. In addition to being inducted into the American Theater Hall of Fame (2013), she has received the Award for Literature from the American Academy of Arts and Letters (2004) and an Obie for Lifetime Achievement (2017). In 2015, the Beinecke Rare Book and Manuscript Library acquired Vogel's archive, making her the first female playwright included in Yale's Collection of American Literature. In 2020, she was awarded an honorary doctorate from Yale, four years after she received her PhD from Cornell. Vogel's original thesis on Restoration comedy was rejected on the grounds that it was not sufficiently scholarly, which is to say it was a pioneering example of lesbian feminist dramatic theory and criticism. She left the university in 1976 with an MA, but 40 years later this egregious wrong was righted by a new committee, comprising three openly queer faculty. Along with her diploma, Vogel received a Cornell hoodie embroidered with the phrase "the greater delayed, the greater delighted."

NOTES

1 José Esteban Muñoz, *Cruising Utopia: The Then and There of Queer Futurity* (New York: New York University Press, 2009).
2 Julia Jordan, "The Count 2.0," 2018. *Dramatists Guild.* www.dramatistsguild.com/advocacy/the-count. See also Jenny Lyn Bader, "A Brief History of the Gender Parity Movement in Theatre," *Howl Round*, March 4, 2017. https://howlround.com/brief-history-gender-parity-movement-theatre

FURTHER READING

Greene, Alexis, ed. *Women Who Write Plays: Interviews with American Dramatists* (Hanover, NH: Smith and Kraus, 2001), 425–448.

Johnson, Katie N., and Warner, Sara L. "Indecent Collaborations in/and Queer Time(s)," in *Critical Perspectives on Contemporary Plays by Women: The Early Twenty-First Century*, ed. Penny Farfan and Lesley Ferris (Ann Arbor, MI: University of Michigan Press, 2021).

Mansbridge, Joanna. *Paula Vogel* (Ann Arbor, MI: University of Michigan Press, 2014).

RON WHYTE
(Black Eagle, Montana, 1941–1989)
Patrick McKelvey

Queer, Italian American, and self-described "radically disabled" writer Ron Whyte worked across seemingly every genre and medium—comics, children's books, literary criticism, pornography, film, and video art, among them—before his premature death after a decades-long battle with debilitating lower-leg prosthetics.[1] Whyte is now largely forgotten within received histories of disability, queer, and late twentieth-century US theatre, but it was through his impossibly prolific work as a playwright that he would offer his most compelling, and politically ferocious, examinations of disability and sexuality. His earliest theatrical forays included childhood tap-dancing recitals completed with the support of homemade leg braces that his enterprising father hoped would afford him greater mobility, but Whyte's relationship to the stage would ultimately prove to be anything but therapeutic. For Whyte, who lived most of his life with both lower legs amputated, a "withered" left arm, and who experienced deafness, vision loss, and mental illness, theatre offered the opportunity both to confront audiences' ableist fantasies and to cultivate desire for disability embodiment, history, and aesthetics.

Whyte's politics and writing were profoundly shaped—albeit sometimes resistantly—by the educational institutions where he studied and produced work. Following a brief stint at Whitworth College in Spokane (WA), Whyte attended San Francisco State College from 1961 to 1964, where he participated in student protests and witnessed the rising tides of disability rights activism throughout the Bay Area. With financial support from Connecticut's state vocational rehabilitation agency, he studied playwriting with John Gassner at the Yale School of Drama. In the years following graduation, Whyte, newly based in New York, met with early (if still intermittent) success, both off-Broadway and in regional theatre. His early dark work about a quadriplegic and his nurse, *Welcome to Andromeda*, was developed and produced at American Place Theatre (1969) and Cherry Lane

(1973), spurred two sequels, and remains one of his most-produced works. And *Horatio*, his musical biography of Horatio Alger (with music by Mel Marvin), was mounted at The Repertory Theatre of St Louis (1970), Arena Stage (1974), and American Conservatory Theater (1974). During this time, he also continued his education at Union Theological Seminary (UTS), where studying with Black liberation theologian James H. Cone fostered some of his most radical disability politics.

As these early works suggest, Whyte was at once interested in magnifying disability's theatrical force and in exploring the mythos of American identity. He sometimes described himself as purposely alternating between plays committed to each of these projects, although his historical interests often took him further away from the US, more firmly anchored instead in theatre history and histories of disability representation, as in his morality play, *Everyman-Cripple-Everyman* (1973), and his stage adaptation of Victor Hugo's *The Hunchback of Notre Dame* (1979). Whyte drew inspiration both from disabled artists past, from Milton to Sarah Bernhardt, and a desire to challenge the specter of tragedy and pity that lurked in mainstream representations of disability, sometimes through subterfuge. (He once likened himself to Tiny Tim masquerading as Neil Simon masquerading as Godzilla.) Whyte's plays frequently met with mixed critical reception, but they also earned him comparisons to Edward Albee, Alfred Hitchcock, Arthur Kopit, and Kurt Vonnegut. Critics frequently situated Whyte's work within the proliferation of seemingly infinite representations of disability on stage in the 1970s and 1980s, what Mel Gussow of the *New York Times* called "The Times of the Wounded Hero" and Tom Nugent of the *Baltimore Sun* called "The Theater of Paralysis."[2] These same critics, however, often failed to notice what distinguished Whyte's plays from *Wings*, *Whose Life Is It Anyway?*, *The Fifth of July*, or *The Shadow Box*. Such critical mishaps no doubt derived in part from the fact that, when speaking with reviewers, Whyte was all too happy to champion the popular appeal of his plays by coyly capitulating to critical assumptions about disability as a universal metaphor for powerlessness and shame, divorced entirely from the material experience of disability. Whyte was concerned, in part, with developing more complex portraits of disability, roles he hoped would eventually be played by disabled actors, although most productions during his lifetime cast nondisabled actors in these roles. But he was just as concerned with the right of disabled artists to control negative representations of disability. He even cited this as one of the primary purposes for founding his activist organization, The National

Task Force for Disability and the Arts (1978). These sometimes competing desires—for complex representation and to reclaim ownership over familiar narratives from which nondisabled writers profited—resulted in works that confronted audiences with ableist fantasies of the horror of disability they thought they already knew. *Disability, A Comedy*, for example, ends with parents forcibly paralyzing the journalist their disabled son meets through a personal ad in *Screw*, upon learning that she has been faking her own disability.

While committed to disabled writers' ownership of disability representation, Whyte loved toying with audience expectations for his plays to be "authentic" representations of disability experience reducible to "autobiography or 'confession'." In a preface to *Everyman-Cripple-Everyman*, Whyte explained that his use of a character named Ron was a dramaturgical device akin to "gossip" he used to maintain audience interest. In *The Extinction of Alexander Pope* (1980), a minor figure named Ron, understood by at least some of the play's characters to have written the narrative in which they find themselves, even appears in Whyte's signature work uniform of leather, denim, and boots. Whyte further complicated these experiments in challenging demands for fidelitous representation by including in his expansive oeuvre several plays that he explicitly framed as autobiographical, including *Yankee Doodle Boy* (no date) and *Mother and Child* (which premiered posthumously in 1990, following Whyte's memorial service at St. John the Divine).

Refusing the sincere and the sentimental in favor of the acerbic and the irreverent, as his campy adoption of the sobriquet "Vicious Cripple" would attest, Whyte's repertoire offers what we might think of as a crip politics of disability representation, a politics steeped in the aesthetic and political conviviality of disability and queer sexuality. "Not unlike *queer* at its most radical," writes Robert McRuer, "*crip* often has the potential to be simultaneously flamboyantly identitarian (as in, we are crip and you will acknowledge that!) and flamboyantly anti-identitarian (as in, we reject your categories or the capacity of languages saturated in ableism to describe us!)."[3] Whyte thought often about the relationship between disability and queer sexuality, even dedicating a section of his UTS thesis, "Life Deformed," to a consideration of "Sex and the Radically Disabled," in which he argued that homosexual oppression and disability oppression were linked through systems dedicated to denying the body. "Social change" first required "affirming the physical body." Sex acts and expressions, solo and communal, Whyte understood, were crucial tools for realizing these pleasures.[4] Many of Whyte's plays featured gay characters, representations of same-sex eroticism, and, more broadly, explorations of the intersection of disability and antinormative sexuality. Whyte's politics and aesthetics of sexuality emerged not only from his perspective as a queer disabled man, but also from his experience as a sex worker and his participation in queer artistic communities in New York. In addition to his longtime partner, Paul William Bradley, and queer colleagues from his time at Union, including photographer and documentary filmmaker Ted Yaple, these influences included, perhaps most prominently, art critic, gossip columnist, and all-around notorious homosexual Gregory Battcock. Until Battcock's murder in 1980, the two men were neighbors, close friends, and regular collaborators, developing, among other projects, an unnamed, campy epistolary performance collaboration that featured some of Whyte's queerest aesthetics and (if, at times, confounding) politics.

Whyte's ambitious *The Extinction of Alexander Pope*, which premiered at Posthus Teatret in Copenhagen in 1980, elucidates what queer sexuality offered to Whyte's theatrical and historical excavations of disability, narrative, and form. The play stages an intimate friendship between the "crippled" titular Pope and the "mad" Jonathan Swift as they revisit scenes from Pope's life on this, the night of his (seemingly infinitely deferred) death. They cross paths with Joseph Addison, John Gay, and William Wycherly (all to be portrayed by "dummies" physically manipulated by Pope and Swift, and voiced by off-stage recordings) in one of many scenes organized around Pope's unrealized heterosexual romance, purportedly on account of his physical disfigurement. In one key scene, however, a younger Pope makes a sexual advance on his aged self. While insisting that his life included no such perversions, Swift (who proudly cops to his own youthful pleasures in "being buggered") insists that his friend would have been open to such experiences of desire, "were you truly aware of reality in youth." If, as Swift offers earlier in the play, the "everyday acquaintances," even friendships, between men and their "deformities and flaws" are destroyed by "the way other men see them," then homo sex that is also an act of self-love offers a way to be hospitable to one's disfigurement.[5] In a play about disabled men struggling to come to terms with the question of if and how their bodies, and bodies of work, will be remembered, queer sexuality offers a desire for the disabled body that is at once a desire for disability history, a desire for disabled forms that last.

NOTES

1 Ron Whyte figures prominently in my current book project, *Disability Works: US Performance After Rehabilitation*. This chapter is based on extensive archival research in Whyte's papers at Yale. Ron Whyte Papers, Yale Collection of American Literature, Beinecke Rare Book and Manuscript Library.
2 Mel Gussow, "The Time of the Wounded Hero," *New York Times*, April 15, 1979, D1; Tom Nugent, "Theater of the Disabled: A Paralysis of the Times?" *Baltimore Sun*, March 8, 1981, D1.
3 Robert McRuer, *Crip Times: Disability, Globalization, and Resistance* (New York: New York University Press, 2018), 20.
4 Ron Whyte, "Life Deformed: An Approach to the Politics of Disability." Box 43, Folder 22, Ron Whyte Papers, Yale Collection of American Literature, Beinecke Rare Book and Manuscript Library.
5 Ron Whyte, "The Extinction of Alexander Pope." Unpublished manuscript. Box 26, Folder 6, Ron Whyte Papers, Yale Collection of American Literature, Beinecke Rare Book and Manuscript Library.

FURTHER READING

McKelvey, Patrick. "Ron Whyte's 'Disemployment': Prosthetic Performance and Theatrical Labor," *Theatre Survey* 57, no. 3 (September 2016): 314–335.

GEORGE C. WOLFE
(Frankfort, Kentucky, 1961–)
Charles I. Nero

George Costello Wolfe is a playwright, director, and arts administrator responsible for some of the most innovative queer works on the American stage. Born in Frankfort, Kentucky, Wolfe achieved fame for his satirical drama *The Colored Museum* (1986), first produced at New Jersey's Crossroads Theatre, then New York's Public Theater, and subsequently broadcast in 1991 on PBS television. Wolfe made his Broadway debut with the musical *Jelly's Last Jam* (1992) and then directed both parts of Tony Kushner's epic *Angels in America: A Gay Fantasia on National Themes* (1993), winning Tony and Drama Desk Awards for Best Director for *Part One: Millennium Approaches*. In 1993, Wolfe became artistic director and producer of the New York Shakespeare Festival/Public Theater and served in that capacity until 2004. During his tenure at the Public Theater, Wolfe wrote and/or directed groundbreaking works including *Bring in Da Noise/Bring in Da Funk* (1996), *The Wild Party* (2000), Suzan-Lori Parks' *Topdog/Underdog* (2001), and Tony Kushner's *Caroline, or Change* (2003). Since that time, he has continued to work on stage and screen, including writing and directing *Shuffle Along, or the Making of the Musical Sensation of 1921 and All That Followed* (2016) on Broadway, and directing the film adaptation of August Wilson's *Ma Rainey's Black Bottom* (2020).

Wolfe's significant contributions to gay theatre are best understood within a specifically Black and queer context. Wolfe belongs to the Generation of 1986, the first collective of openly gay African American male artists, intellectuals, and activists since the Harlem Renaissance of the 1920s. 1986 marks the publication of Joseph Beam's landmark *In the Life: A Black Gay Anthology*, a work dedicated to making visible the Black gay men who "have always existed" and who are now "creating and naming a new community while extending a hand to the one from which we've come."[1] Beam's statement refers to the experience of its members as part of the transition from communities shaped by legally enforced racial segregation to new racially integrated ones. This transition can be seen in Wolfe's early education in racially segregated schools of Frankfort followed by his transfer to the predominantly white Pomona College, where he majored in Theatre and was mentored by the critic Stanley Crouch.[2]

The Generation of 1986 was also intentionally following in the path of Black and women of color feminists who emphasized the importance of the intersection of identities, rather than submerging all identities under one that was a singularly racial, cis-gendered, heterosexual male.[3] This intersectional focus was also a critique of the gay politics of "coming out" because it rejected the idea that sexuality was unrelated to race.[4] Members of the Generation of 1986—including the novelists Melvin Dixon and Randall Kenan, the poet Essex Hemphill, the filmmaker Marlon Riggs, and the performance collective Pomo Afro Homos—directly challenged "respectability politics," a type of activism that equated an individual's respectable public behavior "with the advancement of African Americans as a group."[5] With their insistence on the right to be visible, the Generation of 1986 rejected the respectability politics that had heretofore silenced the sexuality of queer Black artists such as playwright Lorraine Hansberry, choreographer Alvin Ailey, and musician Billy Strayhorn.

Wolfe threw down the gauntlet at respectability politics in *The Colored Museum*, a collection of 11 "museum exhibits" that resembled the skits in popular American television shows. Philosophically, though, *The Colored Museum* enacts what W.E.B. Du Bois in his 1903 work *The Souls of Black Folk* called "double consciousness," the "sense of always looking at one's self through the eyes of others, of measuring one's souls by the tape of a world that looks on in amused contempt and pity."[6] The two-ness that Du Bois attributed to being "an American, a Negro" appears throughout *The Colored Museum* as contradictions pushing against the boundaries of respectability.

The most articulate commentary on double consciousness is delivered by Miss Roj, a Black drag queen lamenting Black people's abandonment of insurrection for assimilation into the middle classes. "Yeah dance!" Miss Roj says, "But don't be surprised if there ain't no beat holding you together 'cause we traded in our drums for respectability. So now it's just words ... instead of blood 'cause you know that don't work."[7] Miss Roj was a daring reimagining of Ralph Ellison's titular character in his landmark 1952 novel *The Invisible Man*.[8] Echoing Ellison, Miss Roj announces that she "comes from another galaxy," and declares that "I ain't just your regular oppressed American Negro ... I am an extra-terrestrial, and I ain't talkin' none of that shit you seen in the movies."[9] Miss Roj enacts violence on her oppressors with her superpower, the snap. Once, when a man yelled at her, "Hey look at da monkey coon in da faggit suit," she snapped her fingers and gave a man a heart attack.[10] As the lights fade, Miss Roj dances to Aretha Franklin's "Respect."

Into the 1990s and beyond, Wolfe has significantly heightened the queer presence in American theatre in works and activities that challenge respectability politics. As artistic director of the Public Theater, Wolfe mentored numerous queer artists, notably the Black gay playwright Robert O'Hara, who interned at the Public Theater and whose first play *Insurrection: Holding History* premiered there in 1996. O'Hara openly acknowledged that his 2014 play *Bootycandy*, with its episodic structure and campy satire, is "a part of the legacy of *The Colored Museum*."[11] Other significant queer works produced during Wolfe's tenure include *A Language of Their Own* (1995) by Chay Yew, *Stop Kiss* (1998) by Diana Son, *Take Me Out* (2002) by Richard Greenberg, and *Well* (2004) by Lisa Kron. Wolfe also directed the successful one-woman show and career retrospective of a beloved icon to queer audiences, *Elaine Stritch: At Liberty* (2001).

Perhaps it is Wolfe's willingness to confront respectability politics that explains his rare position as a Broadway director of shows with casts that are racially homogenous as well as racially diverse, since directors of Broadway shows typically reflect the race of the author and/or the audience imagined for the production. A notable example of Wolfe's unique position is as the director of Tony Kushner's culture-shifting work, the two-part *Angels in America*, which explored the devastation AIDS had on gay men in the 1980s. Critics raved about Wolfe's direction, and Frank Rich in his *New York Times* review made a connection between Wolfe's work in this play and his earlier productions, writing that "*Angels in America* is an ideal assignment for Mr. Wolfe because of its leaps beyond the bedroom into the fabulous realms of myth and American archetypes, which have preoccupied this director and playwright in ... *The Colored Museum*."[12] Rich's praise affirms Wolfe as that rare director who, like others in the Generation of 1986, learned to move with dexterity between African American and white worlds, all the while "creating and naming a new community while extending a hand to the one from which we've come."

NOTES

1 Joseph Beam, "Introduction," *In the Life: A Black Gay Anthology* (Boston, MA: Alyson Press, 1986), 16.

2 Matt Steib, "George Wolfe on the Audacity of His Late Mentor Stanley Crouch," *Vulture* (September 18, 2020). www.vulture.com/2020/09/george-c-wolfe-on-the-audacity-of-mentor-stanley-crouch.html
3 See the landmark anthologies: Cherríe Moraga and Gloria Anzaldúa (eds), *This Bridge Called My Back: Writings by Radical Women of Color* (Watertown, MA: Persephone Press, 1981), and Gloria T. Hull, Patricia Bell Scott, and Barbara Smith (eds), *All the Women Are White, All the Men are Black But Some of Us Are Brave: Black Women's Studies* (New York: The Feminist Press, 1982).
4 Darius Bost, *The Black Gay Cultural Renaissance and the Politics of Violence* (Chicago, IL: The University of Chicago Press, 2019), 9–12.
5 Evelyn Brooks Higginbotham, *Righteous Discontent: The Women's Movement in the Black Baptist Church, 1880–1920* (Cambridge, MA: Harvard University Press, 1993), 14.
6 W.E.B. Du Bois, *The Souls of Black Folk*, ed. David W. Blight and Robert Gooding-Williams (New York: Bedford/St. Martin's Press, 1997), 38.
7 George C. Wolfe, *The Colored Museum*," in James V. Hatch and Ted Shine (eds), *Black Theater USA: Plays by African Americans; The Recent Period, 1935–Today* (New York: The Free Press, 1996), 459.
8 Charles I. Nero, "Toward a Black Gay Aesthetic: Signifying in Contemporary Black Gay Literature," in Essex Hemphill and Joseph Fairchild Beam (eds), *Brother to Brother: New Writings by Black* (Boston, MA: Alyson, 1991), 245.
9 Wolfe, 458.
10 Wolfe, 459.
11 Jeremy D. Goodwin, "Playwright Robert O'Hara on *Bootycandy* and Being Black and Gay in America," *WBUR News* (March 9, 2016). www.wbur.org/news/2016/03/09/robert-ohara-q-and-a
12 Frank Rich, "*Angels in America: Millennium Approaches*; Embracing All Possibilities in Art and Life" (May 5, 1993). www.nytimes.com/1993/05/05/theater/review-theater-angels-america-millennium-approaches-embracing-all-possibilities.html

FURTHER READING

Pacheco, Patrick. "Bold Voice for the Silent; George C. Wolfe Believes in Theater as Reality Check," *Los Angeles Times* (February 8, 2004), E39.
Vélez, Andrew. "Interview with George C. Wolfe," in *Cast Out: Queer Lives in Theater*, ed. Robin Bernstein (Ann Arbor, MI: University of Michigan Press, 2006), 56–59.

BD WONG
(San Francisco, California, 1960–)
Esther Kim Lee

BD Wong is a Chinese American actor, director, and author. He was born on October 24, 1960, as Bradley Darryl Wong and grew up in San Francisco. His parents, William D. Wong and Roberta Christine Wong (née Leong), who called him Bradd, raised three boys in the Sunset District of the city, and Wong was the middle child. He discovered "the joy and passion of acting" while attending Lincoln High School and did not feel limited by his ethnicity or sexuality.[1] He did not have a strong sense of identity or self-image in any particular way.[2] However, he quickly learned that the kind of nontraditional casting practiced at his school was a rarity. When he was cast as a coolie in a community theatre production of *Anything Goes* instead of the sailor role he wanted, he was shocked and felt ashamed of the role.[3] This experience was a wake-up call and introduced Wong to the reality of the acting industry that typecast minority actors in stereotypical roles.

After graduating from high school, he attended San Francisco University for a year and moved to New York in 1981. In New York City, he was cast in summer stock and dinner theatres as well as in chorus roles in musicals. He was part of the national touring company of *La Cage aux Folles* in Los Angeles in 1985 when he decided to stay in the city to pursue acting. He studied with Donald Hotton and developed the technique and philosophy of acting that he has followed throughout his career. Inspired by Hotton, Wong "believed that actors are mere messengers there to serve the writer's vision."[4] He was in Los Angeles playing bit parts in television shows when his agent asked him if he wanted to audition for a play. He initially declined because he had to pay for his own airfare. But, when he read the script of David Henry Hwang's play *M. Butterfly*, Wong felt that the feeling or the "unique plight" he experienced as an Asian American man was validated.[5] Wong borrowed money from his parents and flew to New York City and landed the part of Song Liling, a Chinese opera singer who pretends to be a woman and has a 20-year love affair with a French diplomat. For the production, Wong changed his name to "BD Wong" to underscore the gender ambiguity of the role, but kept it for the rest of his career.

As the permanence of the name change suggests, *M. Butterfly* was a career-defining role for Wong. The play premiered on Broadway in March 1988 and ran for 777 performances and won the Tony Award for Best Play. Wong received a Tony Award for Best Performance by a Featured Actor in a Play, as well as a Drama Desk Award and an Outer Critics Circle Award. He was described as "a remarkable tour de force" who could undergo a "stunning metamorphosis" on stage from "the perfect woman" into a "brash, cocky, insolent man who ... ridicules both racial stereotypes and conventional sex roles."[6] Wong embraced the duality of his character and said, "I guess part of the reason I can play [the role] is that there's a more developed feminine side of me."[7] He also expressed his willingness to do anything, including taking his clothes off (which is in the play) to say Hwang's words on stage. For Wong, the play allowed him to make a contribution as an Asian American actor in the broader discussions of artistic and political representation. In fact, he actively protested against the casting of white actors in Asian roles and became a vocal advocate for better visibility of Asian American actors in the industry.[8]

Wong's identification as a gay man involved a more complex journey. He knew he was gay since he was a child and grew up in San Francisco, a city known for its progressive attitude toward sexuality, but he was not out publicly even after *M. Butterfly* closed. It was in 2003, when Wong's memoir about the birth of his son, Jackson, was published, that he began to speak publicly about his sexuality. Titled *Following Foo: (The Electronic Adventures of the Chestnut Man)*, the book describes his newborn's ordeal in neonatal intensive care (he had his son through surrogacy). Wong has stated that he needed a "positive reason" to come out publicly and did not want to tell a story "laced with self-doubt or shame."[9]

By 2003, Wong had appeared in multiple films and television shows, including *Jurassic Park* (1993), *And the Band Played On* (1993), *Father of the Bride* (1995), *All American Girl* (1994), *Oz* (1997–2003), and Disney's *Mulan* (1998). But he was best known as a series regular on *Law & Order: Special Victims Unit*, in which he played Dr George Huang, an FBI psychiatrist. He appeared in the show beginning in season 2 in 2001, and the character was a calm, soft-spoken, and empathetic Chinese American man. In season 12, it was passingly revealed that Dr. Huang was a gay man, but by then

Wong had decided to leave the show and the character was not further developed.

While appearing on screen in film and television, Wong continued to work in the theatre. In 1995, he performed the role of Ming, a young Chinese American gay man who is HIV-positive, in Chay Yew's *A Language of Their Own*. He returned to Broadway in 1999 as Linus in *You're a Good Man, Charlie Brown* and, in 2003, he was cast as General Gong Fei in Charles Busch's *Shanghai Moon*. In 2004, Wong starred in the revival of *Pacific Overtures* by Stephen Sondheim and Jon Weidman at the Roundabout Theatre Company and played the role of Reciter, which was originated by the Japanese American actor Mako in 1976. In 2009, he starred in the solo musical *Herringbone* at La Jolla Playhouse and played 11 roles, which allowed him to showcase his versatility as a singer, dancer, and actor. And, in 2014, Wong played the lead role in James Fenton's adaptation of the Chinese epic *The Orphan of Zhao* at American Conservatory Theater in co-production with La Jolla Playhouse. As these examples illustrate, the range of character types Wong has played has been extensive.

Wong sees himself as a character actor who tries to avoid being pigeonholed: "I've always tried to force people to see that I did different things, versatile things, that I have those in my toolbox."[10] This emphasis on versatility has been at the core of Wong's approach, not only to acting but also to his life as a Chinese American gay man. He has described it "very human" that he did not like the "same thing as every other gay person" and that he did not feel deeply connected to the Chinese culture, partly because he does not speak the language. Professionally, he further demonstrated his versatility when he ventured into directing (Lauren Yee's *The Great Leap*) in 2019, stating that he wanted to "prioritize writing and directing for the stage and the screen."[11] In 2020, Wong was cast in the comedy television show *Awkwafina is Nora from Queens*, in which he plays Awkwafina's dad. The significance of the show, for Wong, was how it subverted the stereotype of Asians being not funny, which was yet another way to widen his versatility and humanity.[12]

NOTES

1 Edward Guthmann, "BD Wong Returns to His Hometown for 'Orphan of Zhao'," *SFGate*, June 3, 2014. www.sfgate.com/performance/article/BD-Wong-returns-to-his-hometown-for-Orphan-of-5526105.php
2 "B.D. Wong," *Notable Asian Americans*, ed. Helen Zia and Susan B. Gall (Farmington Hill, MI: Gale Research, 1995), 417.

3 Ibid.
4 Audrey Magazine, "BD Wong Reprises Role from Two Decades Ago in 'Jurassic World'," *Character Media*, June 29, 2015. https://charactermedia.com/bd-wong-reprises-role-from-two-decades-ago-in-jurassic-world/
5 Asian Art Museum, "An Evening with BD Wong," YouTube video, 33:41, March 7, 2019. www.youtube.com/watch?v=43Yc4GD9pCo
6 Leslie Bennetts, "New Face: Brad Wong; Blending Genders in 'M. Butterfly'," *New York Times*, March 25, 1988, C4.
7 Ibid.
8 For instance, Wong was a leading voice during the *Miss Saigon* controversy in the early 1990s. See Esther Kim Lee, *A History of Asian American Theatre* (Cambridge: Cambridge University Press, 2006); Amanda Hess, "Asian American Actors are Fighting for Visibility. They Will Not Be Ignored," *New York Times,* May 25, 2016. www.nytimes.com/2016/05/29/movies/asian-american-actors-are-fighting-for-visibility-they-will-not-be-ignored.html?searchResultPosition=21
9 Asian Art Museum, "An Evening with BD Wong," 36:17.
10 David Reddish, "BD Wong Dishes on Homophobic Producers, Dadhood, and Jumping into 'The Great Leap," *Queerty*, November 11, 2019. www.queerty.com/bd-wong-dishes-homophobic-producers-dadhood-jumping-great-leap-20191111.
11 Ashley Lee, "BD Wong is Taking 'The Great Leap' into Directing," *Los Angeles Times*, November 7, 2019. www.latimes.com/entertainment-arts/story/2019-11-07/bd-wong-great-leap-directing-pasadena-playhouse
12 Audrey Cleo Yap, "'Awkwafina is Nora from Queens' Star BD Wong Was Told 'Asian People Aren't Funny' Early in His Career," *Variety*, March 26, 2020. https://variety.com/2020/tv/news/bd-wong-awkwafina-is-nora-from-queens-season-finale-bowen-yang-1203546130/

FURTHER READING

"B.D. Wong." *Notable Asian Americans*, ed. Helen Zia and Susan B. Gall. Farmington Hill, MI: Gale Research, 1995: 417.
Hess, Amanda. "Asian American Actors are Fighting for Visibility. They Will Not Be Ignored." *New York Times*, May 25, 2016.

CHAY YEW
(Singapore, 1965–)
Dan Bacalzo

As a playwright, director, and artistic director, Chay Yew has expanded notions of what queer theatre in the US looks like, particularly in regard to Asian American representation. His debut play, *As If He Hears* (1987), was banned in his native Singapore due to its sympathetic portrayal of its lead gay character, a Malaysian social worker who befriends a heterosexual man with HIV/AIDS. As a result of the controversy, Yew made edits to excise overt references to the character's homosexuality. But, according to a profile of the playwright published in the *New York Times*, he "encouraged the actor playing the part to hint at the character's sexual preference."[1] This compromise is emblematic of the difficulties Yew faced early in his career regarding the expression of his dual identities as queer and Asian.

His next play, *Porcelain* (1992), tackled this duality head-on. The winner of a London Fringe Award for Best Play, the work centers around a Chinese gay man named John Lee, who was arrested for the murder of a white man in a public lavatory. Scholar Heath A. Diehl notes that, while Yew does not

> offer a model for how to construct and maintain a Queer Asian American identity, he does expose some of the corrosive historical forces (within dominant, Asian, and gay communities) that systemically excise that identity from dominant discourses, public spaces, and social practices.[2]

The play clearly demonstrates how John's actions are shaped by a gay white culture that too often excludes those it deems "other," as well as how Orientalist and homophobic constructs affect the perceptions that other characters have towards him.

Yew's US playwriting debut was *A Language of Their Own* (1995), produced at the Public Theater and recipient of a GLAAD Media Award for Outstanding New York Theater. Directed by

Keng-Sen Ong, the world premiere featured four queer actors: BD Wong, Francis Jue, Alec Mapa, and David Drake. The emotional core of the play is the relationship between Ming, an American-born man of Chinese descent, and Oscar, a Chinese immigrant, who break up after Oscar is diagnosed as HIV-positive, but never quite let go of the love that binds them. Critic Steven Drukman notes: "While concerned with both the Asian-American and gay experience, the play really sounds out the ways we speak ourselves into identity, narrate our lives vis-à-vis the 'master' language and, therefore, are all (literally) sentenced to reality."[3] Ultimately, the play is about how communication can misfire, even when the characters want so badly to express themselves.

In 1996, Tim Dang staged *Porcelain* and *Language* along with a new work called *Half Lives* as Yew's *Whitelands* trilogy at East West Players, a prominent Asian American theatre company based in Los Angeles. *Half Lives* was later retitled *Wonderland*, when reworked for a 1999 production at La Jolla Playhouse. As scholar David Román writes, "The trilogy highlights the lives and experiences of queer Asian-Americans and provided one of the first sustained explorations of this theme in American literature."[4] *Wonderland* tells the story of an Asian American family consisting of a father, his immigrant wife, and their American-born son who runs away from home after his father rejects him for his homosexuality. The play is a meditation on shattered dreams, as none of the characters achieve their full potential and instead engage in questionable acts as they try to improve their situations or to just simply survive.

A Beautiful Country (1998) is Yew's collaboration with the LA-based Cornerstone Theatre. A poetic distillation of decades of Asian immigration history in the US, it begins and ends with the recurring character of Miss Visa Denied, a drag queen who undergoes an interview with an immigration officer. This is a quintessential experience in many immigration narratives, particularly for Asians during the period when many were legally excluded from entering the country.

Yew also made an impact as a stage director, receiving a 2007 Obie Award for helming Julia Cho's *Durango*, a play about familial dynamics between a Korean American father and his two sons that includes a nuanced treatment of homosexuality. In his *New York Times* review of the play, Charles Isherwood emphasized the sensitivity of Yew's direction, noting that "Mr. Yew, a playwright himself, has a graceful sense of pacing."[5] Yew's work as a director bleeds into his work as a curator/producer who founded the Asian Theatre

Workshop at the Mark Taper Forum, served as its director from 1995 to 2005, and helped nurture works by several Asian American playwrights, including queer-identified artists Alice Tuan and Alec Mapa.

Yew continued to nurture a variety of theatre artists in his capacity as artistic director of the Chicago-based Victory Gardens Theater from 2011 to 2020. Among his accomplishments was the establishment of the Directors Inclusion Initiative, begun during the 2015–2016 season, to help "encourage and develop talented and emerging Chicago stage directors who identify as people of color, disabled, women, transgender, gender non-conforming and LGBTQ."[6] His initial production at Victory Gardens in 2012 was *Ameriville*, inspired by the impact of Hurricane Katrina, and which Yew helped develop with the performance collective Universes. He directed several collaborations with African American playwright Marcus Gardley, including *The Gospel of Lovingkindness* (2014), *An Issue of Blood* (2015), *The House That Will Not Stand* (2016), and *A Wonder in My Soul* (2017). Additional works directed by Yew at Victory Gardens include the world premiere of Luis Alfaro's *Mojada* (2013), a reimagination of *Medea*; Lucas Hnath's political satire *Hillary and Clinton* (2016); Karen Hartman's *Roz and Ray* (2016), set in the early days of the AIDS crisis; and Boo Killebrew's *Lettie* (2018), about a recently released female convict. Under Yew's leadership, prominent playwrights Ayad Akhtar, Ike Holter, Samuel D. Hunter, Branden Jacobs-Jenkins, Lisa Kron, Dominique Morisseau, Paula Vogel, and Lauren Yee also received productions of their plays during this period.

Reflecting on his tenure at Victory Gardens, Yew emphasizes how theatre needs to change. "I was once given the idea that there is a table and there's a seat for you at the table," he remarked.

> At some point I said that's not good enough, because at the end of the dinner I'm asked to go home. So the question is: Whose table is it? Do I have a say in the menu? Which guests can I invite, and can we make the table bigger? If we can't, can we share more space with each other? I'm not asking someone to be kicked out. I'm asking us to make room. And if no one gives you that opportunity at that table, you need to break that fucking table and build your own.[7]

Based on the diversity of works mentioned above, it seems Yew succeeded. His proclamation has a very queer sensibility, subverting normative ways of looking at inclusion in favor of changing the narrative in a way that can push the genre of theatre forward.

NOTES

1 Rachel L. Swarns, "An Outsider Determined to Be Someone He's Not." *New York Times*, March 21, 1999, B8.
2 Heath A. Diehl, "Beyond the Silk Road: Staging a Queer Asian America in Chay Yew's *Porcelain*." *Studies in the Literary Imagination* 37.1 (Spring 2004), 151.
3 Steven Drukman, "Chay Yew: The Importance of Being Verbal." *American Theatre* (November 1995), 58.
4 David Román, "Introduction." In *The Hyphenated American: Four Plays by Chay Yew*. New York: Grove Press (2002), xv.
5 Charles Isherwood, "An Immigrant Family's Three Survivors, Traveling Together, Alone." *New York Times*, November 21, 2006. www.nytimes.com/2006/11/21/theater/reviews/an-immigrant-familys-three-survivors-traveling-together.html
6 "Directors Inclusion Initiative." *Victory Gardens*. https://victorygardens.org/directors-inclusion/
7 Jerald Raymond Pierce, "Chay Yew: Break the Table and Build a New One." *American Theatre*, May 27, 2020. www.americantheatre.org/2020/05/27/chay-yew-break-the-table-and-build-a-new-one/

FURTHER READING

Ha, Quan-Manh and Andrew Vigesaa. "The Malleability of Truth and Language in Chay Yew's *Porcelain* and *A Language of Their Own*." *Journal of Contemporary Drama in English* 6:2 (2018), 300–314.

Román, David. "Visa Denied: Chay Yew's Theatre of Immigration and the Performance of Asian American History." In *Performance in America: Contemporary US Culture and the Performing Arts*. Durham, NC: Duke University Press, 2005, 78–108.